VICTORY WITH VACCINES

The Story of Immunization

This book is to be
the last

-2

VICTORY
WITH VACCINES

The Story of Immunization

H. J. PARISH
M.D., F.R.C.P.E., D.P.H., Hon.F.R.S.H.

Former Wellcome Trust Fellow, and Clinical Research Director
Wellcome Research Laboratories. Beckenham, Kent

E. & S. LIVINGSTONE LTD.
EDINBURGH AND LONDON
1968

SBN 443 00579 6

Printed in Great Britain

PREFACE

'By the historical method alone can many problems
in medicine be approached profitably.'
SIR WILLIAM OSLER

THIS book is based on my *History of Immunization* (1965),
which was written during my tenure of a Research Fellow-
ship and grant from the Wellcome Trust, and was intended
for the expert and the advanced student rather than for the
general reader, professional or lay.

Immunization is now a subject of topical importance, and the
fascinating story of *Victory with Vaccines* is told in relatively
simple terms for those who are not specialists. Of necessity, some
chapters are much more interesting than others, mainly because
purely technical information could not be excluded altogether.
Failures and disappointments, as well as successes, are instructive
and have a place in the narrative: all have contributed to
medicine's greatest triumph, which is the overthrow of infectious
diseases.

The field covered in this book is so vast that much has necessarily been left out or all too briefly summarized, perhaps to the disappointment or annoyance of some readers. Further, no mention
is made of the immunological reactions (autoimmunization) involved in the transplantation of organs or tissues, or of certain
problems associated with blood groups, e.g. haemolytic disease.
These are important and complicated topics for research, but
developments are too recent for inclusion in this historical review.

Only a short bibliography is appended to this volume: as explained elsewhere, references to sources of information will usually
be found in my earlier *History*. Moreover, none of the 50 por-
traits or other illustrations from that book could be reproduced,
since my aim was to keep down the costs of publication of this
semi-popular work.

Before I retired officially in 1962, the laboratory and clinical aspects of immunization were my major responsibility for nearly 40 years. Recently I have found, like many others, that 'medical history is a delightful hobby for the retired practitioner'. Of course, as a historian I can claim only amateur status!

Acknowledgments.—Brigadier Sir John Boyd kindly read the final typescript, and the Wellcome Trustees made a generous grant towards the cost of production. In addition, I am grateful to those friends and former colleagues of the Wellcome Historical Medical Museum and Library and of the Wellcome Research Laboratories who contributed to the success of my *History of Immunization.* Their influence on this further monograph has been indirect but obviously of great value. My warmest thanks are also due to Dr. Edwin Clarke of the Sub-Department of Medical History, University College, London, for his encouragement and helpful suggestions. Finally, I was fortunate in having the expert secretarial assistance of Mrs. J. Bewry of the Wellcome Research Laboratories.

Petts Wood, Kent. H.J.P.

CONTENTS

I

HOW IMMUNIZATION BEGAN

II

DEVELOPMENTS FROM EDWARD JENNER TO PAUL EHRLICH (Circa 1775-1900)

III

ANTISERA AND VACCINES: 1900-20

IV

ACCOMPLISHMENTS—MAINLY SINCE 1920: MORE AND BETTER BACTERIAL VACCINES

V

ACCOMPLISHMENTS—MAINLY SINCE 1920 (*Continued*): THE GROWTH OF VIROLOGY

VI

MISCELLANEOUS

VII

THE PRINCIPLES OF IMMUNIZATION

IMMUNIZATION is the process of conferring increased resistance to infection. When disease germs enter the body, say, through a scratch, special defensive cells or *phagocytes* from the blood may be rushed to the spot, where they may surround, engulf and destroy the invaders. (Some kinds of micro-organism are more readily disposed of by this means than are others.) However, besides this local and relatively simple type of conflict, there is a more subtle warfare of chemical products in the blood-stream. This combat in its varied aspects is of great importance from the medical standpoint, and has been the main consideration of this book.

So far as the body is concerned, the micro-organisms of disease are foreign substances and are treated as such. In this process some of their components or products of their activity (which may or may not be poisons known as toxins) pass into the blood and act as *antigens*. Certain of the blood cells react by acquiring the new skill of producing or manufacturing their own special antidotes or *antibodies*—part of the immune response of the body. For example, one characteristic form of antidote called diphtheria antitoxin (from any source, human or animal) is able to withstand the poisonous assault of the diphtheria bacillus—it robs the toxin of its sting, thus preventing damage to vital centres. However, it is specific in its action and is no good against tetanus toxin for which a tetanus antitoxin has to be manufactured by an essentially similar process.

The business of antibody formation, in which the body itself is trained to produce its own protection, is *active immunization*. It is in many cases a *natural* process, possibly associated with recovery from a clinical illness. However, readers will soon appreciate and understand that it can also be induced *artificially* for many diseases, and that the aim of immunologists is to bring this about by safe means (vaccines), with a minimum of inconvenience to the patient. Immunity against attack is obtained without the danger of leaving it all to nature.

There is also *passive immunization,* in which an immune serum (or antiserum) containing antibodies obtained from another individual (human being or animal) is given in order to confer protection—usually as early as possible in a medical emergency. Irreversible damage may then be prevented and recovery promoted. The antibodies may be antitoxic (as in diphtheria or tetanus), antibacterial (as in typhoid, although suitable drugs or chemotherapy has now replaced antisera in this group), or antiviral (as in rabies or smallpox).

Active immunity takes some time to develop, and is long-lasting: although it may wane with time, it is lost even more slowly than it is acquired, and it is capable of rapid restoration. *Passive immunity* is rapid in onset and is of short duration—at the most, a few weeks. It may be transferred from mother to offspring. In passive immunization the body of the recipient is not conditioned to the mechanism of production of antibody, and the 'foreign' antibody is thrown out without replacement.

The term *vaccine* is used frequently in this book. Its original scope was material employed by an Englishman, Edward Jenner, to infect a person with the viral disease known as cowpox or vaccinia (Latin *vacca,* a cow). The antigens present in the inoculum give rise to neutralizing antibodies, which are effective against both the minor infection, cowpox, and the major allied one, smallpox. Louis Pasteur broadened the scope of the term by first calling the modified anthrax cultures used to produce immunity 'vaccines', as a tribute to Jenner. Later, suspensions of many other microorganisms or of tissues infected with micro-organisms (e.g. rabies virus) were all referred to as vaccines. Finally, in 1958, there was a further extension of the scope of vaccines to include *toxins* and *toxoids* (see p. 63). According to the new, comprehensive definition, vaccines are preparations of *any* antigen which induces a specific active immunity to the corresponding infecting agent.

PROTECTION AND PREVENTION

The principles of artificial immunization, both active and passive, can be put very simply as follows:

Protection with an efficient vaccine ensures that the person has antibody in his blood and is forearmed against infection. His tissues have been trained to produce antibody more quickly and in larger amounts than is possible with untrained cells; in fact his body cells behave towards the vaccine (whether organisms, toxin or toxoid) like the yokel who said—'Here's a foreigner, let's heave a brick at him'. A child who has not been immunized actively with, say, diphtheria toxoid, may contract the disease and require urgent treatment passively with antitoxin made in the horse. On the other hand, an immunized person will usually remain well, or may suffer from a modified illness, when exposed to attack. He is much better equipped to meet the menace of the invading micro-organisms, as he is likely to have in his circulation sufficient antibody, made in his own personal 'factory'. In the case of diphtheria, once toxin is dealt with by antitoxin, whether of horse or human origin, safety is assured since the attacking force is disarmed.

Infectious diseases can now be largely prevented by immunization—and prevention is safe, usually painless, cheap and extremely effective. In the words which King Edward VII applied to consumption, 'If preventable, why is it not prevented?' The fundamentals are quite clear, but the subject is vast and complex and our knowledge is still incomplete. Against diseases like diphtheria a high degree of active immunity can be induced by toxoids or their derivatives, and useful protection provided by antitoxic sera. Against other bacterial diseases it may be possible to obtain active immunity by killed or living attenuated (weakened) bacterial vaccines, although, for treatment, antibiotics and other chemicals have largely replaced antibacterial sera. Against a number of viral infections, a high degree of active protection, which is longlasting, can now be induced by means of either killed (inactivated) or, more generally, living attenuated viral vaccines. These preparations have nearly ousted antiviral sera, which give only temporary passive immunity.

The reader should return to this Introduction with better understanding after he has become familiar with other sections of this book.

I

HOW IMMUNIZATION BEGAN

CHAPTER 1

DISEASE AND IMMUNIZATION IN THE PRE-SCIENTIFIC AGE

VIEWS ON CAUSATION OF DISEASE

FROM the beginnings of time, primitive tribes have ascribed disease to malign supernatural forces or spirits which had to be warded off, placated or overcome—the demonic theory. Secondly, the Old Testament illustrates the development of the religious standpoint, whereby suffering was believed to be a manifestation of divine wrath and a just punishment for sin: nevertheless the earlier demonic view also persisted, for we read in the New Testament that Christ cast out devils. A third belief of great antiquity, and even today a popular cult in some quarters, is that man's welfare is centred round the heavenly bodies. Only three centuries ago horoscopes based on their movement were cast by astrologers to select 'critical days' for purgation and bleeding. It may be noted that a surprising regard for magical influences of various kinds is still present in the modern scientific era.

About the fifth century B.C., there was a revolution of thought in Greece: a universe of natural law replaced one of supernatural control. Hippocrates, the most celebrated physician of antiquity and a leader of Greek medicine, played an important rôle in this movement. He is universally known for the Hippocratic oath, a code of conduct to which doctors have long subscribed, and for at least the first of his *Aphorisms*, prized in classical and mediaeval times: it runs, 'Life is short, and Art (of medicine) is long; the occasion fleeting, experience deceitful, and judgment difficult'. Diseases were attributed, not to magical and metaphysical influences, but to disturbances of bodily 'humours' caused by climatic and atmospheric changes. Details of his conclusions were often wrong and are unimportant: the main contribution of his teachings was to establish the scientific principle of deduction from observation and experiment.

Next to Hippocrates as a physician of renown in ancient times came Galen, of Pergamum and Rome, who lived in the second century A.D. His writings on medical and philosophical subjects furthered the evolution of epidemiology: atmospheric changes, individual predisposition or susceptibility and, to a less extent, contagion all played a part. This conception of contagion was only vaguely appreciated until the time of the Frenchman, Louis Pasteur, in the nineteenth century. In essence it assumed the existence of a living contagium which explained the transmission of infectious disease. It was responsible for the leper laws. Notwithstanding the discovery of bacteria and protozoa by the Dutch microscopist, Leeuwenhoek, in the seventeenth century, the 'seeds' of contagion were long regarded as chemical gases rather than biological substances. Diffusion of these gaseous vapours was held to explain dissemination from person to person.

The discoveries of Louis Pasteur, and the German, Robert Koch, laid the foundations of the modern science of bacteriology or microbiology and are discussed in later chapters. The prevention and treatment of microbic diseases by immunization were a further development, which has led to results of tremendous benefit to mankind.

Early History of Immunization

Immunization seems to have been practised in crude form in antiquity. King Mithridates of Pontus in the first century B.C. is said to have protected himself against poisons by drinking the blood of ducks that had been given them in sub-lethal doses, presumably as a means of increasing their resistance. About one century later, the Roman Pliny the Elder recommended the livers of mad dogs as a remedy for rabies: this treatment is strangely suggestive of the protective vaccination to which Pasteur gave his name (see p. 25). To give a third example of primitive practices, many tribes in Africa have developed something akin to immunization against snake venoms and other poisons.

However, by far the oldest form of the artificial induction of immunity is *variolation*, the term given to inoculation with the virus from mild cases of variola or smallpox: the inoculated person developed smallpox often, but not invariably, in mild form and was subsequently immune or protected against even major attacks. This disease is mentioned in sacred Sanskrit writings, from which it would appear to have existed in China and India for thousands of years before it was observed in Syria around A.D. 300. There is some evidence that it may have occurred in Egypt much earlier: the mummified head of Rameses V indicated that he may have been the victim of smallpox (1160 B.C.). Be that as it may, from the third century A.D. onwards the spread of smallpox followed the movement of armies and of populations. The crusaders in the tenth and eleventh centuries and the American colonists, including their Negro slaves from Africa, were all responsible for outbreaks. Many millions of persons have died from smallpox in every continent, and whole tribes of Indians in the New World have been exterminated by it.

Variolation or Inoculating the Smallpox.—The procedure of protective inoculation probably goes back nearly as far as smallpox itself, although it was not actually recorded till about A.D. 590 by the Chinese. Variolation was practised also in India in ancient times. In China smallpox was communicated artificially by blowing into the nose through a tube dried crusts or scabs which had fallen from various pustules: this was referred to as 'sowing the smallpox' on a 'lucky day'. An alternative technique was the nasal implantation of the dried crusts on a pledget of rolled cotton. In India Brahman priests inoculated, into parallel scratches in the skin, cotton pledgets infected with smallpox matter and then stored for a year. Unlike the nasal route, the skin wounds or scratches were an unnatural portal of entry for the infection. For this reason, possibly helped by ripening of the inoculum during long storage, the resulting attack tended to be much milder than when contracted naturally. Religious and folk-lore ceremonial, including worship of a smallpox goddess and sprinkling of the variolation site with water from the sacred River Ganges, was long believed to be an essential contribution to a successful outcome. Skin inoculation was also the method carried out for the most part in ancient Persia, although in that country the ingestion or swallowing of prepared scabs is recorded as an alternative. Finally, in India and elsewhere children were sometimes wrapped in the clothing of smallpox patients!

After these beginnings in eastern countries various forms of variolation, like smallpox itself naturally spread westwards into Europe, Africa and later America. As the practice was introduced into Britain from Turkey, certain details taken from the correspondence of Lady Mary Wortley Montagu, wife of the British Ambassador at Constantinople, are both interesting and relevant. In 1717, she wrote to friends in this country: 'The smallpox, so fatal and so general amongst us, is here entirely harmless by the invention of *ingrafting*, which is the term they give it. There is a set of old women who make it their business to perform the operation every autumn. . . . People send to one another to know if any of their family has a mind to have the smallpox; they make parties for this purpose, and when they are met (commonly fifteen or sixteen together), the old woman comes with a nutshell full of the matter of the best sort of smallpox . . . and a large needle (which gives you no more pain than a common scratch). . . . The French Ambassador says pleasantly, that they take the smallpox here by way of diversion, as they take the waters in other countries.'

Notwithstanding Lady Mary's claim, the practice of variolation was anything but safe. As already mentioned, the aim was to obtain protection against severe smallpox by deliberately trying to induce a mild attack. In practice, however, the good intentions miscarried: persons inoculated with supposedly mild smallpox sometimes became seriously ill and possibly 2 to 3 per cent. died. Of course, this was a ten-fold improvement on the 20 or 30 per cent. mortality of naturally-occurring smallpox. It was such a rife and dread disease that people were prepared to accept voluntarily a procedure which was far from devoid of risk to those who were inoculated. Another drawback of variolation was the chance of spread of the smallpox to contacts: isolation of artificially infected persons was often overlooked altogether or, if attempted, was incomplete. Moreover, the virulence of the infection might be enhanced on further spread, and the ravages of the disease in the community thus increased. In retrospect, with all its defects variolation was certainly worth while, but only until something better—Jennerian vaccination (see p. 14)—was available to replace it.

It has been said that the main objective of variolation by the women of Constantinople was the base, commercial one of putting up the market value of female circassian slaves for harems: variolated girls who had few or no blemishes after mild attacks fetched high prices, and were a better buy than either badly marked slaves or those who had not been protected and might still suffer a severe attack.

However, Lady Mary had entirely worthy motives for her brother had died of smallpox and she herself had had the disease mildly. She had her son variolated by a Greek female inoculator under the supervision of Charles Maitland, surgeon to the embassy. On her return to England in 1721, she also submitted her daughter to inoculation.

Lady Mary had established a friendship with Caroline, Princess of Wales, through whom she was able to arouse the interest of George I. Sir Hans Sloane, in collaboration with Maitland, induced six condemned criminals at Newgate Prison to submit to the risk of the operation on condition that they would go free if they survived. When subsequently exposed to natural smallpox, they showed themselves immune. Their freedom was deserved. In another successful experiment the 'guinea-pigs' were six orphan children. King George I was then persuaded in 1722 to permit the inoculation in the Turkish fashion of two of his grandchildren. Once again there were no untoward effects. The practice was extended to other members of the royal family, and subsequently to the court and the whole country. Inoculation centres were set up for the purpose. Understandably opposition increased when some variolated persons died, or when the disease spread to contacts, but the consensus of opinion was that the hazards had to be accepted until a more dependable method could be found. In 1754 variolation was commended by the Royal College of Physicians of London.

Although Lady Montagu deserves full credit for her efforts in popularizing variolation in Britain from 1721 onwards, she was antedated: lay persons in the Scottish Highlands and in Wales performed a process of inoculation before the end of the seventeenth century. A letter by a Greek physician, Timoni, drawing attention to the method used in Turkey, was also sent to the Royal Society in 1714. The contents of an early vesicle before it had become pustular were recommended for the inoculations in order to produce a mild attack.

The introduction of variolation into the American continent

is another story of unusual interest. From the beginning of the eighteenth century there were repeated reports from immigrant Negro slaves about a process which gave 'something of the small-pox and would forever preserve from it'. The Reverend Cotton Mather acquired one of these variolated slaves as a present from some of his congregation, and he also read the publications of Timoni, the Greek who practised in Constantinople. In consequence, he began his advocacy of inoculation, in which he was joined by a physician, Zabdiel Boylston of Boston, in 1721. It should be appreciated that in those early days many American (and British) clergymen included healing in their pastoral activities.

Boylston began by variolating his teen-age son and two servants, and then used the method in his practice. Inevitably, some deaths resulted and were publicized. Thereafter, both Mather and Boylston encountered much opposition from some doctors and clergy, although others gave them encouraging support. In 1724, Boylston visited England and presented a pamphlet in which he reported that six deaths occurred among 286 persons inoculated in Boston (1 in 47).

In America, as in England, variolation continued to have a mixed reception till the nineteenth century when the much safer vaccination (the transfer of cowpox or vaccinia) began to take its place. This development is described in the next chapter.

For generations historians have been concerned with wars and politics, often to the exclusion of the rôle of pestilences in influencing the fate of nations and even civilization itself. Typhus fever contributed to Napoleon's failure in the Russian campaign of 1812, and smallpox may have preserved Canada for the British Empire. In 1766, General George Washington tried to take Quebec with an American colonial force 50 per cent. below strength on account of the prevalence of smallpox amongst his unprotected men. The British defenders were well variolated and fighting fit, and held out till the arrival of reinforcements. Belatedly, in 1776, Washington ordered variolation for his entire army, by which time the British had established their control of Canada. Subsequently, variolation had a considerable boost in the American colonies, Benjamin Franklin being one of its strongest advocates.

In many countries of Europe, variolation was established more slowly. It was made legal in France in 1755, when it was also being done in the Netherlands, Sweden, Denmark and Germany. In the latter country, there was more consistent opposition than elsewhere, and the method made little headway. It was not practised in Spain until about 1770.

II

DEVELOPMENTS FROM EDWARD JENNER TO PAUL EHRLICH

(Circa 1775-1900)

CHAPTER 2

EDWARD JENNER AND THE DAWN OF SCIENTIFIC ENQUIRY

VACCINATION or Inoculating the Cowpox.—Variolation was expensive, time-consuming, risky and rather ineffective. Something better was required for the control of smallpox. The new development was Jennerian vaccination, the material inoculated being taken from cowpox or vaccinia, a related, pustular infection of the udders of cows. The mild local disease which resulted from this inoculation conferred immunity against smallpox, as well as vaccinia, because the viruses of the two diseases are closely related.

In 1774 there was a severe outbreak of smallpox in the Dorset village of Yetminster, about twelve miles north-west of Dorchester. Variolation was introduced to combat it. However, Benjamin Jesty, a prosperous local farmer and cattle breeder, knew of the general belief among farmers in certain country districts that an attack of natural cowpox afforded similar protection to that obtained by variolation itself. If proof were needed, two of his servants had caught cowpox on their hands through milking cows with infected udders and had subsequently nursed their relatives with smallpox without catching that terrifying fever. Jesty was not afraid of contracting smallpox himself because he too had had cowpox in his youth. However, he was concerned about the safety of his wife, Elizabeth, and their two sons, respectively two and three years old, who had no such protection. Fortunately, some of a neighbour's cows had vaccinia, and Jesty scratched the forearm of his wife and the upper arms of his children with a 'stocking needle' and inserted the cowpox virus from the sores on the animals' udders. There were very good 'takes' in all three cases, and Mrs. Jesty had sufficient fever to need medical attention. Soon she recovered. The neighbours thereupon reproached Jesty for his inhumanity and cruelty in experimenting on members of his family. Notwithstanding the scandal, the experiment was completely successful, for the Jestys were, both then and subsequently, repeatedly exposed to smallpox, without taking the disease. Further, Surgeon Trowbridge of Cerne inoculated the two sons with smallpox fifteen years later, presumably to prove the efficiency of vaccination after this long interval: their immunity had persisted.

On the continent of Europe, there is an account of an experiment on similar lines. In 1791, a Holsteiner named Peter Plett had seen a doctor perform variolation and thought a similar technique might be used for vaccination. He was tutor to a family at Schönwaide, where the milkmaids had discovered that cowpox protected against smallpox. Plett, like Jesty, did three vaccinations. He made incisions with a pocket knife on the backs of the hands of his employer's children and inoculated cowpox from udders. This crude method was entirely satisfactory. Three years later there was an epidemic of smallpox in the neighbourhood, and these children were unique in escaping infection.

Although Jesty and Plett in their respective countries made useful contributions to the history of vaccination, they were not, as has sometimes been claimed, the only pioneers of the inoculation of cowpox as a prophylactic against smallpox. A number of other people had apparently practised it from 1500 B.C. onwards. The Vaccine Pock Institution in London may have eventually recognized Jesty as the 'original vaccine inoculator', but this distinction was unjustified.

THE CONTRIBUTIONS OF EDWARD JENNER

Edward Jenner of Berkeley, Gloucestershire, made a further advance by transferring cowpox in series indefinitely through a number of individuals and thus made communal vaccination practicable. His experiments were conducted some twenty years after Jesty, but he too has been erroneously hailed as the 'inventor' or 'discoverer' of vaccination.

The genius of Jenner must be discussed in greater detail. His contributions were two-fold, and indicate the scientific approach to immunization. In the first place, he deliberately tested and proved the validity of the traditional lore of medical, veterinary and lay persons in Gloucestershire that cowpox, which he regarded as cow smallpox, protected against human smallpox. Secondly, and of much greater importance, were his experiments on the artificial transmission of cowpox, not from cow to human, but from one person to another—a method of prophylaxis which was independent of the existence of the natural disease among the cows in the neighbourhood.

This was a conspicuous achievement for what was in effect a unique research project in general practice. Apparently it all arose out of the assertion of a milkmaid in Gloucestershire: 'I shall never have smallpox for I have had cowpox. I shall never have an ugly pockmarked face.' It is well known to scientists that major discoveries often result from such small beginnings— possibly a chance observation, which is followed through logically step by step by someone with an enquiring and receptive mind.

The Advice of John Hunter.—Jenner was a personal friend and pupil of John Hunter, the great surgeon of St. George's Hospital, London, who was an early experimenter on the causation and differentiation of various diseases. The Hunterian Museum of the Royal College of Surgeons bears his name. Hunter was a source of inspiration and advice to Jenner in his work. Both men were also naturalists and contrived to keep in touch concerning problems of mutual interest. Jenner learned from Hunter the nature and value of experiment. On one occasion, Hunter gave his younger friend the famous words of advice: 'Why think—why not try the experiment?' Jenner awaited his opportunity and patiently collected evidence for some years on the alleged protection apparently afforded by cowpox against smallpox.

It has caused surprise that cowpox was known to very few medical men at this time. The explanation is that only certain country folk were in contact with cows, and that the infection occurred only in some counties and at intervals. Jenner had little opportunity for discussion with other clinicians. However, he did not forget Hunter's precept, and, many years later, in 1796, he made his first experiment with human-to-human vaccination.

Jenner's Experiments.—A healthy eight-year-old boy, James Phipps, was inoculated on the arm with material from a typical cowpox sore on the hand of a milkmaid, Sarah Nelmes. A sore developed at the site of inoculation, but there was little general evidence of disease. About six weeks later and again several months later, the boy was inoculated with smallpox material without the development of any reaction. The mild cowpox sore had protected him from smallpox. A further ten experiments on persons who had contracted cowpox previously confirmed that Phipps's immunity was not a chance observation, and that cowpox almost invariably conferred resistance to smallpox material. Jenner then began his second series of experiments, cowpox being transferred, in series, arm-to-arm from the person primarily vaccinated. These vaccinated persons were later inoculated with smallpox without effect.

Publication and Early Troubles and Successes.—Strange to relate, Jenner's paper giving the results and conclusions of this investigation was refused by the Royal Society on the basis of 'lack of adequate proof'. He then published (at his own expense) in 1798, his book of 75 pages entitled *An Inquiry into the Causes and Effects of the Variolae Vaccinae, a disease discovered in some of the Western Counties of England, particularly Gloucestershire, and known by the name of Cow Pox.* Thus began an agitation to substitute vaccination for variolation.

This treatise, which disseminated widely Jenner's views, had a somewhat mixed reception. Certain leading doctors in London, including George Pearson of St. George's Hospital, soon confirmed his findings. However, trouble arose when William Woodville, physician to the Hospital for Smallpox and for Inoculation, found that over half his patients developed local and general reactions closely allied to those of variolation. The explanation he accepted later was that the cowpox vaccine had been contaminated with smallpox, which had caused many generalized eruptions. In these early days, apart from contamination arising from the errors in diagnosis of cases, the same lancet might be used for both variolation and vaccination—faulty technique which was also likely to give rise to trouble!

As the popularity of vaccination increased, it was customary to hold special sessions for the purpose weekly in London and less frequently in country districts. In addition to direct transfer of material (lymph) from person to person, stocks of lymph were kept at those clinics for short periods on ivory points or on squares of glass. Sometimes the dried lymph on the glass was covered with a thin coat of mucilage of gum arabic, in order to preserve it better.

In the early years, Jenner and vaccination were subjected to crude criticism and caricatures from certain unbalanced persons. Some ignorant people actually believed that the transference of material of animal origin to man had a debasing influence on the recipient. A favourite line among cartoonists was to represent the vaccinated as being transformed into cows. Of course, some physicians were genuinely sceptical, whereas others appear to have been influenced by their vested interests in variolation. The clergy's attitude was rather mixed; many still regarded smallpox as an act of God, the practice of vaccination therefore being sacrilegious. A surgeon named John Birch, whom some might claim to be ahead of his times, cynically objected to vaccination because it reduced most effectively the incidence of smallpox, 'an important method of decreasing the population, particularly in large and poor families'.

In 1802, Jenner was voted a parliamentary grant of £10,000 as a token of the nation's gratitude. It seems odd that payment was postponed for two years, when nearly £1,000 was deducted for taxes and fees! In 1807, a further grant of £20,000 followed. To-day, he would surely have been given at least a knighthood. He received honorary degrees at home and abroad, and learned societies elected him to membership. The Royal Jennerian Institute, which was founded in 1803 to provide further supplies of vaccine lymph, made him its first president.

Jenner died in 1823 at the age of 74. Although vaccination, with all its defects, was flourishing at the time of his death, the much more dangerous practice of variolation was not made illegal in this country till 1840. The delay has been ascribed to official inertia, but a period of seventeen or more years is surely excessive!

The Spread of Vaccination Overseas.—Two years after the publication of Jenner's *Inquiry*, Dr. Benjamin Waterhouse, Professor of Physic at the new medical school at Harvard, U.S.A. read a copy and sent to England for a supply of vaccine. He vaccinated his five-year-old son, Daniel, and six domestic servants in his house-hold. Later, some of those vaccinated were sent to the smallpox hospital, where they were inoculated with smallpox vaccine (vario-lated) and shown to be resistant. Waterhouse became enthusiastic and determined to spread vaccination all over the United States. President John Adams was approached but refused his support. However, Thomas Jefferson, who was then a candidate for the Presidency, praised Waterhouse and offered every assistance. He encouraged vaccination in his home and amongst his neighbours, and then throughout Virginia and other states. He is said to have performed many vaccinations himself. An interesting episode is the introduction of vaccination amongst the Indians—'the last of the Mohicans in their prairie homes'. Chief Little Turtle and several of his warriors were inoculated while on a visit to Washing-ton, D.C., after Jefferson had explained that 'the Great Spirit had made a gift to the white men in showing them how to preserve themselves from the smallpox'.

Sir William Osler, the famous physician and medical historian, who occupied chairs in Montreal, Philadelphia, Johns Hopkins (Baltimore) and finally Oxford, relates that

'in Boston, on August 16 1802, 19 boys were inoculated with the cow-pox. On November 9 12 of them were inoculated with smallpox; nothing followed. A control experiment was made by inoculating two unvaccinated boys with the same smallpox virus. Both took the disease. The 19 children of August 16 were again unsuccessfully inoculated with fresh virus from these two boys. This is one of the most crucial experiments in the history of vaccination, and fully justified the con-clusion of the Board of Health—*cowpox is a complete security against the smallpox*'.

Although Waterhouse has rightly been called the 'Jenner of the New World', he made personal enemies and was dismissed from his post at Harvard in 1812. He kept up his crusade for more vaccination, and his friendship with Jenner, with whom he cor-responded although they had never met. President Jefferson appointed him as Federal Vaccine Agent in the National Vaccine Institute of the U.S.A.

In addition to the U.S.A., other countries were quick to benefit from vaccination. In France, after a few years Napoleon had his troops vaccinated with 'le vaccin jennérien' if they had not already had smallpox. He honoured Jenner and is reported to have remarked that he could refuse him nothing. In Russia, the first child to be vaccinated was given the name of Vaccinof and a life pension by command of the dowager empress. Jenner's system was made compulsory for a time, and a million and a quarter people were vaccinated in 1812, the year in which Napoleon retreated from Moscow: it was estimated that 160,000 lives had been saved. Nevertheless, there was considerable agitation from Russian extremists, and compulsory vaccination was not continued. Other countries, including Bavaria and Denmark, also made vaccination compulsory within a few years of its introduction, and in Sweden, even without compulsion, smallpox virtually disappeared for a time.

Few men have saved more lives than Edward Jenner, exceptions being Louis Pasteur and Alexander Fleming. In a letter, President Jefferson of the U.S.A. paid to him the following tribute: 'Future nations will know by history only that the loathsome smallpox has existed and by you has been extirpated.'

In conclusion, John Hunter, Jenner's famous teacher, gave an interesting description of immunity: 'The body, once affected by some stimuli, never forgets, as it were their action, and thereby is never again affected by that poison, as in the smallpox, measles, etc.'

CHAPTER 3

THE RISE OF BACTERIOLOGY AND PASTEUR'S ATTENUATED VACCINES

JENNER knew nothing about microbes or germs, and he did not understand the modes of action of vaccination as a preventive against smallpox. All the early work on immunization was in fact empiric. The introduction of scientific immunization was brought about by the French School, under the organic chemist, Louis Pasteur, who was neither a doctor nor a veterinary surgeon but selected and inspired devoted colleagues with the professional background he lacked: through his interest in the mechanism for the production of disease, and the recovery therefrom, he became the founder of modern immunology. This science deals with the microbial cause of human or animal infection, how the infected subject reacts to the presence of the organism in the body, how cure takes place, and how prevention of a recurrence or of spread to other individuals can be obtained.

Pasteur's research was made possible by the work of Robert Koch and the German School, whose far-reaching improvements in technique led to the discovery and study of the causal microbes of a number of infectious diseases—the science of bacteriology.

STAINING AND CULTURING BACTERIA

Reference has already been made to the microscopist Leeuwenhoek's demonstration of microbes in the seventeenth century. Living or but recently dead bacteria were observed, unstained, in suspension in the fluid in which they had developed. Staining of bacteria was not introduced till about 1870, but they were still suspended in fluid for observation. A few years later, Koch discovered that films of organisms could be made on glass slides or cover glasses and dried and fixed with heat. This was a major advance, which facilitated accurate microscopic observation of stained bacteria, an essential preliminary to their identification. Koch also introduced improvements in culture media—the food-stuffs used for obtaining cultures of bacteria. Lastly, the new media permitted the isolation of *pure* cultures of given strains for further study.

Koch's genius is well illustrated by reference to *anthrax*, an acute disease of animals, especially sheep and cattle. It also occurs in man in different forms. Strict measures of control are in force in many countries. In 1876, Koch demonstrated the anthrax bacillus and the germination of its spores (forms resistant to adverse conditions, such as heat, dryness, chemical substances and absence of food). While others had grown this organism along with other microbes in mixed culture, Koch obtained *pure* cultures and transmitted anthrax to mice and other laboratory animals. This was the first time a germ was definitely proved to be the cause of an infectious disease. Bacteriology has existed for no more than a long human lifetime.

IMMUNIZATION WITH ATTENUATED CULTURES

Fowl Cholera.—Pasteur, who was already well known for his work on fermentation and the germ theory of disease, then turned his attention to the problem of immunization against fowl cholera, a malady which was a serious menace to the fowl population of France. Cultures of freshly isolated causal bacilli were demonstrated to be very fatal to chickens, but old cultures (used after Pasteur had been on vacation for two weeks) failed to produce the typical disease and a large number of birds recovered. The explanation was that the germs had been transformed by having their virulence reduced or attenuated during storage. Perhaps this was an accidental discovery, but Pasteur was able to profit from it: as Claude Bernard pointed out, 'In the field of observation chance favours only the mind which is prepared'. Pasteur's next discovery was also a lucky accident. He wished to inject fully virulent cultures into fresh birds, but there was none available. His laboratory technician then gave him some fowls which had survived a previous injection of attenuated culture. They were resistant to the virulent culture also; after minor illnesses, they all recovered. The explanation was that they had been vaccinated or immunized by the earlier dose. Pasteur published this work in 1880, and the new attenuated type of fowl cholera vaccine was widely used soon afterwards.

Anthrax.—The next research project which engaged Pasteur's energies was immunization against the cattle-killing disease, anthrax. While he had been encouraged by his success with fowl cholera, he was aware that anthrax was altogether more difficult. He knew that the organisms could form resistant spores which would wait possibly for years in a state of suspended animation and eventually prove dangerous. However, H. Toussaint of the Veterinary School at Toulouse was already investigating the use of anthrax-infected blood for preparing a somewhat crude vaccine for sheep: in 1880, he tried exposure to heat and treatment with carbolic acid, among other procedures, for making this vaccine safer and more acceptable. Pasteur noted these methods, which he employed later in his own researches on attenuating (weakening) pure cultures.

In addition to being influenced by Koch, Pasteur knew about Jenner's work on vaccination and was greatly interested in the relationship of cowpox to smallpox, a topic he had heard debated at the French Academy of Medicine. Here was a naturally occurring immunizing agent, already attenuated for use. Pasteur's conception of attenuation as a scientific method of prophylaxis was the outcome of this clue. He asked himself what factors in the environment of organisms led to modifications of this type. Changes in temperature, exposure to oxygen and other physical factors had to be investigated. The final crucial question was whether dangerous organisms which were reduced in virulence by any of these methods, were still capable of vaccinating and producing useful immunity.

Pasteur found that aged cultures of anthrax bacilli were dangerous, and therefore unusable, due to the spore formation he had feared. With his medical and veterinary colleagues, Roux and Chamberland—the latter was a superb bacteriological technician —he eventually discovered that cultures kept at 42°-43°C. for upwards of a week, instead of at the temperature of the human body (37°C.), were reduced in virulence, and also lost the power of producing spores. The attenuation was in direct relationship to the length of time used for growth. Two doses of vaccines thus prepared were used as the course for immunizing susceptible farm animals. The first was a culture of low virulence ('premier vaccin') and the second was a less attenuated culture ('deuxième vaccin'), given 12 days later.

Pasteur was criticized and abused by many members of the veterinary profession, who regarded him as an arrogant chemist and charlatan who had invaded their domain. The Agricultural Society of Melun challenged him to a public demonstration of his power to prevent anthrax, and he boldly accepted the proposition. On May 5 1881, Pasteur, Roux and Chamberland inoculated 24 sheep, one goat and six cows with a living attenuated vaccine, and on May 17 with a less attenuated culture. A further 24 sheep, one goat and four cows were left uninoculated as controls. On May 31 all the vaccinated animals and the controls were challenged with a fully virulent culture of the anthrax bacillus. By June 2 all the control sheep and the control goat were dead and the four control cows very ill, whereas the immunized animals were without symptoms and well. The experiment was completely successful and was given full publicity in the world press, including *The Times*, whose special correspondent was an interested spectator. In his hour of triumph Pasteur did not forget what he owed to his great predecessor, Jenner. He paid him the tribute of calling the anthrax culture used to produce immunity a 'vaccine'. He thus extended the scope of the word, which was originally restricted to material employed to infect a person with cowpox (vaccinia from Latin *vacca*, a cow).

Living attenuated anthrax vaccines proved very effective and within a few years reduced the mortality of French farm animals from 10 per cent. for sheep and 5 per cent. for cattle to approximately 1 and 0.35 per cent. respectively. Although Pasteur had broken fresh ground, Koch, who had become his rival, was sharply critical of his methods for the prophylaxis of anthrax. The vaccines were not always sufficiently attenuated and sometimes caused deaths among the inoculated animals. Sometimes cultures were impure—a defect which aroused the scorn of Koch, a master of bacteriological technique. It is only fair to add that Pasteur himself was not responsible for these faults. Finally, although the figures were impressive, modern statisticians would not wish to follow

24

Pasteur in comparing the mortality of vaccinated animals in one period with that of unvaccinated animals in an earlier period. Information would be sought concerning the numbers of actual exposures to risk of infection in the two periods. Of course, a carefully planned trial involving equal numbers of vaccinated and control animals in the same period and on the same farms would have been a preferable test of efficacy.

Swine Erysipelas.—This disease, which affects mainly pigs and used to cause serious economic losses, now engaged Pasteur's attention. In 1883, he devised protective attenuated vaccines analogous to those for anthrax. Unfortunately, although the results were on the whole good, some deaths occurred amongst vaccinated animals. Later, other workers introduced a variety of prophylactics, living and dead, and some of these have been most successful.

Rabies.—In 1885, four years after his success with anthrax vaccine, Pasteur produced a living attenuated prophylactic for rabies. This was perhaps his greatest achievement, which entailed much patient and persevering research. An interesting fact is that he began the complex project when he was 59 years of age, and crippled as the result of a stroke.

Rabies or hydrophobia is a typical virus disease, which meant that Pasteur was handicapped by the impossibility at that time of either seeing or growing the causative germ. Once more he showed his courage by being undeterred by these difficulties, and by refusing to abandon the hope of finding a preventive vaccine. He seems to have been specially attracted to rabies, which affects mainly dogs but is also one of the most distressing and lethal of human diseases. He had boyhood memories of a mad wolf charging through the Jura and biting men and animals in its path. (We now know that the reservoir and perpetuation of rabies is mostly in biting animals, as the virus is transmitted via the saliva.) A deep impression was also made when he witnessed the painful cauterization of the wounds of one victim at the local smithy: this patient survived. Altogether eight persons died in the vicinity. Whatever the basic stimulus, at 59 Pasteur gladly took up the difficult research project. He first established that the rabies organism, although it was too small to be seen, existed and multiplied in the brain and spinal cord of infected animals. His name for it was *virus,* meaning simply poison. He now sought a method of attenuating this virus so as to have a safe vaccine. He made a long series of experiments, inoculating small portions of infected nerve tissue from one animal into the brain of another. Passage through a series of rabbit brains increased the virulence for rabbits but decreased (attenuated) it markedly for dogs. As the rabbit virulence of the infected cords increased, the incubation period was shortened progressively to six days, at which point it remained stationary. Pasteur's term for this stabilized virus was 'fixed virus' to distinguish it from 'street virus', the name he gave to virus when found naturally in rabid saliva. Fixed virus was the basis for vaccines, but was used for inoculation of dogs only after further attenuation by drying the spinal cords of the infected rabbits. The drying was done slowly in sterile air over a desiccating agent at room temperature, in order (it was said) to 'allow penetration of oxygen to attenuate the virus'. The duration of the period of drying of the fixed virus determined the degree of attenuation. Rabbit spinal cord dried for 14 days was non-infective and could be used as the first dose of a course. Further daily doses would consist of cord which had been dried for progressively shorter periods—13 days, 12 days and so on. The final dose, the fourteenth, would be fully virulent fresh cord.

So much for Pasteur's rather complicated method of preparation of rabies vaccine! With regard to his experiments on immunization, he obtained promising results by saving the lives of dogs which had been bitten by rabid animals, and had then been immunized with a whole series of injections of the vaccine during the long incubation period in this species—generally a month or more after the bite. In 1884, he announced this successful vaccination of dogs.

In 1885, Pasteur was suddenly faced with the ethical problem of attempting the same type of lengthy immunization of a human being. A boy aged nine years, Joseph Meister, was brought from Alsace for treatment. He was suffering from 14 bites from a rabid dog on hands, legs and thighs, and, without the new treatment, was regarded as certain to die painfully and slowly. With the collaboration of the doctor, Jacques Grancher, a full course of attenuated rabbit-cord vaccine was given. The boy did not develop rabies, in all probability (but not with absolute certainty) on account of the new treatment. He went home to Alsace, but years later he was proud to become the gate-porter at the Pasteur Institute, Paris. Alas, in 1940, he committed suicide, because he did not wish German invading troops to have access to the crypt at the Institute in which Pasteur is buried.

The second famous case treated by Pasteur was Jean Baptiste Jupille, aged 14 years, a shepherd boy from Villers-Farlay in the Jura Mountains. He was with five other boys when a rabid dog sprung among them. In a desperate struggle with the animal to protect the others, Jean eventually wound his whip around its jaws to muzzle it, felled it with his sabot and killed it; he was badly scratched and bitten in the fight, and was later awarded a prize for his bravery. Six days after the incident, a course of vaccine was begun in Paris. Once again Pasteur had a complete success. Later, a commemorative statue to Jupille was erected in the courtyard of the Pasteur Institute.

Towards the end of 1885, Pasteur had his first failure. A little girl, Louise Pelletier, developed symptoms of rabies eleven days after the completion of a course of vaccine, and subsequently died. However, it would have been surprising if she had lived, for she had been bitten on the head by a mountain dog, and 37 days had elapsed before she was brought for treatment. The delay was too long.

In 1888, an official English Commission expressed confidence in the value of Pasteur's work, although attention was drawn to the difficulty of evaluating either the prevalence of rabies or the severity of the cases. However, Pasteur was disappointed that the Commission's only recommendation was that police regulations on dogs should be tightened up. In consequence, imported dogs have been quarantined and kept under observation for six months, and the disease has been virtually wiped out. Specific preventive measures with vaccine have been unnecessary for animals in Britain. (As might be expected, there have been cases of persons developing symptoms after reaching this country from an endemic area where they have been infected.)

The mortality from rabies in persons receiving Pasteur's prophylactic treatment is considerably less than 1 per cent., compared with a mortality of 15 to 20 per cent. of those who are bitten but untreated. These are average figures from a number of sources in France and elsewhere. Unfortunately no treatment is effective once the symptoms of rabies become apparent.

Pasteur's method was in great demand, and bitten persons from many countries flocked to Paris for life-saving inoculations. Nevertheless, as there were some failures, he was much abused and even accused of homicide by his opponents. His health suffered under the strain, and he had two further strokes in 1887. He died in 1895.

It is impossible to assess too highly Pasteur's contributions to humanity. His achievements were commemorated in his life-time by the inauguration in 1888 of the Pasteur Institute in Paris, in which the application of his work and ideals continues.

CHAPTER 4

KOCH AND IMMUNIZATION AGAINST TUBERCULOSIS

BACTERIA AS CAUSES OF DISEASE

THANKS to Robert Koch's improvements in the technique of cultivating and staining bacteria, far-reaching discoveries were made in 1876 in establishing the anthrax bacillus as the cause of anthrax. Thereafter, Pasteur devised attenuated vaccines for the prevention of this, and certain other, infectious diseases, as described in the last chapter.

The measure of Koch's greatness as a bacteriologist is shown by the list given below of the main bacteriological discoveries, bearing on the relation of bacteria to human and animal diseases, made in the last twenty years or so of the nineteenth century. The discoverers were very often German assistants inspired by the master, Koch, himself. Some of the pioneers from other countries were for a time his pupils or associates.

1879	Gonococcus	—	Neisser
1880	Typhoid bacillus	—	Eberth
1881	Staphylococcus	—	Ogston
1882	Tubercle bacillus	—	Koch
	Glanders bacillus	—	Loeffler and Schütz
1883	Cholera vibrio	—	Koch
1883-84	Diphtheria bacillus	—	Klebs and Loeffler
1884	Tetanus bacillus	—	Nicolaier
1886	Pneumococcus	—	Fraenkel
1887	Meningococcus	—	Weichselbaum
	Micrococcus of Malta Fever	—	Bruce
1888	Bacillus enteritidis	—	Gaertner
1892	Clostridium welchii	—	Welch and Nuttall
1894	Plague bacillus	—	Kitasato and Yersin
1896	Clostridium botulinum	—	Van Ermengem
1898	Bacillus dysenteriae	—	Shiga

Of these, the tubercle bacillus is difficult to stain and to cultivate, and it is rather astonishing that it is high up on this list. However, tuberculosis was such a prevalent and lethal disease that it would have been a high priority for any scheme of research. Since ancient times it has killed human beings and also animals by the million. Hippocrates described it as a pestilential disease, 'the most difficult to cure and the most fatal', and John Bunyan aptly called it 'Captain of the Men of Death'. The thoroughness and technical skill of Koch led to the discovery of the causal agent, the tubercle bacillus, in 1882. This achievement definitely established the infectiousness of tuberculosis, and was the peak of his brilliant career.

German research workers under Koch were characteristically concerned with the painstaking discovery and cataloguing of the infective agents of various diseases. In the meantime, the French continued Pasteur's own special investigations into problems of immunity and immunization. It is pointless and unhelpful to discuss whether Koch or Pasteur was the greater genius. Not surprisingly, there was intense national rivalry between the schools, which continued for decades.

TUBERCULIN

Alas, Koch was disillusioned on one occasion when he departed from his work on the classification of bacteria and attempted the control of tuberculosis by immunization. In view of the discovery of the tubercle bacillus, the early development of a vaccine or similar preparation, which would be of immense benefit to mankind, seemed possible. Koch and his assistants made important advances, but the results obtained in the next few years came far short of expectations.

When the tubercle bacillus or its products are injected into tuberculous animals, inflammation or even ulceration is observed, primarily at the site of injection—the 'Koch phenomenon'. As pointed out by Koch, this response could be a mechanism for clearing the area of the invading bacteria—a defensive or immune reaction. (The word 'immune' is derived from a Latin one which signifies freedom or exemption in the military sense.) Animals which have not been previously infected with tuberculosis are insensitive. There was thus a striking difference in their responses between infected animals which gave exaggerated responses—they were said to have developed *allergy* or delayed hypersensitivity— and so-called 'normal' animals which gave no reaction at all.

This difference was the basis or clue for much further research directed towards the cure of tuberculosis, human and animal, by immunization. In 1890-91, Koch claimed that such a cure had been found. Although the formula of the material he introduced, called *tuberculin*, was not disclosed at first, he indicated subsequently that it was a glycerinated extract of the soluble products of the tubercle bacillus. At the outset, he intimated his belief that tuber-culin might prove a remedy for certain *early* cases of tuberculosis. This was a guarded statement, but, in view of Koch's fame and popularity, the excitement and expectation it caused were exces-sive. There was a rush of hopeless cases to Berlin, a complete breakdown of organization and services, and of course unnecessary suffering and tragedy. A disastrous rebound followed, and Koch was subjected to misrepresentation and abuse. It was unfair, for Koch had been cautious in his preliminary announcement, while recognizing that more preliminary trials would have been prefer-able before publication. However, Kaiser Wilhelm II urged and obtained immediate action for the glory of the Fatherland: Ger-many must not be outdone by France!

The original or old tuberculin (O.T.) was followed by a wide variety of other products made from tubercle bacilli. These dif-fered in source and method of extraction, but they all contained break-down products of the bacillary bodies themselves. By 1927, certain American authorities estimated that there were no fewer than 65 'tuberculins' and 'tuberculin ointments', and 36 'vaccines' of tubercle bacilli. Unfortunately, the final verdict must be that none provided a cure for tuberculosis.

The curative use of tuberculin in any of its numerous variants has had a long-continued vogue. The potential dangers were not at first recognized. In 1890, when it was distributed for clinical trial, relatively large doses were considered necessary. Sometimes the local and general reactions were severe, the tuberculosis got worse, and occasionally the patient died. The trial was given up, but the use of tuberculin for treatment was later revived with much more emphasis on a cautious increase of dosage. However, excessive reactions were not excluded by the regimen, and curative tuberculin became generally unpopular, and has been virtually discontinued at the present time.

Although tuberculin has been disappointing in treatment, it has proved to be a most valuable diagnostic aid in medical and veterinary practice. Tuberculin tests, as they are called, depend on the demonstration of sensitization or allergy, the local inflammatory reactions (to tuberculin) in humans or animals previously exposed to tubercle bacilli. The mechanism is that the antibodies to tuberculin which develop in these subjects have the ability to unite with the tuberculin used for test, thereby causing a red patch of inflammation. Only brief references to allergy are made at this stage, because diagnostic tests with tuberculin were mainly developed in the present century and belong to a later chapter. However, Koch himself introduced a subcutaneous test in 1890, whereby graded dilutions of tuberculin were injected into persons suspected of being tuberculous. This was a dangerous procedure, since reactions were sometimes unduly severe and occasionally even fatal. This test is now obsolete.

In conclusion, while Koch discovered the cause of tuberculosis as long ago as 1882, effective preventive vaccines were introduced only in the 1920s (see p. 123), and reliable curative anti-tuberculous drugs only in the last two decades. The long interval must not be allowed to detract from Koch's wonderful contribution to the promotion of human and animal health in discovering the tubercle bacillus and in making possible several, possibly less obvious, bacteriological and immunological advances. Even his discovery of the Koch phenomenon and of tuberculin had unexpected consequences beyond the field of tuberculosis: the delayed type of hypersensitivity has come to be recognized as a fundamental immune reaction, playing an important rôle in many other diseases.

CHAPTER 5

ALMROTH WRIGHT AND 'KILLED' VACCINES

THE British bacteriologist, A. E. (later Sir Almroth) Wright, began his research on vaccines soon after he was appointed professor of pathology at the Army Medical School at Netley on Southampton Water in 1892. He did not hold army rank, because he remained a civilian in this post—one of the army's earliest experiments in 'civilianization'. His main interest at once became centred on Malta fever and later on typhoid fever which were scourges of armies in various parts of the world.

THE INFLUENCE OF PASTEUR AND KOCH

Every research worker is influenced by his contemporaries or immediate predecessors in allied fields. Wright was no exception. As has been told in an earlier chapter, the fertile genius of Pasteur had succeeded in using preventive immunization for anthrax in cattle and rabies in dogs and man. His vaccines were attenuated *living* cultures or virus-containing tissues, and Wright was suitably impressed. Pasteur in his turn had followed Jenner, and firmly believed that any vaccine likely to prove effective must consist of *living* organisms.

At this time, also, owing to the influence of Koch and his school, great strides had been made in medical bacteriology. The stir which resulted from Koch's discovery of the tubercle bacillus in 1882 had not yet died down: on the contrary, the problems of infection and control in other diseases looked nearer solution. There was a feeling of optimism which was frequently encouraged by fresh discoveries and triumphs, including those of Roux, Behring, Kitasato and many others which will be discussed in this book.

At the Royal Victoria Hospital at Netley, Wright saw many cases of typhoid fever and of men invalided home with Malta fever.

How could the *control* of these diseases be effected? Could Pasteur's achievements be applied to these diseases by the inoculation of bacterial vaccines? Prevention seemed feasible by such methods.

MALTA FEVER AND TYPHOID FEVER: THE PUBLIC HEALTH PROBLEM

Malta Fever was a disease of garrison troops on Malta, and of sailors visiting the island. It was characterized by a low typhoid-like fever, with partial remissions of symptoms between a series of two, three or even ten febrile attacks. The illness was usually prolonged and very debilitating. In 1861, a British army doctor, Jeffery Allen Marston, recognized it as a disease entity, to be differentiated from typhoid fever and certain other fevers to which it was not easy to attach a diagnostic label. Many years later, as a result of tests in the laboratory, Wright and others demonstrated that Malta fever was not confined to the island, but occurred in various parts of the Mediterranean littoral, all over the African continent, in India and China, and even in some parts of America.

In the pre-bacteriological era, *typhoid fever* was much confused with other long-continued fevers, such as typhus, malaria or tuberculosis. Moreover, it was impossible to differentiate between typhoid and paratyphoid fevers. There were also mild cases of typhoid or the closely related paratyphoid which were undoubtedly overlooked altogether. In the early 1890s, typhoid-like fevers were killing 5,000 persons a year in England and 15,000 in the U.S.A. In some years at least, the latter figure rose to 35,000.

As professor of pathology at Netley, Wright had access to army records of casualties and various diseases in important campaigns. Data relevant to his proposed research included the following: In the Crimean war, The Guards lost only 449 men 'by ordinary warfare' and 1,713 died from disease. For this reason, *Punch*, in 1861, was moved to make the pungent suggestion that the Guards Memorial in Waterloo Place, London, should bear the names Fever, Dysentery and Cholera instead of Alma, Inkerman and Sebastopol. Wright must also have known that in the American Civil War of 1861-66 and in the Franco-Prussian War of 1870-71, battle casualties again played a secondary rôle: from 60 to 75 per cent. of all deaths were from disease, mainly typhoid-like fevers. In the latter war, the German army had 73,393 admissions to hospital from such fevers, with 6,965 deaths.

The infectious nature of typhoid had ceased to be a controversial topic during the last quarter of the nineteenth century, as a result of the work of William Budd, the country doctor and public health pioneer, who became a lecturer in the department of medicine in the Medical School of Bristol. He studied numerous outbreaks of typhoid and reached the conclusion that the disease was spread, from case to case, mainly through the agency of contaminated water. His monograph on *Typhoid Fever* was published in 1875 and develops the controversial views he propounded between 1856 and 1860. This work was certainly remarkable because Budd did not have the aid of bacteriology at his disposal: the pioneer discoveries of Koch and his associates were still to come.

By 1892, the year of his appointment, Wright was thus able to read the publications of the Pasteur school; the Koch school, Marston, and Budd; the Army records; and of course David Bruce's account of his discovery of the causative organism of Malta fever in 1887, and Carl Eberth's of his discovery of the typhoid bacillus in 1880. The stage was set for research on preventive immunization with bacterial vaccines.

WRIGHT'S WORK ON MALTA FEVER

Leonard Colebrook, the friend, pupil and biographer of Almroth Wright, states that Malta fever was his first objective. After some experiments with a few monkeys injected with living and killed vaccine, Wright backed his belief in immunization by vaccinating himself with killed organisms and afterwards, as Pasteur might have considered necessary, with a living culture. 'Unfortunately', writes Colebrook, 'protection in his case was not adequate, and he went down with a very unpleasant attack of fever, which lasted several weeks. He often told me of the misery of those weeks.' For obvious reasons, the research was discontinued, although work was resumed under the auspices of the Maltese Commission some ten years later: dead cultures were injected and a minor degree of protection was obtained.

WRIGHT'S WORK ON TYPHOID FEVER BEFORE AND DURING THE BOER WAR

During Wright's convalescence from Malta fever, he made plans to experiment with typhoid vaccine. He received encouragement in this project when Waldemar Haffkine, a Russian bacteriologist who was associated with Pasteur in Paris, visited him at Netley. Haffkine told him that he intended to use a killed vaccine against cholera in India. There appeared to be a possibility that a similar type of vaccine might be effective against typhoid fever. After his own unfortunate experience with a living culture of Malta fever vaccine, Wright was ready to break with the Pasteur tradition and use the obviously safer vaccine of dead typhoid organisms.

The first trials of Wright's typhoid vaccine were carried out on himself and other volunteers, including 'surgeons on probation' in the laboratory of the Royal Victoria Hospital, Netley. As some of these faithful 'guinea-pigs' were very sick, the War Office expressed disapproval. By this time sufficient work was on hand to show that the blood-serum of inoculated animals, and of Wright and his co-workers, developed protective substances (antibodies) which were able to disrupt and destroy typhoid bacilli. This research was based on the results of analogous work about this time by the German bacteriologist, Richard Pfeiffer, using living cholera organisms as the vaccine for animals. Wright used *killed* typhoid vaccine for this investigation—again a departure from Pasteur's principle of using living material. He also introduced various ingenious laboratory devices at this early stage of his career—he was famed as a superb craftsman.

In view of the rather severe reactions, further tests in the field were necessary with different types of vaccine and also varying dosage: how small a dose of vaccine would produce the protective substances or antibodies in large amount (high titre)? An opportunity was presented to Wright in an outbreak of typhoid in a Kent asylum. Later, work was begun on the inoculation of volunteers in the Indian Army. The vaccine usually consisted of cultures of typhoid organisms in broth, which were killed by exposure to 53°C. and by the further addition of 0.4 per cent. of lysol. The early reports showed that local and general reactions were still rather severe, but that, in most cases, there was a considerable increase in the power of the blood to kill typhoid bacilli. This enhanced power was sufficiently impressive for Wright to urge upon the War Office the desirability of inoculating the troops embarking for the Boer War of 1899-1902 in South Africa. The task of persuasion was indeed formidable. Apart from the reluctance of a government department to introduce a relatively untried procedure, some influential advisers of the hierarchy were unimpressed by the results of tests that measured new-fangled changes in blood. They demanded statistical data, which of course were then unobtainable, that inoculated persons were protected against the disease itself. A golden opportunity was thus missed, for typhoid was known to be virtually an occupational disease of armies and was soon to become extremely common in the South African campaign.

Although compulsory inoculation was not introduced, Wright was instrumental in having 12,000 to 14,000 men vaccinated—alas, less than 4 per cent. of those who enlisted for this war. The available data are unreliable, since records of inoculations were often lost. In connection with the follow-up, Colebrook writes that 'when a man was admitted to hospital it was necessary to rely upon his own statement as to whether he had been inoculated or not—and he was inclined to say "yes" in order to avoid any further inoculation or because he was thinking of smallpox vaccination. And ignorance or partisan feeling about inoculation often loaded the dice against it. . . . Moreover, the diagnosis of typhoid fever under active service conditions usually could not be verified by bacteriological or post-mortem evidence'. During the three years of the war, the British Army had nearly 58,000 cases of typhoid (15 per cent. of the troops), with about 9,000 deaths—more deaths than resulted from enemy action (about 8,000). All that can be claimed about the value of inoculation is that Wright's typhoid vaccine apparently reduced the incidence of the fever among the inoculated. However, it is impressive, on the basis of the actual figures, that the incidence among 10,529 uninoculated soldiers during the siege of Ladysmith was 14·0 per cent., whereas among 1,705 persons inoculated it was 2·0 per cent. In 1904, Wright published a monograph on the value of anti-typhoid inoculation.

The War Office had again to consider whether compulsory immunization was desirable, and referred the matter to various committees. There were differences of opinion among the experts.

Open opposition came from Sir David Bruce, the discoverer of the organism responsible for Malta fever and an authority on trypanosomiasis, and from Karl Pearson, the mathematician and statistician. The latter asserted that Wright's figures proved nothing. The dispute between Pearson and Wright was aired in the correspondence columns of *The Times* and the *British Medical Journal*. Wright could assert that his adversary did not fully appreciate the difficulties involved in conducting the trials. On the other hand, Pearson was certainly correct in his criticism of how the trials involving morbidity or mortality rates were conducted. On the basis of his requirements, he may justifiably be regarded as one of the pioneers of the statistical techniques used in present-day medical science.

The decision of the War Office was very sensibly to nominate Colonel W. B. (later Sir William) Leishman to carry out a properly conducted trial in India. Leishman had worked under Wright in the Military Hospital at Netley, where he was Assistant Professor of Pathology. When Wright resigned his Chair to go to St. Mary's Hospital, London, in 1902, Leishman was his successor.

The investigations of Leishman in India belong to a later chapter. At this stage it is only necessary to state that the series of reports which appeared over many years showed that Wright's claim could be substantiated: typhoid vaccine did in fact protect against the disease.

CHAPTER 6

THE MECHANISM OF IMMUNIZATION: SOME CONTROVERSIES

EARLIER chapters have dealt with the artificial induction of immunity by the use of living virus by Jenner, living attenuated bacteria or viruses by Pasteur, and 'killed' bacteria by Almroth Wright. Although Koch's work on immunity was a disappointment, indirectly his successes in bacteriology encouraged and made possible the discoveries of others, including those of Pasteur himself.

The results and theories that commenced to flow from laboratories in different centres in the 1880s were rather bewildering. From the time of the pioneer discoveries of Pasteur, questions were asked about the mechanism by which the body protected itself against the onslaught of micro-organisms, and, in particular, about the method of destruction of dangerous bacteria which might gain access to blood.

Pasteur was convinced that, to produce immunity, living organisms were essential. For a time he maintained that the protection was in some way related to the disappearance of some essential foodstuff which was used up during the first attack of the invaders (living vaccine, or disease-producing bacteria or viruses). However this 'exhaustion hypothesis' soon became obsolete.

CELLULAR AND HUMORAL THEORIES

The first major theory, was the *cellular* or *phagocytic*, which was concerned with the rôle of body cells and dated from about 1884. It was predominantly the result of the work of Elie Metchnikoff, a Russian zoologist who was a pupil of Pasteur. In the previous year he had described certain cells in the starfish which took foreign particles into their interior and then digested them. The theory he developed was that immunity to bacteria was likewise due to this process of phagocytosis (Greek *phagein*, to eat and *kutos*, cell) and intracellular digestion. He observed that the cells themselves or phagocytes were of two varieties: either they were 'fixed' cells in the spleen, lymphatic glands, bone marrow and liver, or they were 'wandering' cells which entered the blood stream from these organs and were carried to the invading micro-organisms. In acute infections, the wandering polymorphonuclear leucocytes were the phagocytes mainly concerned. The German pathologist, Julius Cohnheim, had previously shown that the process of migration of these leucocytes (white blood corpuscles) is the essence of inflammation. When pus is formed, leucocytes die and disintegrate.

Difficulties arose at once. Since the phagocytic cells disposed of offensive material, both living and dead and including bacteria, Koch and others likened the phagocytes to scavengers rather than defensive agents. The controversy about their exact function continued, and need not be described in detail here. Metchnikoff was right in drawing attention to the importance of phagocytes as an essential part of the defence mechanism against many diseases. He was wrong in failing to appreciate, however, that these cells, when deprived of the assistance of the blood plasma, are almost incapable of ingesting micro-organisms and other material.

The rival theory was the *humoral*, which was introduced by George Nuttall of Cambridge, who was working at that time (1888) in collaboration with Carl Flugge in Göttingen. They were interested in the property which blood possesses of killing bacteria —the so-called bactericidal action of blood. They demonstrated that chemical products of cells, present in the blood serum and body fluids, were defensive or protective against certain organisms. Bacteria were devitalized by these 'humoral' influences, which were also designated antibodies (antidotes) or antibacterial substances. Up to this stage, Metchnikoff's phagocytes were not required in the operation. However, after the bacteria had been killed or at least prevented from being harmful, the action of the phagocytic cells might be interpreted as merely that of scavengers, which played a part in their removal. Thus, Nuttall's view about their rôle was identical with that of Koch, who had been openly contemptuous of Metchnikoff's theory. In 1894, Richard Pfeiffer, a pupil of Koch, was able to bring forward fresh evidence in support of the humoral standpoint. Cholera organisms, which had been introduced into the peritoneal cavity of a guinea-pig immunized against them, disintegrated and passed into solution without the aid of any cells. Also, the blood serum of animals immunized against typhoid by inoculations of typhoid bacilli, dissolved these bacilli specifically: the blood serum of persons recovering from typhoid had a similar action.

Neither the cellular nor the humoral doctrine afforded a full explanation of the mechanism of protection.

ALMROTH WRIGHT'S OPSONINS

At the outset of his long research on the mechanism of immunization, Wright was influenced mainly by the work of Pasteur and Metchnikoff. The former had demonstrated that preventive inoculations could be successful in the case of rabies even when the patient had been bitten by a mad dog several days before the first dose of the course was given; presumably the patient's tissues were still capable of responding to ensure recovery. Similarly, Wright argued, the men he saw at Netley, who were suffering from boils, must be capable of cure by appropriate doses of vaccine. However, his early tests of the blood of these men showed nothing which would disintegrate and destroy the causal organisms—in technical terms, there were no 'bactericidal antibodies to the staphylococci'.

Wright also pondered over Metchnikoff's claims for phagocytosis. This was the starting point for rather more than 20 years of work on *therapeutic immunization*. He tried to find a method for ascertaining whether the blood of a sick man had less capacity for phagocytosis than that of a healthy man. Thereafter, it might be possible to increase his phagocytic activity by a course of vaccine. Very soon Wright discovered that 'when he collected leucocytes from his own blood and washed them free of serum (by the centrifuge) and then mixed them with microbes, there was almost no phagocytosis, but when serum was present in the mixture it was abundant'. Apparently there were specific antibodies ('opsonins') in the serum which reinforced the destructive action of the leucocytes: bacteria were 'prepared' in some way by opsonins (from the Greek *opsono* = I prepare victuals for) before they were engulfed and digested.

With considerable technical ingenuity, Wright devised a method for measuring the opsonic factor. He was thus able to collect data for the serum of different individuals and for the serum of the same individual before and after an injection of vaccine. On the basis of these opsonic tests, staphylococcus vaccines were given to patients with boils, and tuberculins to tuberculosis patients; the dosage had to be sufficient to encourage and maintain the production of phagocytic antibody. Vaccine therapy was also tried on a similar basis, for septicaemia, erysipelas, arthritis, lupus, and various infections of the urinary and respiratory tracts. As no attempt was made to assess the findings (and their vagaries) by statistical methods, Wright's work on opsonins was vitiated in the long run by others. No evidence was produced by Wright that variations in the amount of phagocytosis were due to corresponding variations in antibody level. Moreover, according to Leonard Colebrook, there were 'many cases in which it was difficult to be sure how much the patient's recovery had been assisted by our treatment'. No figures are available: there were many cures, but many more failures.

In conclusion, Wright's long, persistent and dedicated research on phagocytosis drew attention to the merits and also the defects of Metchnikoff's cellular theory. On the debit side, it misled many of his contemporaries, for it was the subject of numerous, somewhat verbose, lectures and publications. In retrospect, the story of this lamentable project underlines the need for properly controlled investigations. In biological research, there are so many variable factors that statistical considerations can never be disregarded. Perhaps the verdict of history on Almroth Wright and his phagocytes may appear to be harsh, but this failure should be considered alongside his great success of preventive vaccination against typhoid fever. Unfortunately, we still do not know how typhoid and other bacterial suspensions which are used as vaccines work.

Exciting developments in the study of other organisms will now be considered.

ANTITOXIC IMMUNITY AND THE SCIENCE OF IMMUNOLOGY

In diseases like diphtheria and tetanus, the causal organisms remain at a local site of infection, from which they attack by means of a powerful, specific and diffusible toxin. As will be seen in the next chapter, the most important mechanism in prevention is to provide an antidote to the specific toxin, which is termed an anti-toxin. The toxin can thus be neutralized and the toxaemia counter-acted. Knowledge in this field is on a firmer scientific basis, and truly belongs to the modern science of immunology. It is more easily understood than some of the complex mechanisms of the rival cellular and humoral theories which it influenced. In fact, the discovery of diphtheria and tetanus antitoxins around 1890 provided limited support to the humoral protagonists, although it was realized that different protective agents varied in importance in many different infections. Once again, this story of dramatic conquest had its beginnings in workers from the French School of Louis Pasteur and the German one of Robert Koch—there was intense rivalry, but it was also in a special sense a combined operation!

CHAPTER 7

DIPHTHERIA AND TETANUS—TO 1900:
RESEARCH ON ANTITOXIC IMMUNITY: I

THIS is the story of laboratory research into disease mechanisms, which led to the conquest of diphtheria in the first instance and contributed eventually to that of other infections.

DIPHTHERIA IN THE PRE-ANTITOXIN ERA

Towards the end of the last century diphtheria was a killing disease, which explains why it was studied intensively by workers in Germany and France soon after the discovery of the causal organism by Theodor Klebs of Zurich and Friedrich Loeffler, an assistant of Robert Koch, in 1883-84. It is difficult for the present generation to realize the prevalence and severity of this grim infection in earlier times, when treatment also was very crude. Thus, in 1799, George Washington, general, statesman and first President of the United States of America, was thought by some to have died of diphtheria, but more probably he suffered from an acute streptococcal pharyngitis and laryngitis. He was given gargles of molasses, vinegar and butter and of vinegar and sage tea, bled 'heavily', and a blister of cantharides was placed on his neck, 'his strength meanwhile rapidly sinking'.

Pierre Bretonneau, the famous French clinician of Tours, first recognized diphtheria as a specific contagious disease with membranous exudation (1826), which he termed diphtérite (diphtheritis), since modified by his pupil, Armand Trousseau to diphtérie (diphtheria). The name comes from the Greek word for skin or membrane. It is recorded that the village of Elcour, comprising about 40 families, lost 42 children in one winter: this grim experience was by no means exceptional in their practice. Bretonneau also performed the first successful tracheotomy in a case of diphtheria (1825). He had witnessed the death from diphtheria of three of the four children of a friend, and obtained permission to open into the trachea of the apparently moribund fourth child. The patient lived to the age of 71.

Up to 1850, blood-letting persisted and cantharides blisters or other counter-irritants might be placed on the neck. After the acute phase had passed, purgation might be drastic. Within the next two or three decades, emphasis was placed on supporting the patient's strength; depletion (bleeding), blisters and counter-irritants were altogether discontinued. The throat was swabbed with some styptic mixture. It is difficult to appreciate that these were the only measures available for treating diphtheria before the days of antitoxin: of course, they were of doubtful efficacy.

THE DISCOVERY OF TOXIN AND ANTITOXIN

The diphtheria bacillus is still sometimes called the Klebs-Loeffler bacillus after its two discoverers. As befitted an assistant of Koch, Loeffler was a master of bacteriological technique and grew the organism from the throats of cases of diphtheria on a special solid medium containing inspissated blood serum, which still bears his name. On the basis of experiments on animals, he suggested that the bacillus elaborated a powerful poison or toxin which caused illness and death: there was local multiplication of the organism at the site of inoculation where a characteristic membrane formed, but he could find no evidence of dissemination throughout the body. The obvious inference was that the toxin diffused from the local site into the blood and did all the damage, the heart and nervous system being specially vulnerable.

Proof of Loeffler's suggestion came from Paris, where it will be recalled that Louis Pasteur pioneered research on immunization, notably in connection with anthrax and rabies. Since his health was now failing, Emile Roux, his greatest pupil and collaborator, and Emile Yersin, a young assistant, took over the diphtheria project and demonstrated the specific soluble toxin or 'exotoxin' (culture filtrate) of the causal organism. In essence, they grew the bacilli for several days in broth, which they then filtered through unglazed porcelain; the filtrate was sterile, but killed laboratory animals in the same manner as the living bacilli themselves; the filtrate was therefore the crude toxin and was specific to diphtheria because it often reproduced in these animals the 'membrane' characteristic of human diphtheria, and the intense local inflammation, oedema and haemorrhage. Moreover, the paralysis, which is a late manifestation of the disease, was also noted.

Diphtheria toxin was first demonstrated in Paris in 1888, and two years later the scene moves again to Germany where we have the first inkling of an antidote or antibody to this toxin, appropriately called *antitoxin*. It is not at all surprising that some assistants of Robert Koch at the Institute of Infectious Diseases, Berlin, were the successful team. In the first instance, Carl Fraenkel made some preliminary observations by injecting a toxic substance, extracted from diphtheria cultures, into animals. He observed that, if they recovered from its effect, they could then tolerate an injection of living diphtheria bacilli. The degree of immunity obtained was very slight. One day after Fraenkel's paper was published, his colleagues, Emil Behring and Shibasáburo Kitasato, a German and a Japanese, published a joint paper on artificially produced immunity in animals against tetanus. One week later Behring was the sole author of an article enumerating five methods he devised for obtaining a similar immunity against diphtheria. These two investigators found that sublethal doses of living or killed broth cultures of diphtheria or tetanus bacilli, each containing the corresponding toxin, produced a new property or antidote—namely, diphtheria or tetanus antitoxin which gave protection from the damaging effect of many lethal doses of the corresponding bacilli or toxin. They observed later that even minute amounts of broth-culture filtrates of diphtheria bacilli produced a specific immunity in laboratory animals. The antibody protected the directly immunized animal against the organisms or their toxic products: moreover, when the blood serum of this animal was injected into another animal, this protection was transferred. If the second animal was already showing symptoms due to the diphtheria toxin, the protective blood serum could sometimes be curative. This was a far-reaching discovery. Behring soon realized its implications. His earlier experiments had been on guinea-pigs, but obviously much larger animals—sheep, goats or even horses —would be needed if antitoxic serum was to be prepared in quantity for the treatment of diphtheria (or tetanus) in man.

EARLY USE OF DIPHTHERIA ANTITOXIN IN MAN

Germany.—Behring's discovery attracted much attention and was followed up rapidly in his own laboratory. Diphtheria antitoxin prepared in a sheep was ready for clinical trials in December 1891. It was first cautiously used in the treatment of diphtheria by Geissler in von Bergmann's clinic in Berlin on the night of Christmas. The patient, who was a little girl, recovered. After further successes, which seemed miraculous—and, of course, a few deaths—the large chemical firm of Meister, Lucius and Bruning began to make the antitoxin (1892), mainly in herds of sheep but also in goats. Within three years some 20,000 children had been injected in Germany.

In 1892, Behring and his colleague, E. Wernicke, were able to improve methods of preparing the antitoxin in animals. The process could be speeded up by using increasing doses of living cultures after a protective dose of antitoxic serum. Later, the method was further improved by giving increasing doses of toxin partially neutralized by antitoxin.

It will be recalled that Behring and Kitasato demonstrated the passive transfer of protection from one directly ('actively') immunized laboratory animal to another animal which was unprotected (non-immune). Behring and Wernicke showed that passive immunity to diphtheria could likewise be transferred to man by means of the injection of a protective dose of antitoxin: this procedure became common-place for the protection of the close contacts of clinical cases of the disease. Later, other workers found that this type of (passive) immunity is short-lived, lasting only for about two weeks.

In 1893, Behring published the first series of cases of diphtheria in man treated with antitoxic serum.

France.—Emile Roux, with his co-workers, Emile Yersin and Louis Martin, enter the field once more. They were pioneers in the large-scale production of horse antitoxic serum, which was used at the Hôpital des Enfants Malades in Paris between February and September 1894. The case mortality in children suffering from diphtheria was 52 per cent. in the months before antitoxin was used, whereas that of the first 300 cases treated with serum was 25 per cent. Roux gave these encouraging data in a classical paper (1894) presented at the International Congress of Hygiene and Demography at Budapest. In the next few years the antitoxin treatment of diphtheria became orthodox all over the world. In France itself Roux founded and directed large serum laboratories at Garches on the outskirts of Paris, which are affiliated to the Pasteur Institute. Finally, the average mortality from diphtheria for the years 1886-94 in Paris was 146.9 per 100,000 persons, whereas for 1895-1900 it fell to 35.4.

England.—Edward W. Goodall (*A Short History of the Epidemic Infectious Diseases*, London, 1934 and in some of his papers) stated that the first cases to be treated in England were about 20, in the early summer of 1894, at the Eastern Hospital, Homerton. The serum had been supplied to him by the then Sir Joseph Lister, the famous surgeon, who had obtained it from Roux. He also stated that in the autumn of the same year Armand Ruffer prepared antitoxin at the British Institute of Preventive Medicine, now the Lister Institute, London, and this serum also was used at the Eastern Hospital on October 23, 1894. However, the first patient to be treated for diphtheria with serum manufactured in this country (October 15, 1894) was a boy of eight years who lived at Lewes in Sussex: the antitoxin was obtained from a preliminary bleeding of a horse which was being immunized by Ruffer and C. S. (later Sir Charles) Sherrington, who became the leading physiologist of the nervous system. Here is Sherrington's own account from *Science, Medicine and History*, edited by Underwood: Oxford, 1953. 'Ruffer . . . almost as French as English. Bouchard, the eminent Paris physician, was a brother-in-law. Ruffer was often in Paris and constantly brought us news of the Institut Pasteur. Returning from one of these visits he spoke of the treatment of diphtheria which was being tried out there. Injection of the serum of an immunized horse. He would like us to try it. I had a spare stall in the stable at my Veterinary Hospital (at the Brown Institution, south of the Thames), and we got a horse and began inoculating it with gradually increasing doses of diphtheria cultures. We had been at this a week or two, and had a serum at least partially effective in guinea-pigs. We were badly in the dark about dosage. Then oddly enough, one Saturday about seven in the evening, came a telegram from my brother-in-law in Sussex. "George has diphtheria." George, a boy of eight was the only child. The house, an old Georgian house, was some three miles out of Lewes, set back in a combe under a chalk down. There was no train that night. I did not at first give thought to the horse, and when I did, regretfully supposed it could not yet be ripe for use. However, I took a cab to find Ruffer—no telephone or taxi in those days. Ruffer was dining out, I pursued him and got a word with him. He said "By all means, you can use the horse, but it is not yet ripe for trial!" Then by lantern light at the Brown Institution I bled the horse into a great four-litre flask duly sterilized and then plugged. I left it in ice to settle. Then after sterilizing smaller flasks and pipettes, drove home, to return at midnight and decant the serum, and sterilize needle-syringes. By Sunday's early train I reached Lewes. Dr. Fawsset of Lewes was waiting at the railway station in a dog-cart. I joined him, carrying my awkward package of flasks and such-like. He said nothing as I packed them into the dog-cart, but, when I climbed up beside him, he looked at me. "You can do what you like with the boy, he will not be alive at tea-time." We drove out to the old house. Tragedy seemed to shroud it. The boy was breathing with difficulty. He did not know me. The doctor helped with injecting the serum. The syringes were small and we emptied them time and again. The doctor left. Early in the afternoon the boy was clearly better. At three o'clock I sent a messenger to the doctor. Thenceforward progress was uninterrupted. On the Tuesday I returned to London and sought out Ruffer. His reaction was that we must tell Lister. The great surgeon had visitors, some Continental surgeons, to dinner. "You must tell my guests," he said, and he insisted.'

In an earlier account of this dramatic episode, Sherrington added that 'the boy had a severe paralysis for a time. He grew to be 6 feet and had a commission in the first World War.'

Ruffer subsequently contracted diphtheria himself. The attack was severe and was followed by paralysis, and he had to resign his post as director of the British Institute of Preventive Medicine.

He emigrated to Egypt where he became a professor of pathology at Cairo, and later was a prominent egyptologist and palaeopathologist.

There was a second early source of supply of diphtheria antitoxin in England, namely the Wellcome Research Laboratories. They were founded by H. S. (later Sir Henry) Wellcome in London in 1894, who used his increasing wealth to encourage medical and pharmaceutical research and to indulge his passion for collecting objects, books and manuscripts bearing on the history of medicine. At that time it was a new conception for the owner of a pharmaceutical firm to seek to further fundamental research in the medical sciences in addition to routine production matters. Other firms in the pharmaceutical industry have now followed this lead. Wellcome declared 'I like to support a research laboratory much as another man might like to support a racing stable.' It is relevant to this chapter that the new laboratories, as one of their first activities, were engaged on the problems of preparing diphtheria antitoxin, almost simultaneously with the British Institute of Preventive Medicine. Towards the end of 1894, the serum was the first to be exported to the American continent: it was used at the Belle Vue Hospital, New York.

The gradual introduction of diphtheria antitoxin around 1895 led to a decline in the case fatality from diphtheria in fever hospitals throughout this country. In London hospitals, for example, the rate of 29.7 per cent. for 1890-94 fell to 17.0 per cent. for 1895-1899, and still further to 11.2 per cent. in 1900-04.

United States of America.—In 1894, not only was British antitoxin used in New York, but a significant appointment was made: William H. Park, a nose and throat specialist in Manhattan, became head of the diphtheria diagnostic laboratory in New York City. For the next 45 years Park and various collaborators gave devoted service to the cause of disease prevention. He was early promoted to the direction of all the research laboratories in the City. In collaboration with Anna Williams, he discovered the classical 'Park Williams 8' strain of diphtheria bacillus, which has continued to be used for potent toxin production all over the world. He was the first person outside Europe to produce diphtheria antitoxin. From 1897 onwards, horses were immunized with mixtures of toxin and antitoxin in variable proportions. Park also tried for a time the injection of 10,000 units of antitoxin, so as to permit larger doses of toxin and thus speed up the immunization of the horses. Park's other achievements in the control of diphtheria and other diseases are described in later chapters.

CHAPTER 8

DIPHTHERIA AND TETANUS—TO 1900: RESEARCH ON ANTITOXIC IMMUNITY: II

PAUL EHRLICH: During the last decade of the nineteenth century, another great German, Paul Ehrlich, made a series of discoveries which established immunology as a new and rapidly growing science. His work on diphtheria put certain findings of Behring on a more quantitative basis. In 1892, he described the differences between active and passive immunity, which were briefly mentioned in the last chapter. However, the standardization of toxins and antitoxins was his main contribution to immunology. This had the important consequence that it ensured the supply of consistently good antitoxins; his new methods of exact measurement eliminated the inconsistencies and uncertainties of much of the early work. Ehrlich also became an exponent of the humoral theory of immunity. Lastly, he devised a 'side-chain' or 'receptor' theory, which had a chemical basis and would explain the interaction of toxins and antitoxins. It was in essence 'a pictorial conception of interlocking parts on the surface of molecules'.

The hypothesis that the union of toxin and antitoxin was of a firm chemical nature, is no longer accepted. For the record, the general idea of side-chains was widely acclaimed for many years, although progressive alterations in the plan of receptors were necessary to meet criticism: it also stimulated much fundamental research.

THE STANDARDIZATION OF ANTITOXIC SERA

As sera differ widely in potency, the need for a numerical expression of their respective values was early appreciated. Diphtheria antitoxic sera were first standardized in accordance with their capacity to neutralize known quantities of diphtheria toxin. For this purpose, Behring introduced an antitoxin unit or 'yard-stick', which depended on the amount of serum required to protect a guinea-pig against 100 fatal doses of toxin. Unfortunately, the results were not consistent, the main difficulty being all the variables involved in the toxin batches used for test. The key to the inconsistencies was discovered by Ehrlich, who demonstrated in the toxin solutions the presence of toxoids—immunizing substances which had lost their harmful toxic properties but still retained their power of combining with the antitoxin, which was thus rendered unavailable for combination with still active toxin. The presence of a varying proportion of toxoid in toxin solutions used for test purposes vitiated the results of Behring's assays in terms of his original unit.

Ehrlich next introduced a new unit of diphtheria antitoxin, which was defined as a precise weight of a carefully dried, stable antitoxic serum, preserved *in vacuo* and in the cold. This batch of diphtheria serum became Ehrlich's serum standard. All sera to be tested prior to human use were compared with it for antitoxic value. This was preferable to Behring's method of expressing the potency of a serum in terms of the number of fatal doses of a variable toxin against which it would protect a guinea-pig. Ehrlich's most important paper on the subject was published in 1897.

From time to time other batches of serum were standardized and stored in the same way for reference purposes. For years samples were issued from Frankfurt to form the basis for evaluating diphtheria antitoxin in other countries—a step towards the large-scale production of potent antitoxin everywhere. It is not the function of this history to give details of the methods used for testing, which may be found in books and articles on immunology—the study of the mechanisms of the reactions of immunity.

Altogether three modern sciences were found largely on Ehrlich's researches, viz. chemotherapy, haematology, and, of course, immunology. He is perhaps best known for his discovery of salvarsan or '606' for the treatment of syphilis. He was unquestionably one of the greatest medical pioneers of all time.

TETANUS: THE DISCOVERY OF TOXIN AND ANTITOXIN

Tetanus or lockjaw has a world-wide distribution, and is most prevalent in areas and under conditions where manured soil is likely to contaminate wounds. It is an infection characterized by distressing contractures or spasms of muscles, and used to be one of the most fatal of maladies—probably at least 85 per cent of cases died. Antitoxic serum and other modern measures have reduced the case mortality rate, although the disease is still serious. Prevention by a suitable vaccine (toxoid) is very effective and is being used increasingly.

The causal organism is the tetanus bacillus or *Clostridium tetani*, which was first described by Arthur Nicolaier of Göttingen in 1884. It was sometimes called Nicolaier's bacillus. Although he produced tetanus in mice, rabbits and guinea-pigs by injecting them with garden earth subcutaneously, it should be noted that he failed to grow the organism in pure culture. In the same year, two Italians, Carle and Rattone showed that tetanus could be transmitted from an infected lesion in man to rabbits.

S. Kitasato, the Japanese pupil of Robert Koch, was the first to grow the tetanus bacillus in pure culture and to describe its biological characteristics. He also produced tetanus in laboratory animals by inoculating them with pure cultures. The next stages were reminiscent of the diphtheria story all over again. Kitasato and his co-worker, Behring, suspected that the signs and symptoms of tetanus were due to the effects of a very powerful chemical poison or toxin rather than to the organisms themselves, which were confined to local lesions: the disease was obviously an intoxication and not the result of spread or dissemination of the bacillus throughout the body. It was the toxin which upset the nervous system and led to violent and painful muscular spasms, and eventually death in many cases.

Knud Faber, a Dane, reproduced tetanus with the toxic filtrates of cultures containing tetanus organisms. However, this work is open to criticism because these cultures were impure. About the same time (1890), Behring and Kitasato published more exhaustive and far-reaching studies, which became the basis of the serotherapy of tetanus. They immunized animals actively and artificially with small and progressively increasing doses of tetanus toxin. The blood serum of these animals had acquired protective and curative properties—an antitoxic or toxin-destroying action which was not possessed by the serum of non-immunized (so-called 'normal') animals. Animals could be protected passively from tetanus by the previous or simultaneous injection of this antitoxic serum, provided it had been obtained from a thoroughly immunized animal. It was soon found that antitoxin was valuable in the prophylaxis of human tetanus. However, it was rather disappointing in the treatment of established cases, because several hours had often elapsed *after* the onset of tetanic symptoms, when toxin had become firmly fixed to cells of the central nervous system and could not be effectively displaced or neutralized. Prevention was thus much easier than cure.

The early work on the immunization of animals was done with rabbits and mice. The first antitoxic sera to be used in the treatment of human tetanus were prepared in rabbits (Germany) or in dogs (Italy). In 1892, Behring obtained considerable amounts of antitoxin from sheep and horses.

We shall see in later chapters how the knowledge acquired from studying diphtheria and tetanus was applied to other antitoxins, and also how these diseases can be successfully controlled.

HYPERSENSITIVITY TO SERUM

From 1894 onwards a number of workers drew attention to reactions of different kinds, duration and severity which were sometimes associated with the injection of diphtheria antitoxin and other preparations. The trouble was a hypersensitive state or allergy (literally, 'altered reactivity') to the protein content of the serum; this allergy was either inherent or acquired. Skin eruptions ('serum exanthems') were the most frequent manifestations in human subjects.

The essential mechanism seemed to be that injections of foreign materials (such as horse serum into man) gave rise to reactions which were damaging to the cells of the body. In 1894, Simon Flexner, an American who acquired fame as a bacteriologist, showed that rabbits were rendered hypersensitive to dog serum when a second dose was injected some days or weeks after the first. (It is of interest that in 1890, Robert Koch had demonstrated a specific sensitization, sometimes fatal, to another protein he was investigating, namely, tuberculin.)

The various phenomena of the allergic state were intensively studied in the present century (see also p. 68). Some of these allergic responses were immediate in their onset, whereas others were 'delayed'—the technical term used to describe them. In reviewing the earlier and somewhat scattered communications, reference should be made to the work of A. Johanssen in 1895. He studied hypersensitivity to diphtheria antitoxic serum of equine origin, and was able to prove that the responsible factor was the horse serum itself and not the specific antitoxin for which it was a vehicle: the same complex of symptoms was produced in non-diphtheria patients with normal horse serum as in diphtheria patients treated with antitoxic serum.

Although more is known today about allergic reactions of various kinds and their prevention, the troubles arising from foreign proteins are still a hazard of immunization. Where possible (as in the prophylaxis of tetanus), active immunization with vaccine should replace passive immunization with horse antitoxic serum.

CHAPTER 9

SMALLPOX VACCINATION:
FURTHER PROGRESS TO 1900

B ETWEEN 1810 and 1840 it became obvious that Jenner had
been over-optimistic when he claimed life-long protection
following vaccination. This was simply not true. [Attacks
of smallpox, usually mild, sometimes occurred in persons who
had certainly been vaccinated successfully: the criterion of success
was that these people had at one time demonstrable reactions to
vaccination which had been performed with matter from typical
pustules in previous vaccinees. Nevertheless, their immunity had
obviously waned.] After much recrimination and argument, it was
established that there were two rather simple remedies for any
failures in protection, namely, the use of good-quality lymph and
revaccination at periodic intervals. With regard to the former
many so-called 'humanized' strains of vaccine virus, which were
being carried on from arm to arm, showed a progressive loss of
potency as a result of this repeated passage. New strains of high
potency had to be sought from affected cows or milkers directly
infected from such cows. Regarding the second remedy, the need
for revaccination in order to counter any waning immunity was
appreciated by some vaccinators, but there were long delays in
taking effective action.

Great Britain

With all its defects, vaccination flourished in many parts of this
country. By 1825 nearly 50 per cent. of children in large towns
were being inoculated. In some parishes, before 1840, about 70 per
cent. of persons were vaccinated. Unfortunately, as in the 1960s,
a considerable section of the population was apathetic. Not surprisingly, from 1839 to 1842, there was a great epidemic of smallpox. In 1840 the State was forced to intervene to try to control
the infection by more vaccination. The practice of variolation,

57

which was dangerous both to the individual and to the community was at last made illegal. In its place legislation empowered Boards of Guardians to vaccinate the children of the poorer classes at the ratepayers' expense.

In 1853, the State intervened again. Vaccination of infants was made *compulsory* in the United Kingdom, under penalty of a fine of 20 shillings. However, owing to counter-propaganda and distortion of facts, the law was not enforced till 1871, when Boards of Guardians were compelled to appoint public vaccinators for their districts. The explanation for the enforcement was that 1871 and 1872 were major epidemic years, when 42,084 deaths occurred. Between 1853 and 1898, 80 to 85 per cent. of infants were vaccinated: the figure was seldom below 70 per cent. However, it should be noted that the statute of 1853 was concerned only with compulsory powers for *primary* immunization. No provision was made for revaccination in childhood. It is now established that this further procedure is necessary in order to counteract the waning protection which tends to occur with the lapse of time.

Progress is illustrated by the following figures: Before vaccination was introduced, the mean annual death-rate from smallpox *per million* living in England and Wales was probably not less than 3,000 to 4,000 in the eighteenth century. Between 1847 and 1853, it was 305 per million; between 1854 and 1871, it was 223 per million; from 1872 to 1891, when vaccination was better enforced, it was 89 per million; from 1891 to 1900, it was as low as 13 per million, although the disease had greater facilities for spread owing to the growth and congestion of the cities.

TABLE

Mean Annual Death-rate from Smallpox per Million living: England and Wales

	All ages
Pre-vaccination	3,000-4,000
Vaccination optional (1847-1853)	305
Vaccination obligatory, but not efficiently enforced (1854-1871)	223
Vaccination better enforced by vaccination officers (1872-1891)	89
1891-1900	13

In 1898, a Vaccination Acts Amendment Act was passed. It laid down that, if a child in Britain had not been vaccinated before it was four months and one week old, the public vaccinator must visit its home and offer free vaccination: this official was usually a general practitioner on a part-time salaried basis. Unfortunately the legislation also introduced a 'conscience clause', which was a relaxation of compulsion and a retrograde step: objectors could make a declaration of conscience before a magistrate and thus escape the provisions of the Act of 1853. However, the Act of 1898 was memorable in another direction, for it gave official approval to the use of vaccine lymph prepared by propagation of virus in the skin of calves. A new Government Lymph Establishment was set up under F. R. Blaxall, Chief Bacteriologist. Vaccination with the glycerinated calf-lymph advocated by Monckton Copeman of the old Local Government Board (later a Senior Medical Officer, Ministry of Health) soon became the standard procedure at the Establishment. Glycerine had been added to lymph in Germany in order to kill many extraneous bacteria, and the treated lymph had been adopted by a Commission of which Koch was president. Copeman visited the vaccination centres of Germany, France and Switzerland, and then he and Blaxall also carried out experiments on the best method of control of dangerous bacteria, while safe-guarding the lymph's protective properties. Prolonged treatment of the lymph with sterile 50 per cent. solution of glycerine in water or normal saline was the procedure they recommended. With the introduction of glycerinated calf-lymph, arm-to-arm vaccination was no longer necessary.

From 1899 onwards the supply of humanized lymph also ceased.

The passing of the arm-to-arm technique was a cause for satis-faction, because a number of diseases had been attributed to it, including syphilis (very rare), cellulitis, erysipelas and many skin conditions. An anti-vaccination movement, which had started about 1800, became more active towards the end of the century, and also alleged the transfer of tuberculosis, leprosy and even cancer: according to the Royal Commission on Vaccination of 1889-97 there was no evidence of any connection with this latter group. It was rightly appreciated that Copeman's new glycerin-ated calf-lymph was the safest lymph, and that it eliminated the possible transfer of secondary infections from a diseased donor to a healthy recipient. Moreover, in the interests of safety, the calves were maintained in good general health and nutrition, and their past history was investigated. An abundant supply of potent vaccine could be ensured by the method.

OTHER COUNTRIES

Some random observations concerning the progress of immunization in countries overseas are of interest.

United States of America.—The first compulsory law was passed in 1855. Compulsion was not enforced, however, until 1872.

France and Germany.—During the Franco-Prussian War of 1870-71, the German Army was much better vaccinated than the French. Many of the Germans had been revaccinated within two years' time: there were 4,835 cases of smallpox, with only 278 deaths. The revaccination of the French troops had been permitted to lapse in the national emergency. French prisoners produced 14,178 cases of smallpox, with 1,963 deaths.

In Germany, the adoption of glycinerated lymph, mainly as a result of the influence of Koch, has already been mentioned. In 1869, Müller in Berlin had found that the addition of glycerine to lymph did not lead to deterioration. A few years later vaccination was made compulsory.

Austria.—From 1875 to 1894, 239,800 persons died from smallpox alone. This was almost 30 times as high a smallpox mortality as was recorded in the neighbouring country, Germany, where there was compulsory vaccination.

CHAPTER 10

NINETEENTH-CENTURY PROGRESS:
A SHORT GENERAL SURVEY

SINCE about 1800, social medicine has made rapid advances in many spheres. At the beginning of the period improvements in health were mainly the result of the rising standard of living. However, as the century progressed, disease could no longer be accepted passively, but was opposed actively with the utmost vigour. Sanitary measures had an effect from about 1870, and many medical measures came later. In consequence people are now healthier and are living longer. This book is concerned with only one aspect of the fight, namely immunization.

Before reviewing the advances (and some failures) made in this amazing period, the following data serve to show progress in perspective: they have a bearing on the control of infectious disease, and indeed on the state of the public health right through to the present day.

The average expectation of life was only about 22 years in Roman times and, according to Sigerist from 20 to 25 years in Europe in the fifteenth century. To quote from a 'Lancet' editorial (1964), it was 'above 36 at the end of the eighteenth century in western countries, and then *accelerando* from about 40 to 70 years in the last golden century of preventive and curative medicine'. In amplification of the last statement, the life expectation for a male at birth in England and Wales in 1876 was 41 years and for a female 43 years, in contrast to 68 years for a male child and 74 for a female in 1964.

I do not know the origin of the following table which I found amongst my papers: it reflects dramatically on life in the 'good old days' in this country.

Period	Children dying under 5 years of age
1730-49	75 per cent.
1811-29	32 ,, ,,
1915-24	13.8 ,, ,,

Although the control of smallpox by variolation had a limited success, the beginnings of immunization in the modern sense may be linked with Jenner's *Inquiry*, published in 1798. The flood of discoveries in the scientific era (from about 1875) was ushered in by Pasteur and Koch. While we pride ourselves on the speed at which advances are made in so many fields in modern era, it is salutary to contemplate and summarize some of the basic discoveries made in medical knowledge during the last two decades or so of the nineteenth century.

FROM PASTEUR AND KOCH TO EHRLICH

The new factors in this period were the rapid progress of the new sciences of bacteriology—the cause of at least one important infection was revealed almost yearly at first—and immunology. *Living and killed vaccines.*—Thanks to the bacteriological triumphs of Koch, Pasteur developed living attenuated (weakened) vaccines against fowl cholera, anthrax and swine erysipelas, which were all diseases of veterinary importance. The word immunity began to be used in 1880 in connection with this work on fowl cholera. Later, Pasteur applied the 'living attenuated' principle to vaccination against rabies or hydrophobia. The causal organism of this infection is a virus, which passed through the pores of a porcelain filter and was too small for him to see. (The electron microscope had not yet been invented.) Dogs were protected in the first instance by nervous tissue containing living attenuated virus. Ethical considerations made the next stage from animals to human beings somewhat difficult at first: however, Pasteur took the correct decision, and very fortunately the early human vaccinated cases did not develop rabies. The method was successful. Vaccination services for suspected cases were then established in several countries.

Pasteur, influenced to some extent by Jenner, was convinced

that *living* organisms were essential for the production of immunity. Continuing the story, his great rival, Koch, discovered the tubercle bacillus but failed to immunize against tuberculosis: effective preventive vaccines—once again, *living* attenuated organisms—were introduced only in the 1920s.

It was found that living organisms, even when attenuated, of certain diseases carry a danger of causing serious infection. Thus, an early experiment with living Malta fever vaccine produced the disease, and the method had to be abandoned. Fortunately, towards the end of the century, *killed* cultures of cholera organisms were being tried in the prevention of cholera, and Almroth Wright investigated dead typhoid vaccine, which was used in the Boer War in South Africa. This was a valuable contribution to disease prevention.

There was prolonged controversy about the mechanism of immunity between Metchnikoff, Nuttall and others. Almroth Wright also took part and developed his views about the rôle of cells known as phagocytes.

Filtrates (toxins and toxoids) as vaccines.—In the case of diphtheria and tetanus, the cellular or phagocytic theory of Metchnikoff was inapplicable. In 1888, Roux and Yersin, two of Pasteur's disciples, produced a bacteria-free filtrate of a broth culture of the diphtheria bacillus. This contained a powerful, soluble poison or toxin which produced the same symptoms in animals as a culture of the living bacillus itself. Other workers prepared the analogous toxic filtrate for the tetanus bacillus. Koch's pupils and associates, Behring and Kitasato, first produced the antidotes (antitoxins) for diphtheria and tetanus. In the 1890s antitoxic sera were coming into use for the control of these two diseases in man. A new type of vaccine (viz. formalinized toxin or toxoid) for human immunization, was developed many years later: modified toxins of this type have been conspicuously successful in preventing diphtheria and tetanus.

Ehrlich furthered the science of immunology, and therefore the consistent supply of good antitoxic sera, by introducing methods of exact measurement (1897). Reliable units and dried standard sera for reference purposes were essential requisites. Someone has said that Behring forged the sword of serotherapy, but Ehrlich ground its edge. Immunization as an exact science had begun, and was to have an increasing effect on the trend of mortality in the twentieth century, notably from 1920 onwards.

The beneficial effects of immunization on man (and animals), which are being unfolded in almost every chapter of this wonderful story, could only have been attained by experiments on animals, carried on from early times and still required today. Those who oppose further advances by this means incur a heavy moral responsibility, which is no longer excusable on the grounds of ignorance of the relevant facts. Are the vivisectionists (a misleading term) really cruel and callous, as sometimes depicted? Of course they are not. Let it be appreciated that bacteriological and virological research entails certain obvious risks to the workers themselves: some have even died. Further, in immunological investigations, there must come a stage when human experimentation takes over from tests on various laboratory animals. The author has been privileged to know many medical scientists who have run the calculated hazards of being human guinea-pigs for clinical trials of antisera and all kinds of vaccines for preventing human infections.

III

ANTISERA AND VACCINES: 1900-20

CHAPTER 11

IMMUNIZATION AGAINST DIPHTHERIA, TETANUS, GAS GANGRENE AND BOTULISM—DISEASES IN WHICH ANTITOXIC IMMUNITY IS OF VALUE

IN the period from 1900 to 1920 there were more important advances in this group of diseases, in which we are concerned with antitoxic immunity, than in other groups. It is fitting that the antitoxic infections should be considered first.

DIPHTHERIA

The Discovery of Toxoid.—From the beginning of the century the use of antitoxin had become established in the prevention and treatment of diphtheria throughout the world. The serum was made almost exclusively in horses, which were immunized mostly with toxin-antitoxin mixtures of variable proportions. However, as long ago as 1904, Alexander Glenny in London and E. Loewenstein in Vienna were using formalinized toxin (now known as toxoid in this country and anatoxine in France) in the immunization of horses and other animals. Glenny was concerned with diphtheria toxoid, but Loewenstein made his discovery primarily in connection with tetanus toxoid. It was worthy of note that nearly 20 years elapsed before toxoid came into use for human immunization: this is a surprisingly long latent period, which is unfortunate as toxoid now forms the basis of very successful diphtheria vaccines, rendering all earlier preparations obsolete.

Glenny told me that he produced toxoid by a very lucky chance. He was puzzled by the finding, that a particular batch of diphtheria toxin was of low toxicity but nevertheless immunized animals just as efficiently as the highly toxic batch that preceded it. He remembered that formalin had been used for chemical sterilization of the large earthenware butts which were used as containers in the toxin laboratory at that time. The anomalous differences between the successive batches of toxic filtrates were explained by the unforeseen action of residual formalin: the chemical had been responsible for conversion of toxin into 'detoxicated' toxin, which was still of full immunizing power or antigenicity. A toxic filtrate, which has been rendered harmless without destroying its capacity to induce antitoxin formation on injection into man or animals, is called toxoid. Moreover, according to modern nomenclature, it is one form of vaccine.

The rôle of toxoid in the conquest of diphtheria, tetanus and staphylococcus infection is discussed mainly in Section IV of this book (p. 89).

The Beginnings of Human Immunization.—With Toxin-Antitoxin.—In 1901, Behring was deservedly awarded a Nobel prize in Physiology and Medicine, and thereafter changed his name to von Behring. He continued to work on more or less balanced mixtures of toxin and antitoxin (T.A.) for producing immunity in animals. In 1907 and again in 1909, Theobald Smith, an American pathologist, suggested that such mixtures might be useful for human immunization. This project was not followed up till 1913, when von Behring used mixtures which were nearly neutral, and obtained relatively safe, rapid (usually some weeks) and durable immunity in man.

Both 1909 and 1913 were momentous for other advances also. In the former year, Paul Römer, who was a disciple of von Behring at Marburg, Germany, introduced an intradermal method in guinea-pigs for the quantitative estimation of the antitoxin content of specimens of blood serum. This convenient method of measurement gave a fillip to research in finding the best diphtheria vaccines for human immunization campaigns. Römer's discovery also served as a stimulus to Bela Schick—at that time a Hungarian paediatrician at the University of Vienna, but later an American citizen of New York—who published (1913) an account of the intradermal test in man which later bore his name: the Schick test involves the injection of a measured amount of diphtheria toxin, the local reaction to which is dependent on the antitoxin content of the blood. While not completely reliable, this harmless skin test provides a rough clinical method of determining a person's state of immunity to diphtheria.

Hypersensitivity to Serum.—In the period before the 1914-18 war, there was some anxiety over local and general reactions due to hypersensitivity to diphtheria antitoxic serum. As often happens, investigations were going on concurrently in different countries. In 1902, Bela Schick of Schick test fame collaborated with Clemens von Pirquet in studying the symptoms following injection and re-injection of horse serum. They published their classic *Die Serum-krankheit* (Serum Sickness) in Vienna in 1905. They explained the clinical manifestations as evidences of an antigen-antibody re-action in vivo. The foreign serum is an antigen to which antibody is elaborated. The appearance of symptoms is evidence of the harmful union of antigen and antibody after a variable interval, long or short. Full consideration of the mechanism is outside the scope of this book.

Also, in 1902, Charles Richet, Professor of Physiology at Paris, began a long research on allergies to foreign protein substances in dogs, rabbits and other animals. Reinjection of protein some-times gave rise to violent symptoms of poisoning and possibly death. This is the phenomenon which Richet called *anaphylaxis*, meaning the opposite of prophylaxis or protection: in one sense all serum allergy is a disorder of the antibody-forming mechanism or protection 'gone wrong'. In 1903, Nicolas Arthus, at the instigation of Richet, observed and studied the signs of local anaphylaxis (Arthus phenomenon) in rabbits injected at intervals with sub-stances like horse serum and milk. Fortunately this type of very severe reaction is rare in man.

A third country in which abnormal reactions to horse serum were being investigated was the United States of America, where Theobald Smith (previously mentioned in this chapter in con-nection with toxin antitoxin) made independent observations on what has been called the Theobald Smith phenomenon but is essentially anaphylaxis. When testing diphtheria antitoxin in guinea-pigs, second injections of the serum administered after a long interval produced severe symptoms including convulsive seizures. More than half the animals died within 30 minutes.

There were of course other workers in various countries who made useful contributions to the problem of untoward reactions. The constituent of a serum responsible for serum allergy was proved to be independent of the antitoxic antibodies, as normal horse serum yielded exactly the same results as an antiserum.

Finally, in 1910, the incidence of serum sickness after injections of horse serum was reduced by Robert Gibson and Edwin Banzhaf in America, who concentrated serum by a process of fractional precipitation with ammonium or sodium sulphate. As the diphtheria antitoxin is intimately associated with the pseudo-globulin fraction of the serum, these chemists were able to devise a practical method of eliminating many non-antitoxic protein constituents. Their process of purification and concentration was generally applied to antitoxins for upwards of 30 years. The quality of sera was improved by the removal of much non-essential protein, and reactions were less troublesome than with unconcentrated preparations.

The New York Immunization Campaign.—In 1914, William Park, the bacteriologist and Director of Hygiene Services and his associate, Abraham Zingher, began to use toxin-antitoxin mixtures extensively in New York City. Susceptible children were selected by means of the Schick test. In the first year of the campaign approximately 10,000 children and adults were injected. The results were most successful and will be reviewed in a later chapter (p. 94).

Behring was a pioneer in immunization with toxin-antitoxin, and Park deserves credit for the practical application of his discovery on a large scale.

TETANUS

Prevention with Antitoxic Serum: Independence Day Celebrations.—At the beginning of the century antitoxin was already being used prophylactically in the treatment of wounds. The best example of its success was the annual records of the injuries received during the celebrations on July 4 (Independence Day) in the U.S.A. From 1904, due to the initiative of the American Medical Association, serum prophylaxis was encouraged, and there was a consistent fall in the mortality from tetanus. The following data illustrate this improvement: Of 3,983 Fourth of July injuries in 1903, 406 resulted in death from tetanus, equivalent to 102 tetanus deaths per 1,000 injuries. Of 3,986 injuries in 1904, the first year of the campaign, 91 resulted in death from tetanus, equivalent to 23 deaths per 1,000 injuries. There was no further improvement till after 1910—still 24 tetanus deaths per 1,000 injuries—but the results from 1911 to 1914 were quite dramatic. In 1914 the incidence of injuries was reduced to 1,506 with no mortality from tetanus.

From 1910 onwards there was a fall in the numbers of injuries: this is readily explained by success in a further campaign to restrict the sale of fireworks—an aim which made little or no impact in the early years (1904-09).

Prophylaxis in Warfare.—The effectiveness of tetanus antitoxin in prophylaxis was also demonstrated in the British Army on the Western Front in the World War of 1914-18. In the early months of the war (August-October, 1914) the incidence of tetanus reached the alarming figure of 8 cases per 1,000 wounded, and some 85 per cent. of these died. There was a shortage of antitoxin during these months and the available serum was naturally reserved for treatment rather than prevention. Ample supplies of antitoxin were ordered urgently and were hurried to the Front during November 1914. The incidence of tetanus soon fell to about 1 case per 1,000 wounded at the end of the year, and the mortality to less than half. In 1918 the incidence was about 0·6 per 1,000 wounded.

During the 1914-18 war there were 2,500 cases of tetanus in the British Army, with 550 deaths. It has been suggested that, if there had been no antitoxic serum, there might have been 25,000 cases with 20,000 deaths.

It is interesting to compare the incidence of tetanus (per 1,000 wounded) in the 1914-18 war with that of certain other campaigns.

TABLE

INCIDENCE OF TETANUS

Campaign	Per thousand wounded
Peninsular War (British Legion in Spain)	12·5
Crimean War	2·0
American Civil War	2·0
Franco-Prussian War	3·5

ANTITOXIN USED

1914-18 (British Army-Western Front)　　　　　　1·47

TOXOID USED (SUPPLEMENTED BY ANTITOXIN)

1939-45 (Different British Armies or Theatres of War)　　0·04-0·43

It will be seen that the control of tetanus was best in the 1939-45 war when tetanus vaccines, supplemented by antitoxin, were the specific measures employed (see p. 119).

GAS GANGRENE

This disease has no connection with gas warfare, as its name might suggest. It is simply a special type of bacterial infection of wounds characterized by spreading swelling, gangrene or death of tissues, and gas formation.

According to the official *History of the Great War* of 1914-18, the incidence of gas gangrene among the British troops in France was 1 to 5 per cent. of all wounds, with a death-rate of about 22 per cent. It is not surprising that the causal anaerobic bacilli and their toxins were studied intensively in different countries, with a view to the preparation of potent antisera. These were available for the British, French and German medical services only towards the end of the war.

The organisms mainly responsible for the local necrosis, cellulitis and gas formation, and, in fatal cases, death were *Clostridium welchii* (Welch's bacillus), *Cl. septicum (Vibrion septique)* and *Cl. oedematiens (Cl. novyi)*. The first and most important of these organisms was discovered (1892) by William Henry Welch of Baltimore, the famous American pathologist: it is significant that he had attended lectures by Koch in Berlin, and was doubtless inspired by that great pioneer. His collaborator in research on infection was George Nuttall, who has already been mentioned as the first scientist to describe the bactericidal properties of normal horse serum. Welch's bacillus is also known as *Cl. perfringens*. In the war of 1914-18 it represented about 70 per cent. of the anaerobic spore-bearing bacilli associated with wound infection: the contributions of *Cl. septicum* and *Cl. oedematiens* were about 15 per cent. each.

In 1917, Carroll Bull and I. W. Pritchett, and M. W. Weinberg and P. Séguin of the Allied Armies showed that these organisms produced soluble toxins: specific antitoxins could therefore be prepared by immunizing horses with formol toxoids. Weinberg of the Pasteur Institute, Paris, was for many years the leading French authority on this group of organisms.

Starting early in 1918, considerable quantities of mixed tetanus and welchii antitoxins were used by the British Army in France. At first, the proper dosage and the best route of injection had to be investigated. This research was difficult as the various gas-gangrene antisera differed widely in potency. However, where serum was given early, its value in prophylaxis was unquestioned, according to the observers of a Committee set up by the Medical Research Council. In treatment, the results 'exceeded expectations —in view of the numerous factors which militated against success'.

If the war had lasted into 1919, it is almost certain that a mixed tetanus, welchii, septicum, oedematiens antitoxin would have been employed. Supplies were ready for use.

Readers should appreciate that in the 1914-18 war there was less efficient wound surgery than was developed subsequently. Further, there were no antibiotics. The gas-gangrene problem never attained such magnitude again.

BOTULISM

This rare but severe type of food poisoning was given its name from *botulus*, the Latin word for sausage, because German physicians who first studied it found that it often developed after the consumption of spoiled sausages. In 1896, E. M. van Ermengem of Ghent isolated the causal spore-bearing anaerobe (now known as *Cl. botulinum*) from a pickled ham which had been responsible for 34 cases of botulism, 10 of which were severe, with three deaths. The disease is due to the ingestion of toxin—apparently the most potent of all poisons—which is already formed by this bacterium in contaminated meat or canned vegetables. The relative rarity of serious trouble is mainly explained by the observation that this toxin is destroyed by boiling for four to 20 minutes.

Soon after the discovery of the organism and of its extremely toxic filtrates, potent antitoxic sera were prepared by the immunization of goats (1897). Many years later (1910), L. Leuchs prepared antitoxic sera in horses. All this early work was done on the continent of Europe.

The disease also became a problem in America. In 1915 and again in 1918, Ernest Dickson reported many cases of botulism in the United States. Outbreaks also occurred in Canada, and in both these countries the case mortality was approximately 66 per cent.

There was an interesting development in 1919 when the American bacteriologist, Georgiana Burke, studied a number of strains of *Cl. botulinum*, which she placed in two groups, Types A and B, on the basis of toxin-antitoxin neutralization tests. (Other types were identified later.) She found that Type A antitoxin neutralized the filtrates of Type A strains but not of Type B strains—and vice versa. This observation had a practical bearing on prophylaxis and treatment: monotypical serum would obviously be expected to give better results when the type of the intoxicating organism is known. In practice this is a rare event, because laboratory investigations are time-consuming and the disease runs a rapid course.

In the period under review (1900-20), some apparently favourable results were reported in the treatment of human cases of botulism. Large doses of serum were advised, although they were not very effective when quite large amounts of toxin might have been ingested, causing profound toxaemia and collapse. Prophylaxis with antitoxin, or preferably with mixed toxoids, is much more likely to be successful than is the treatment of established botulism. There is an analogous situation in connection with tetanus which is discussed in a later chapter (p. 117).

CHAPTER 12

IMMUNIZATION AGAINST ENTERIC FEVER, CHOLERA AND BACILLARY DYSENTERY: THE 1914-18 WAR

THIS and the next chapters are concerned mainly with infections (other than tetanus and gas gangrene) which were of importance to the armed forces of different countries before and during the World War of 1914-18. Although the period under review is 1900-20, there is an obvious disadvantage in too rigid an adherence to these dates: some overlap into the previous century has been inevitable in order to assist the reader.

We have already seen (p. 37) that soldiers on active service are particularly vulnerable to epidemic diseases and that in large campaigns more men used to die from infections than from enemy action. War therefore affords excellent scope for the introduction of immunization and controlled research. Unlike civilians, troops can be organized, and if necessary compelled, to be inoculated against certain well-known scourges of armies, of which enteric (typhoid and paratyphoid) fever is one of the most important.

ENTERIC FEVER

Vaccination in India.—In 1904 an antityphoid Committee of the British War Office, of which Almroth Wright and William Leishman were members, stated that typhoid vaccine had caused 'a substantial reduction in the incidence and death-rate from enteric fever among the inoculated'. It was also recommended 'that the practice of voluntary inoculation against enteric fever in the Army be resumed'. Leishman, who had become Professor of Pathology at the Royal Army Medical College, was asked to supervise further research. Troops proceeding to India and other foreign stations were systematically inoculated, and by 1909 practically all the soldiers stationed in that country had been done. There was a reduction in the enteric fever admissions to hospitals from 8·9 per 1,000, with a death-rate of 1·58 in 1909, to 2·3 per 1,000, with a death-rate of 0·25 in 1913.

The First World War: British Armies.—In 1911 Leishman ordered a reserve of vaccine sufficient for the personnel of six divisions to be held in readiness in case of hostilities. At the outbreak of the 1914-18 war there were 200,000 doses available for use, and the skeleton organization existed for a greatly expanded vaccine department.

Britain owes a great debt to Leishman, one of the most distinguished army medical officers of all time. Thanks to his foresight, about 97 per cent. of the British armies in France were inoculated on a voluntary basis: there was said to be no compulsion. The vaccines were all prepared at the Royal Army Medical College in London. Altogether 20 million doses of vaccine came from this source during the war period.

The following data of cases and deaths due to enteric fevers throughout the four years of war illustrate the progress made since the Boer War in South Africa:

TABLE

	Annual incidence per 1,000 strength	Annual death rate per 1,000 strength	Total cases	Total deaths	Mean strength
1914-18	2·35	0·139	20,139	1,191	2,000,000 (approx.)
South African War 1899-1902	105·00	14·6	57,684	9,022	208,226

If this grim experience of the British and Colonial troops in the South African War were applied to the British Armies in all theatres in the 1914-18 war, it would have resulted in the enormous totals of 1,000,000 cases and about 125,000 deaths. These figures could easily have been higher, having regard to the type of warfare. The fighting on the Western Front was mostly in insanitary trenches along the Franco-German frontier where typhoid fever was endemic: yet, thanks to the medical services, typhoid was not a major problem—there were only 7,500 cases, with 266 deaths, on this front, which had an average British strength of one and a quarter million. Even unhealthy Gallipoli failed to produce the very high incidence that was expected. The contribution of preventive inoculation to these striking figures is a matter for speculation. The use of vaccine was certainly an important factor, but another was the improvement (even under difficulties) in military hygiene, with special regard to the water supply.

The vaccine used from 1914 to 1916 was typhoid only. It was changed to a mixed typhoid, paratyphoid A and paratyphoid B (T.A.B.) vaccine early in 1916, because paratyphoid A and B infections were occurring in some theatres of war. Triple vaccination helped to prevent serious outbreaks.

The First World War: Other Armies.—The results obtained by Leishman in India and elsewhere attracted attention in many countries. In the United States of America, the British procedure was copied. Vaccination was even made compulsory for all soldiers in 1911, and two years later only one case of typhoid was reported among over 80,000 men. During the 1914-18 conflict there were 1,529 cases, with 227 deaths, in an American force of 4,129,478 in all theatres of war. The figures for the Western Front were 488 cases, with 88 deaths, among perhaps 2,000,000 troops. These data were most satisfactory.

In France, the unexpected outbreak of hostilities left the army incompletely protected for more than a year; under field conditions, speedy inoculation was not possible. During the first 16 months of the war, 96,000 cases occurred, with nearly 12,000 deaths. As soon as the vaccination of the troops had been effected, however, the French figures showed a dramatic improvement and were similar to the British.

The German Army also suffered through failure to give priority to typhoid vaccination in 1914. An alarming epidemic of typhoid fever occurred early in 1915, which subsided following the hurried inoculation of the soldiers.

The British Army Pathology Advisory Committee.—After the 1914-18 war, various wartime consultative committees were wisely merged into the A.P.A.C. The function of this body was primarily to supervise research to meet the needs of the Armed Forces, but it speedily acquired influence and authority outside the confines of the Services. A Pathology Directorate was also set up under the chairmanship of Major-General Sir William Leishman.

CHOLERA

This much-dreaded and fatal disease used to spread in Britain and is believed to have killed 1 in 131 of its population during the pandemic of 1831. It has already been mentioned in this book in connection with the Crimean War (p. 34), but its relative prevalence was unknown; inevitably, in the pre-bacteriological era, cholera was confused with enteric fever, dysentery, ulcerative colitis and other infections of the bowel. Water-borne diseases might occur together. For the bulk of people sanitation was non-existent, and many even believed that the smell from ordure purified and disinfected their living quarters!

John Snow, the famous anaethetist who administered chloroform to Queen Victoria at the birth of Prince Leopold, was also a pioneer in epidemiology and preventive medicine. He studied cholera epidemics in London in 1848-49 and again in 1853-54, and adduced that there was an association between cholera deaths and the drinking of infected water. He believed that cholera was propagated by means of intestinal discharges. The epidemic of 1848-49 is said to have caused 54,000 deaths in England, and Snow's work drew attention to the need for public and domestic sanitation. Alas, nothing more definite came of it.

In 1883, Robert Koch supplied definite proof of the infective nature of cholera by identifying the causal organism, *Vibrio cholerae* or the 'comma bacillus'. In order to clinch his discovery he made a special journey to Calcutta, where he found the vibrio (which had aroused his suspicions on a previous expedition to study cholera in Egypt) in the corpses of all of forty cholera victims examined: he could not demonstrate it in hundreds of healthy Hindus nor in any animal species from elephants to mice. He also learned to grow this organism on a beef-broth jelly. Incidentally, cholera is endemic in the warm, humid delta of the Ganges, and from there it spreads from time to time in various directions, usually along the trade routes.

77

Jaime Ferran, a Spanish bacteriologist, who had worked under Pasteur, was the first to attempt vaccination (1884), but his living attenuated cultures caused too much reaction on injection. The method was abandoned, but his practical studies stimulated Waldemar Haffkine, another pupil of Pasteur, to try to do better. From 1892 for many years Haffkine worked intensively in India on problems of immunization against cholera and plague. Like Ferran, he failed with attenuated vaccines. He eventually showed that protection could be obtained safely by using cultures of the cholera vibrio which had been killed by heat. In 1896, Wilhelm Kolle, who worked in Koch's laboratory in Berlin, also introduced a heat-killed, phenolized vaccine. The adverse reactions to killed vaccines were negligible.

One disadvantage of the killed type of cholera vaccine is that the immunity conferred is short-lived, further doses of vaccine having to be given every six months. This may be feasible in the Services, but civilian members of any community cannot be persuaded to attend twice yearly to have their protection revived or 'boosted'.

The First World War.—In 1915, two British statisticians, Major Greenwood and George Yule, analysed the accumulated data of Haffkine and many others. Although many of the available figures were worthless from the statistical standpoint, vaccination was apparently 'a prophylactic step of importance'. This study encouraged the use of cholera vaccine for the Armed Forces serving in certain eastern theatres of war, where there was a likelihood of the spread of infection from the civil population to the troops. Allied and German armies in these countries were given preventive inoculation. Experience showed that the selection of the cholera strains for the vaccine had some influence on its efficacy: some were better than others. By and large, the results were satisfactory: isolated cases occurred among the vaccinated troops, but there was no epidemic spread. Reactions were slight and much milder than with enteric vaccine.

During the war, a so-called 'tetravaccine' was used on the Serbian Army. It was a mixture of typhoid, paratyphoid A and B and cholera vaccines, and was similar to one prepared in 1910 by Aldo Castellani, an Italian specialist in tropical diseases, who practised for many years in London: he had mixed agar cultures of the different organisms in saline emulsion. Combined immunization reduced the number of injections, and was a convenient advance especially under field conditions.

BACILLARY DYSENTERY

Bacillary dysentery resembles enteric fever and cholera in its epidemic spread from person to person when proper sanitation cannot be enforced. In civil life it has broken out in mental hospitals, jails and nurseries. It tends to be prevalent in armies, especially under war conditions when the weather is warm.

The causal organisms of the bacillary variety of dysentery (to be distinguished from the amoebic type) belong to a group of bacilli, of which certain species are relatively common and important. The only type of major immunological interest is *Bacillus dysenteriae* or, as it is now named, *Shigella shigae*. Its discoverer was Kiyoshi Shiga, a pupil of Kitasato, who in turn was a disciple of Koch himself. In 1896 there was an enormous epidemic of dysentery in Japan, causing 90,000 cases and 20,000 deaths. While investigating this outbreak, Shiga isolated the organism from the stools of patients, and also showed that it was agglutinated or clumped by the blood serum of other patients.

In 1900, Shiga prepared an antiserum—as Kitasato would have done. The animals were immunized with killed cultures of his bacillus, and their serum was useful in treating the human disease. The case mortality rate of the serum-treated group was 12 per cent., whereas from 28.5 to 37.9 per cent. of other groups of patients which were treated without serum died.

While this work was in progress, bacteriologists in other countries studied their dysenteric patients, and isolated strains which are now broadly classified into either the Shiga or Flexner group. The latter was named after the American investigator, Simon Flexner.

In a number of dysentery cases there is necrosis or death of the lining mucous membrane of the colon. L. Rosenthal in Moscow and C. Todd in London showed independently in 1903-04 that this damage was caused by a soluble toxin (culture-filtrate) of Shiga's bacillus, analogous to the toxins of diphtheria and tetanus. How-

79

ever, there was one interesting difference: Shiga culture-filtrates were most toxic when the cultures were old and the bacilli were broken up or autolysed, whereas diphtheria culture-filtrates were highly toxic without any need for ageing and the presence of autolysed bacillary bodies. Rosenthal and Todd also showed that Shiga toxin gives rise to a neutralizing antitoxin on injection into animals.

Flexner bacilli rather surprisingly do not produce a soluble toxin, and therefore there is no antitoxic serum.

The First World War.—Bacillary dysentery due to the Shiga bacillus was the commonest disease on the Gallipoli Peninsula and caused the greatest number of deaths. It contributed appreciably to the ultimate failure of the British and Australian troops, whose commander, General Sir Ian Hamilton, is reported to have remarked from his bed of sickness that it explained to his satisfaction why the Greeks took ten years to capture Troy.

Shiga dysentery was also prevalent on the Macedonian front, which was based on Salonica. Antitoxin of Shiga type was used and proved beneficial in proved cases. The effect was sometimes only temporary. In these early days the control of dysentery was hardly a success story.

Shiga and Flexner vaccines.—Although a wide variety of dysentery vaccines were used from 1903 onwards, there is no conclusive evidence that any preparation was of value for either prevention or treatment.

CHAPTER 13

IMMUNIZATION AGAINST PLAGUE, BRUCELLOSIS, CEREBROSPINAL MENINGITIS, TYPHUS FEVER AND INFLUENZA—OLD MENACES IN PEACE AND WAR

PLAGUE

PLAGUE or pestilence caused the Black Death in Europe in the fourteenth century, when there were perhaps 33 million deaths out of a total population of 100 million—possibly the greatest single disaster ever to befall mankind. In this country it may have been responsible for 2 million deaths—said to be a quarter to a half of the population at that time. In the sixteenth and seventeenth centuries there were frequent importations from the Continent to Britain. The last of these was the Great Plague of London of 1664-65, when 80,000 deaths occurred (an average estimate) out of a population of 460,000, a quarter of whom fled from the City.

The rat is the main carrier of plague, which is essentially a disease of rodents and *not* a disease of man: the improvement of city drainage and the use of stone and brick as building materials instead of wood helped to eliminate the rat and consequently the threat of this disease from this country. Although the last major epidemic on the Continent of Europe was in Constantinople in 1803, millions of persons in India, China and elsewhere in Asia were still dying from plague in the 1890s and the early years of the present century. These epidemics stimulated research on the control of this ever-present menace.

Bacteriology: early vaccines: rôle of rats.—S. Kitasato and A. Yersin (respectively disciples of Koch and Pasteur) discovered independently the causal bacillus, now known as *Pasteurella pestis*, during an epidemic in Hong Kong in 1893-94. They also transmitted the disease to rats—a line of research suggested to them by the heavy

81

mortality of rats at this time. In epidemics since 1894, numerous rats have died from plague *before* human cases have been recognized. In China and the Himalayas, plague was commonly called the 'rats' disease'. Kitasato established the rôle of the rat-flea in the transmission of plague (1897-98). The infection was transmitted from rat to rat by their fleas, but occasionally the rat-fleas left their dying hosts and climbed on to humans, carrying the plague bacilli with them. An important British Commission eventually decided that the elimination of rodents and fleas was the most important measure in the prevention of plague.

Vaccines.—Yersin, Albert Calmette and Amédée Borrel prepared the first plague vaccine, killed by heat, in 1895. In the following year, there was an outbreak of plague in Bombay. In consequence, the Indian Government engaged Waldemar Haffkine to investigate and prepare plague vaccines—really an extension of the work on which he was already engaged on cholera vaccines. Once again he used killed cultures. After the first 8,000 persons were inoculated, the Plague Research Laboratory was set up to produce vaccine for many millions. In 1925, this Laboratory became the Haffkine Institute as a tribute to its founder.

Haffkine's work had a serious set-back in 1902, when 19 persons died from tetanus, after being inoculated with his vaccine at Mulkowal. In 1902-03 there was a tremendous strain on the manufacturing laboratory—more than half a million persons were inoculated against plague—and some lowering of standards had been inevitable. The official view was that responsibility for the disaster lay with Haffkine's laboratory, but Haffkine himself always maintained that the contamination had been introduced elsewhere. For a time he was suspended, but was subsequently reinstated as Director-in-Chief of the Biological Laboratory in Calcutta.

With regard to the results of inoculation, a typical finding was a reduction in case incidence from 7.7 per cent. among the uninoculated to 1.8 per cent. among the inoculated. The case mortality was reduced from 60.1 per cent. to 23.9 per cent. in the same groups. These statistics came from the Punjab during the cholera season of 1902-03, and were from selected villages where 10 per cent. or more of the population had been immunized.

From 1905 onwards a Plague Commission under the joint auspices of the Royal Society, the Indian Office and the Indian Medical Service supervised research work on all aspects of the prevention and control of epidemics, and issued numerous valuable reports. We have already referred to its pronouncement on the rôle of rats and rat-fleas.

Towards the end of the 1914-18 war this Commission reported that plague vaccine reduced the incidence of the disease to about one-fourth and case mortality about one-half. The death rate was thus reduced to one-eighth.

BRUCELLOSIS

This is the name given to a group of diseases of man and animals, which are due to three species of very small, related bacilli, now known as *Brucella melitensis, Br. abortus* and *Br. suis.*

Malta Fever.—This is the manifestation of brucellosis, which first attracted attention after British forces captured Malta from the French in 1799. The disease has already been mentioned in an earlier chapter (p. 34). The causal organism was discovered (1887) by David Bruce, later a Surgeon-General in the British Army. Almroth Wright's research on vaccination, including his own illness after an injection of a living culture, has also been described (p. 35).

In 1904, a Commission was set up to investigate Malta fever, with Bruce as chairman. Their main finding was to incriminate the goats on the island, which excreted the organism in milk sold for human consumption. When the drinking of unboiled milk was prohibited, the incidence of Malta fever fell dramatically. From 1906 onwards, dead cultures of *Br. melitensis* were sometimes used for the prophylaxis of persons exposed to risk. Two doses were advised, and some protection was obtained.

Contagious Abortion of Cattle.—An illness causing abortion in cattle was shown (1895) to be due to a species of small organism now known as *Brucella abortus.* Its discoverer was Frederick Bang of Copenhagen. About 1910 it was suggested that Bang's bacillus could also give rise to an intermittent but persistent type of illness in man. The kinship of Bruce's and Bang's micro-organisms was not recognized till many years later.

In 1906, Bang successfully used a living vaccine for the protection of cattle: killed vaccines were useless. This work was confirmed in Great Britain, although it was noted that the choice of strain was important. If cultures were too virulent, pregnant cows might abort, and, if such virulent organisms in protective vaccines happened to be excreted in milk, human cases of brucellosis might result. Obviously the melitensis germ was not the only pathogen which might infect man: the abortus variety constituted a potential danger also.

Brucellosis in Swine.—Abortion in swine may be caused by the porcine type of organism, now called *Brucella suis*. It was discovered (1914) by Jacob Traum of the United States Bureau of Animal Industry. Direct infection with this organism has long been recognized as a hazard in swine abattoirs in America, but it is very rare in Britain.

All three types of *Brucella* can infect many species of domestic animals and also man, and all the diseases due to them are included under the term Brucellosis or Undulant Fever.

Further developments with vaccine in prophylaxis and treatment are discussed in Chapter 21. There were conspicuous successes in the veterinary field where live vaccines could be used. In man, all vaccines were given up.

CEREBROSPINAL MENINGITIS

Epidemics with 'stiffness of the neck' have been recorded for centuries. Although in the pre-bacteriological era there was inevitably much confusion with such diseases as poliomyelitis, typhus and influenza, some of these outbreaks were undoubtedly a contagious form of meningitis. One of the many organisms which can cause infection of the meninges (membranes covering the brain) is the meningococcus or *Neisseria meningitidis*, first cultivated (1887) by Anton Weichselbaum of Vienna.

An antimeningoccal serum was first prepared in 1905 in Germany. Thereafter intensive research was carried out on serum therapy in many countries, notably by Simon Flexner and James

Jobling of the Rockefeller Institute, New York. Good results were claimed in the early years, when the antiserum was injected intrathecally (into the lumbar spine) after a quantity of cerebrospinal fluid had been withdrawn. Thereafter doubts arose, and there was no general agreement about the actual worth of any antiserum. The product was never given to alternate cases in an epidemic, and the effect of lumbar puncture and the withdrawal of fluid, on the serum-treated cases was never assessed. As this procedure appeared to be of value, a similar number of control cases should also have been subjected to lumbar puncture. In clinical trials, both treated and control groups should be maintained under conditions as identical as possible in order to meet the requirements of the statistician.

In recent chapters, special attention has been paid to events in the 1914-18 war. Like other infections, cerebrospinal meningitis came to the fore possibly due to adverse, overcrowded conditions. In this country, there was a considerable epidemic amongst the troops and later amongst civilians in 1915. In that year there were 712 notifications in London with 241 deaths, the case mortality rate being 34 per cent. Mervyn Gordon and George Murray did valuable bacteriological work during the epidemic and classified their strains into four types on the basis of agglutination tests. Much antiserum was used, mostly polyvalent and made from recent strains of representative types, which was later administered intravenously as well as intrathecally. In retrospect, although it was considered to be useful at that time, serotherapy may not have been of much value. It was subsequently replaced by effective chemotherapy.

TYPHUS FEVER

Many of the pestilences throughout the ages must surely have been typhus fever, although this disease was often confused with plague and enteric fever in the pre-bacteriological era. Inevitably, as mentioned elsewhere, there must also have been the co-existence of various dire infections in major military campaigns and other circumstances. Predisposing causes of typhus included overcrowding, poverty and filth. Synonyms such as 'famine fever', 'jail fever', 'ship fever', and 'hospital fever' reveal much.

Napoleon's expeditions, including the disastrous Russian venture of 1812, were much upset by typhus. Armies in other campaigns have also suffered a heavy toll. Medical writers such as Zinsser and Hobson have drawn attention to the major part played by disease in influencing the course of history: Hobson criticizes generations of historians for having too little to say about a factor of such far-reaching importance as pestilence.

In the 1914-18 war, Serbia suffered severely from typhus, which affected both the retreating army and the civilian population. It is significant that when the outbreak was at its height in 1914-15, all of 400 Serbian doctors contracted the disease, with 126 deaths. The disorganization in Eastern Europe during and after the war also facilitated epidemic spread. Between 1918 and 1922, according to one estimate there were 30 million cases of typhus in Russia, with three million deaths. In 1920, there were 3,216,000 notifications in Russia, and 200,000 in Poland.

In 1909, Charles Nicolle of the Pasteur Institute in Tunis showed that the vector of epidemic typhus was the body louse, *Pediculus corporis*. The causal agent, *Rickettsia prowazeki*, was discovered in 1916 by Henrique da Rocha Lima, a Brazilian working in Germany, who named it after Ricketts and von Prowazek, two research pioneers who had died of the disease. (The rickettsiae are a group of organisms usually included among the viruses, although they are slightly larger than the viruses proper.) The rat (with its rat fleas and lice) is a reservoir of the typhus rickettsia between epidemics.

Antisera and vaccines against louse-borne typhus were developed much later (p. 173).

INFLUENZA

Apart from the acute respiratory infections between epidemics that are popularly called 'influenza', there is a more virulent and widespread form which occurs every few years as epidemics. The virus of 'true influenza' was demonstrated in 1933, but the clinical data of many previous epidemics strongly suggest the typical disease, although this probability cannot be confirmed.

In 1892-93, Richard Pfeiffer, who had been associated with Robert Koch in Berlin, isolated a bacillus, *Haemophilus influenzae*, during an epidemic. At first it was present with great constancy in typical cases, but in the 1918-19 pandemic it was often absent. It has now been relegated to a subsidiary rôle.

The 1918-19 pandemic was one of the worst plagues in history, and was doubtless an unforeseen consequence of all the rigours of four years of war and its aftermath. The virus suddenly broke loose and swept through vast disorganized populations. There were probably 500 million cases all over the world, with 25 million deaths—more than all the battle casualties of all nations throughout the war. In London alone it killed 18 thousand persons.

Naturally, many bacterial vaccines were tried in the control of influenza at this time. A favourite one was a mixture of *H. influenzae*, the pneumococcus and the streptococcus, all of which were common 'secondary invaders'. Notwithstanding some favourable claims, it would seem that no bacterial vaccine had a significant effect on either the incidence or the mortality-rate. No immunity was conferred.

Vaccine work of this nature has also a bearing on other acute respiratory infections, including the common cold (p. 164). However, progress in virology, which began with the discovery of the virus of influenza in 1933, led to a new era for preventive vaccination against diseases of this group (p. 159). Considerable progress has been made, but much remains to be done.

IV

ACCOMPLISHMENTS—

MAINLY SINCE 1920:

MORE AND BETTER BACTERIAL VACCINES

CHAPTER 14

THE CONQUEST OF DIPHTHERIA BY ACTIVE IMMUNIZATION: I

INOCULATION against diphtheria is the classical example of primary prevention in medicine.

Early Work on Immunization in Britain.—In the 1920s, a backroom British scientist, Alexander Glenny, rapidly came to the fore for a series of important contributions to the principles and practice of immunization. His work in the laboratory was first applied clinically by Richard O'Brien and his colleagues of the Wellcome Research Laboratories, and it also influenced opinion and practice all over the world. It will be recalled that Glenny and Loewenstein were independently using formalinized toxin (toxoid) for the immunization of horses and other animals as far back as 1904: this practical utilization of toxoid was Glenny's first major discovery—more important in retrospect than was appreciated at the time.

His second valuable contribution was concerned with the essential principles of the control of infections by immunization. In 1921, Glenny and his colleague, H. J. Südmersen, enunciated the laws of primary and secondary stimulus responses to an antigen (a preparation of diphtheria toxin) injected into a variety of non-immune and immune animals and applicable also to men. The first dose of an antigen produced only minimal antibody or basic protection (*primary response*) in a completely non-immune subject. However, it served to condition or educate the body so that a second dose, given after a suitable interval, would produce large amounts of antibody rapidly (*secondary response*). In effect, Glenny and Südmersen were studying differences in the speed and extent of responses after different antigenic stimuli. The most advantageous spacing of injections, and to a less extent the optimal size of dose, in human and animal immunization in general have been based on this fundamental work.

Schick-testing and *toxin-antitoxin mixtures,* T.A. were used in 1921-22 by O'Brien and his team. Although such mixtures were employed extensively in the U.S.A. and Germany, they were never issued commercially in Britain: both O'Brien of the Wellcome Laboratories and Monckton Copeman of the Ministry of Health considered that any vaccine containing unmodified toxin as one of its constituents was potentially unsafe. In any event, Glenny was soon preparing (1923) *toxoid antitoxin mixture, T.A.M.* This was obviously a much safer preparation because toxoid was substituted for toxin, thus ensuring complete non-toxicity without the addition of antitoxin. Unfortunately both the American T.A. and the safer British T.A.M. shared the disadvantage of containing a small amount of horse antitoxic serum, which sufficed to sensitize a very few persons to subsequent injections of tetanus antitoxin and other preparations of horse serum. Incidentally, T.A. and T.A.M. were weak and slow-acting in comparison with modern diphtheria vaccines.

The next prophylactic of importance was undiluted, unpurified *toxoid, F.T.* which caused rather frequent local and general reactions and was soon given up (1924-25). A similar prophylactic called 'anatoxine' in France seemed to have the same incidence of untoward reactions, but this was not regarded as a serious drawback in that country. Later, the British toxoid was diluted 1 in 10 and was tried on a small scale as *toxoid, M.T.* It caused fewer reactions but was too weak for general use—it was quite impracticable to give early and repeated reinforcing doses in order to compensate for the low potency. Accordingly, this diluted vaccine was soon withdrawn.

P. (later Sir Percival) Hartley of the National Institute for Medical Research, London, prepared *toxin-antitoxin floccules* by suspending the flocculant deposit which forms when toxin and antitoxin are mixed in neutralizing proportions. He showed that this suspension produced immunity in animals, but he did not recommend its use for human immunization because the toxin constituent was a potential hazard. However, Glenny and C. G. Pope introduced (1927) washed *toxoid-antitoxin floccules, T.A.F.,* which was based on Hartley's prophylactic and was completely safe. This was a useful but rather slow-acting vaccine, requiring three doses for the primary course. It caused very little reaction, but unfortunately could cause sensitization to horse serum because it contained a small amount of this serum itself.

Clinical Trials: 1920-35.—During this period O'Brien and his colleagues accepted invitations to control outbreaks of diphtheria in a number of institutions and training centres. Opportunities were taken for testing out new techniques or variations of old ones, in accordance with the indications provided by research in the immunological laboratory. The following representative list of seven of the places visited is now of general historical interest: (1) the Holborn Poor-Law Schools, Mitcham, and (2) the Lambeth Poor-Law Schools, West Norwood. (Subsequently both these schools came under the control of the London County Council, and the poor-law stigma was dropped.) (3) Dr. Barnardo's Girls' Homes at Barkingside, Ilford.

Here, some digression may be permissible. The children at Barnardo's were grouped in separate houses, each with a foster mother; they retained their individuality and were obviously happy. They also welcomed the visits of the immunization team. One day the research doctors were puzzled, and not a little worried, by some unusual reactions on the forearms of children they were sure they had never injected. One child, bolder than the others, then confessed she had been playing at Schick testing—with mud and a pin! Fortunately there was no sepsis!

The immunization campaign at Barnardo's halted diphtheria and was so successful that a prominent representative of the Ilford staff drew attention to it in a letter to *The Times*. The reaction of a small section of contributors to the Homes was unexpected. Letters were received calling for a halt to experimentation on defence-less children under penalty of discontinuing some quite substantial subscriptions. So the good work was stopped! There was of course a recurrence of diphtheria amongst newcomers a few months later. After due consultations immunization was resumed and again brought the disease under complete control. Wisely, there were no further letters to the press—and no more interruptions of the programme!

(4) and (5) the naval Training Ships 'Exmouth' and 'Cornwall', which were stationed in the Thames estuary off Grays and Gravesend respectively. (6) the Foundling Hospital during the

transition period after the governors had sold their valuable site in central London. After a temporary stay at Redhill, the children were again transferred to new buildings at Berkhamsted. Some readers may recall that the composer, Handel, took an interest in this Foundation, which still possesses one of the organs on which he played. (7) the Rachel MacMillan Schools at Deptford. This charitable institution was the pioneer of Nursery Schools in this country.

All these projects were successful from the standpoint of diphtheria prevention and control. All the salient features of the research projects, bacteriological as well as serological, were published in the medical and scientific journals.

In addition to participating actively in this research work, O'Brien encouraged full co-operation with the Superintendents of many British Infectious Diseases Hospitals and Medical Officers of Health, and he also kept in close touch with leading scientists overseas. Clinical research in a very wide field was thus a major activity of the Wellcome Laboratories.

An immunization campaign sponsored by the government was a late development in Britain, and is discussed in Chapter 16.

Some Early Campaigns Overseas

France.—In France, Gaston Ramon began to advocate the use of *anatoxine* (toxoid) in 1923, and continued to press for its use, to the exclusion of other vaccines, till the outbreak of the 1939-45 war and beyond: the disorganization of this war was an impeding factor for seven years, but the campaign was intensified in 1946.

Ramon's prophylactic was safe, easily prepared and efficient in use. Notwithstanding unpleasant reactions, especially in adults, considerable headway was made with it after some preliminary trials among both children and adults in 1923. The Academy of Medicine gave the method its blessing in 1927. Combined diphtheria anatoxine and typhoid-paratyphoid vaccines were introduced in 1929, and were used compulsorily in all the armed forces in 1936. Two years later, immunization with diphtheria anatoxine became compulsory for children aged one to fourteen years.

As might be expected, the French campaign had its vicissitudes. We have mentioned elsewhere that in general the Services of a country are ideal for implementing immunization procedures: compulsion succeeded in all the land, naval and air forces in France also. On the other hand, the immunization of the child population was bedevilled by unco-operative persons who were opposed to the laws and regulations.

Here are some statistics, which incidentally reflect how ineffective French civil 'compulsion' must have been before and during the 1939-45 war. Between 1919 and 1945, an average of 20,000 cases of diphtheria occurred annually. In 1946, when it was possible to intensify the post-war immunization programme, the yearly average fell in a few years to 2,000 to 2,500 cases. Before 1924 there were approximately 3,000 deaths per annum, in 1946 there were still 2,000, and in 1957 there were only 39.

Canada.—Ramon's persistent advocacy of anatoxine encouraged the authorities in other countries of Europe and in Canada to introduce their own scheme, mostly from 1925 onwards. The Canadian teams were led by John FitzGerald and later by Donald Fraser, both of the Connaught Laboratories, Toronto. In 1926-27, the incidence of diphtheria in Canada amongst 9,000 unimmunized controls was 11·44 per 1,000, whereas amongst those who had been immunized, it was only 1·55 per 1,000. The success of the campaign in the city of Hamilton was spectacular and attracted world attention: it was reported in 1938 that immunization was introduced in 1925, that diphtheria deaths ceased after 1930, and that no cases were notified after 1933. In Toronto there were no diphtheria deaths between 1934 and 1940; since then the morbidity has been nil or only a few cases annually. In Canada as a whole, 1,300 diphtheria deaths occurred in 1921, approximately 300 in each of the last three years of the 1939-45 war, and only six in 1958—it is said in an area where immunization had been neglected.

United States of America.—Park's toxin-antitoxin mixture, T.A. (see p. 69) was still being employed routinely in New York and most of the United States of America in 1924. In that year toxoid began to be substituted for it in New York City. T.A. continued to be used elsewhere for many years but was finally given up in favour of toxoid as late as 1933 in New York State.

TABLE

Diphtheria: U.S.A. and New York City

Year	Deaths in U.S.A.
Before 1925	15,000 approx.
1940	1,457
1951	302
1955	150

Year	Deaths in New York City
1917	1,158
1926	425
1931	198
1936	less than 80
1952	1
1953	1
1954	1

In 1933, William Park, who was Professor of Bacteriology and Hygiene at New York University, immunized the millionth New York City child against diphtheria. At the same public ceremony, Bela Schick, originator of the Schick test, who had left Vienna and become a leading paediatrician in New York, immunized the first child of the second million. This was indeed a great occasion for two men who had done so much to conquer diphtheria.

There is one final point: diphtheria immunization always leads to an enormous saving in hospital beds. In 1920, the cost of hospital treatment in New York exceeded 1,000,000 dollars, and in 1939 only 44,000. Obviously this figure has now fallen further, and is low also in other large American cities where cases of diphtheria are extremely rare.

CHAPTER 15

THE CONQUEST OF DIPHTHERIA
BY ACTIVE IMMUNIZATION: II

IN the previous chapter, it was shown that considerable progress
was made in immunization campaigns in countries overseas,
notably France, Canada and the United States of America. In
Britain, official action was delayed for many years owing to a series
of unfortunate early accidents reported from abroad, none of which
were in any way due to the carelessness of British manufacturers.
These disasters, which are discussed below, emphasized the need
for the maintenance of the highest possible standards of expert
staff and laboratories, and a full knowledge of methods, including
all the pitfalls possibly involved in processing.

SOME UNFORTUNATE SETBACKS

(1) In 1919, an American firm prepared a *toxin antitoxin mixture*,
T.A., by adding the requisite volume of toxin to the antitoxin in
two stages instead of *at one time*: a considerable interval was
allowed to elapse between the additions. We now know that the
fractional addition of the toxin to the antitoxic serum could lead to
a very dangerous toxic mixture, as in fact it did. This particular
batch certainly contained free diphtheria toxin. Ten deaths and
74 cases of severe reactions occurred after injections of the vaccine
at *Dallas* in Texas.

(2) In 1924, there was a second American disaster due to T.A.
(How wise we were in this country not to market a vaccine made
from toxin and therefore potentially hazardous!) On this occasion
the mixture had been correctly prepared. It contained phenol
(carbolic acid) as a preservative—it was thought as an added safe-
guard! Unfortunately some of the batch of vaccine was stored at a
temperature below freezing point: this was based on the supposi-
tion that low temperature storage must be a commendable pro-

cedure on all occasions. However, it was shown subsequently that, in the presence of phenol, freezing alternating with thawing can cause destruction of the antitoxin, leaving a toxic mixture. The vaccine which had been frozen caused severe local and general reactions—luckily there were no deaths—in all of 43 children injected in the towns of *Concord* and *Bridgewater*, Massachusetts. Material from the same batch which had not been frozen was not toxic and caused no trouble on injection.

(3) Owing to carelessness in the laboratory of manufacture, toxin alone was issued as a vaccine. The antitoxin, which would have ensured a safe mixture, was omitted in error. Moreover this mistake was not detected, as it should have been, before the material was released for general use. Seven infants died at *Baden*, near Vienna. For a time immunization was forbidden in Austria as a dire consequence of this laboratory error.

This Austrian disaster was in 1924, and in 1929, E. Loewenstein of Vienna introduced an ointment containing diphtheria toxoid and dead diphtheria bacilli—an obvious attempt to get rid of all the dangers and inconveniences of giving vaccines. The ointment was rubbed into the skin of the back, chest or abdomen at weekly intervals. Sometimes there were local skin eruptions at the site of application. The method was little used outside Austria, because good immunity could not be achieved with any certainty. This was a pity, but the point is emphasized that no vaccine or method can be acceptable in the long run unless, in addition to safety, a high proportion of persons used as guinea-pigs can attain the objective of well-established, solid protection.

(4) In 1926, a *Russian* laboratory was at fault. *Toxin* was supplied instead of toxoid. Of the fourteen children injected 'eight of them died within two weeks, four of polyneuritis within a month and two recovered after symptoms of general intoxication'.

(5) Also in 1926, a disaster was reported from *China*. For some reason a *toxin antitoxin mixture*, which had presumably been correctly prepared in the laboratory of origin, was diluted with water before use. At this stage a dangerous contamination (haemolytic streptococci) was introduced. Of 89 persons injected, five died and 37 had local or general reactions of varying severity. The organisms were demonstrated in specimens from the patients.

(6) The tragedy at Concord and Bridgewater in 1924 was recalled

by manufacturers of *toxin antitoxin mixture* in *Australia*, who issued some of their own material to Queensland in 1928. They assumed they were on reasonably safe ground when they intentionally omitted to add preservative, which might cause damage to the antitoxin, leaving a toxic mixture, as had been the case in the previous disaster. However, they did not issue any warning about precautions to be observed during storage and subsequent use. In consequence, a large multi-dose container of vaccine was stored at room temperature in a tropical climate, and it was used on four different occasions. A dangerous contaminant, a strain of *Staphylococcus pyogenes* of exceptional toxicity, was introduced into this bottle at an early stage and multiplied under favourable conditions for bacterial growth. This led to the much publicized disaster at *Bundaberg*, Queensland: of 21 children inoculated from this bottle, 12 died (within 48 hours), six were seriously ill but recovered, and three were unaffected. This accident was deplorable, but some good resulted in the long run. It became an incentive to research on the properties of the causal microbe, and also on measures for the safety and control of antisera, vaccines and other therapeutic substances.

(7) *Medellin*, in Colombia, South America was the scene of the next tragedy. In 1930, *toxin*, which had stupidly been kept in the same store as toxoid, was given in error to 48 Schick-positive (susceptible) children, who had already received the first two doses of the usual immunizing course of three injections of toxoid. One-third (16 out of 48) died, and many others were seriously ill but recovered.

All these dire events, between 1919 and 1930 had their adverse publicity, but the consequences were fortunately only temporary. Of course antisera and vaccines have their pitfalls like other medicaments, and a full knowledge and appreciation of the risks has had a salutary effect in the long run. Partly as a result of these disasters, British legislation was introduced which has served as a model for similar measures in Commonwealth countries and elsewhere.

THE BRITISH THERAPEUTIC SUBSTANCES ACT

Although this Act was passed in 1925, the Therapeutic Substances Regulations which were framed to meet its requirements, did not become effective till 1931. Their purpose was to control the purity, potency and quality of all the antisera, toxoids, vaccines, etc., prepared for sale in this country. Naturally, the best manufacturing firms had already introduced their own high standards, which they were constantly reviewing in the light of further experience. Senior scientists from these companies assisted the staff of the Ministry of Health in drawing up the official Regulations, to which they willingly conformed themselves—this is an apt illustration of the application and rule of law under a democratic form of government!

One of the main safeguards of the Act was the emphasis on the suitability of the expert staff and of the premises placed at their disposal by the manufacturing firms. The licensees were all accredited by the Ministry of Health, and the professional training and standards of those in control of processes and of their laboratories had to be maintained at a high level. The human element was wisely recognized as of first importance: the safety and quality of the various substances had to conform to the detailed legal provisions, but full implementation of the rules clearly depended on experts with a sense of responsibility and vocation.

A British biochemist, Percival Hartley, was a leader in preparing the British Regulations and in research on the principles and practice of biological standardization. He introduced many 'yardsticks' (as he called them) or Standards of potency of products, which were also acceptable as International Standards, and were held for the League of Nations and later for the World Health Organization: where appropriate, many of these standard preparations were maintained in the dried state in order to ensure their stability on prolonged storage. It was fitting that Hartley should be the first Director of the new Department of Biological Standards, National Institute for Medical Research at Hampstead, London.

The Regulations under the Act of 1925 have been subject to continuous review since they first became effective in 1931. Many modifications and additions have been issued from time to time.

In the United States, the corresponding authority for the standardization and control of biological substances had its headquarters at the National Institutes of Health, Washington. G. W. McCoy was its able director for many years.

It is fitting to end this section with the general comment that no vaccine or antiserum is completely safe, although some are safer than others. Moreover, the potential risk for an individual vaccine may be greater in one set of circumstances than another. Sir Graham Wilson aptly points out that there is no insurance without premium and that 'our business is to provide a greater and more comprehensive cover and to diminish the size of the premium'.

THE IMPORTANCE OF STERILE SYRINGES AND NEEDLES

Although the Therapeutic Substances Regulations went a long way towards eliminating trouble from faulty manufacture, they could not have any influence on what happened subsequently. There was always the possibility of contamination of a product at the time of use.

In November 1936, 38 children were inoculated with *toxoid antitoxin floccules, T.A.F.* at Ring College, County Waterford, Republic of Ireland. In April 1937, a girl aged 12 years died from miliary tuberculosis, and 23 other children had local tuberculous lesions but recovered. All these children were inoculated from the same 25 ml. bottle of T.A.F. The manufacturing firm was blamed in the first instance but gained the verdict in a legal action brought by the father of the deceased child in 1939. It was shown that the large batch contained phenolic preservative, which was most effective in killing tubercle bacilli—not immediately but in several hours. Attention was drawn to the ease with which faulty technique at the time of inoculation could contaminate an entire bottle. Evidence was also adduced, both in the 1930s and subsequently, that sterile needles and syringes are essential for the administration of biologicals and other medicaments and that slipshod inoculation technique carries serious risks. The tubercle bacillus is only one of a wide variety of disease-producing microbes which have been introduced on apparatus at the time of injection.

The Medical Research Council subsequently published an important war-time Memorandum on 'The Sterilization, Use and Care of Syringes'. This document has been brought up to date from time to time. (A recent development has been the increasing use of cheap, sterile, disposable syringes and needles.)

CHAPTER 16

THE CONQUEST OF DIPHTHERIA
BY ACTIVE IMMUNIZATION: III

MUCH of the previous chapter was taken up with a brief survey of some unfortunate mishaps, which took place overseas and delayed progress in this country and elsewhere. In contrast, this chapter deals with a series of advances which originated in immunological laboratories and were applied clinically, often with initial difficulties but ultimately with very successful results. In diphtheria prevention progress had been slow in the early stages, but we now come to the final period of triumph.

ALUMINIUM-CONTAINING VACCINE

Toxoid or anatoxine has the disadvantage of being a fluid preparation which is absorbed rapidly from the site of injection and is eliminated rapidly. The stimulus it affords to the cells of the body which produce antibody is therefore rather short. Naturally research workers tried to prolong the action of toxoid by making it less 'soluble'—more of a 'depot' type of preparation. They investigated the addition of substances which aggregate the antigen and are now known technically as 'adjuvants'. The French scientist, Gaston Ramon, added tapioca to his anatoxine, mainly for horse immunization, and he certainly delayed elimination; unfortunately, this improvement was off-set by unduly severe reactions in these animals. In this country, C. G. Pope worked on the precipitation of toxoid with alum, a chemical with greater appeal to the scientist than the crude substance, tapioca! Glenny, Pope, Waddington and Wallace then found that the antigenic value of toxoid was enhanced by the addition of alum. Thus began, in 1926, a series of observations which culminated in *Alum Precipitated Toxoid, A.P.T.*

In preparing this vaccine for human use, the precipitate formed in the mixture was washed thoroughly with saline and resuspended to the required volume, thiomersal being used as preservative. The more usual preservative, which the team considered, was of course phenol: however, phenolic antiseptics caused rapid deterioration of the antigen and had to be excluded at all stages of manufacture.

Glenny and Barr first recommended washed alum-toxoid precipitates for human immunization in 1931. There was a temporary hitch because some of the earlier preparations used for clinical trials in Britain were insufficiently purified and gave rise to untoward reactions. General release of the vaccine was not possible at this stage. However, after Park in New York had commented most favourably on other batches of Glenny's A.P.T., Glenny and his co-workers carried out further purification as a matter of urgency; irritant substances were removed to a large extent, without impairing the efficiency of the prophylactic in the process. The improved vaccine was now generally acceptable. Two doses spaced by four weeks gave the best results.

It will be recalled that *toxoid antitoxin floccules, T.A.F.* (see p. 91) had the disadvantage of containing a small amount of antitoxin, which could cause sensitization to horse serum. A.P.T. caused rather more reaction, local and general, than T.A.F., but it did not give rise to serum-sensitivity (which might be manifested when, say, tetanus antitoxin was required for injection into an injured person months or years later). As in other respects T.A.F. was the mildest diphtheria vaccine known, there was a place for both A.P.T. and T.A.F. The former was preferred for child immunization and the latter for adolescents and adults.

The British National Immunization Campaign

Before the 1939-45 war, immunization against diphtheria was undertaken by several enthusiasts—medical officers of health, superintendents of hospitals for infectious diseases and the staff of the Wellcome Research Laboratories under the direction of R. A. O'Brien. The Ministry of Health adopted an attitude of benevolent, but not very active, encouragement from 1922 onwards. We have seen that mishaps of various kinds overseas between 1919 and

1930 acted as a deterrent to an all-out immunization campaign in this country. The further disaster of 1937, at Ring Irish College, followed by the legal action of 1939 at Dublin, was observed closely by officials of the Ministry and many others. The success of the manufacturers in defending this action was re-assuring, and it was widely felt that the time was ripe for implementing a national scheme. Prophylactics could obviously be prepared which were safe and effective.

In the early months of the 1939-45 war, there were considerable movements of the population. The evacuation of children from the London area in particular led to the fear of widespread epidemics. It was the right psychological opportunity and timing for immunization to be pressed. The Ministry's scheme was ready towards the end of 1940, but was not applied on a large scale until 1941-42. A major factor in its ultimate success was the free issue of materials by the Government: the cost ceased to be borne mostly by the local rates, as had been customary previously. The main emphasis was on immunization in infancy, partly because diphtheria was most severe in early life and partly owing to the relative ease of contacting the very young at child welfare clinics and elsewhere. *Alum Precipitated Toxoid A.P.T.* was the prophylactic most used. The chief medical officer of the Ministry of Health, Sir Wilson Jameson, frequently came to the microphone to urge on parents the necessity of immunization for their children. Attendances increased after each broadcast.

A Severe Test for Immunization

Between 1927 and 1931, there were reports of a highly toxic and lethal type of diphtheria in Leeds and elsewhere in the British Isles. The most severe attack was characterized not only by unexpectedly scanty membrane formation in the throat, but also by much oedematous swelling and dead tissue locally, 'bullneck' from massive cellulitis of the neck, various haemorrhages, and palatal and other paralyses from the intense toxaemia. J. W. McLeod and his colleagues of Leeds University described a special epidemic strain of the diphtheria bacillus, which was associated with this outbreak. It had distinctive bacteriological properties, which enabled McLeod to differentiate it from two other cultural types of the diphtheria organism. The Leeds classification of the types was *gravis* for their own special strain at that time, and *intermedius* and *mitis* which were often predominant elsewhere. However, the *mitis* strain was not always associated with mild diphtheria and it could be lethal, nor was the *intermedius* strain always intermediate between the other two. The correlation between the name gravis and clinical severity certainly applied to Leeds itself and to certain other cities, but could not be applied universally.

From the standpoint of immunization, many of the gravis cases were unusually difficult to treat with antitoxin. Much larger doses of the serum had to be given, mostly into a vein of the arm in order to ensure more rapid distribution of the antidote throughout the body. However, cases continued to be lost in spite of intensive treatment. Undoubtedly in some cases there had been considerable delay in administering the serum, because the appearance of the throat did not at once suggest diphtheria to the family doctor —we have seen that the characteristic membrane was often scanty or even absent. This unfortunate experience emphasized the old dictum that the earlier antitoxin is injected in treating a case of diphtheria, the better the outlook for the patient.

There was another interesting development just before the outbreak of the 1939-45 war, viz. a new method for the purification and concentration of antisera, which involved treatment with proteolytic enzymes. A comparison of old and new products was made and the results were eagerly awaited. However, gravis cases of diphtheria were relatively refractory to treatment not only with antitoxin concentrated by the old method of fractional precipitation with ammonium or sodium sulphate (Gibson and Banzhaf, 1910) but also with antitoxin purified by the new Pope process, developed in 1936 by the English biochemist, C. G. Pope, and later used all over the world. (We have already referred in this chapter to Pope's essential contribution to the discovery of A.P.T.) This valuable method depended on proteolytic enzyme action plus heat denaturation. It reduced the quantity of protein to be injected and therefore the risk of serum sickness. On this basis it was to be preferred to other methods for concentrating antitoxins. Enzyme-treated antitoxin is now generally known as *refined antitoxin*.

So much for *passive* immunization with antitoxin, which was not wholly successful in the event of any delay in administration or the appearance of an epidemic strain similar to the one at Leeds. The real answer was the intensification of campaigns for the *active* immunization especially of the child population with a toxoid preparation. Once again a policy of prevention is so much better than treatment of the established disease.

During the last World War, there was a steady fall in the diphtheria incidence and mortality in Britain due to the national policy to ensure protection of the majority of children. However, in sharp contrast, immunization was allowed to lapse badly under war-time conditions on the continent of Europe, with the inevitable consequence that there was a recrudescence of epidemic diphtheria. The areas worst affected were Norway, the Netherlands and parts of Germany. When the war was ended and more attention could be paid to immunization campaigns, considerable success was achieved almost everywhere.

In this country also, after the war, we had a salutary reminder of the need to maintain protection at a high level everywhere. In 1950, Hartley, Tulloch and their associates gave an account of epidemic infections with the gravis type of diphtheria bacillus in Gateshead and Dundee. The disease was often fatal among the uninoculated, but very seldom serious or lethal among those who had had some inoculations: 'the higher the circulating antitoxin (in the patient's blood) had been raised by immunization, the less likely was infection to result in disease, and the smaller was the possibility of complications or death.'

Much light has indeed been thrown on this question of protection. Observations in man, as well as in laboratory animals, make it certain that immunity depends on antibodies or antidotes which are developed in the blood or tissues, preferably actively by the injection of the appropriate vaccine—in the case of diphtheria, a toxoid preparation. This is more effective than immunizing passively (catching up, as it were, on the infection) by injecting 'foreign' antiserum—preformed antibodies, which are present in the serum of another species, usually a horse, which has been given a course of doses of vaccine. In an earlier chapter, units of antitoxin were discussed: the present reference to this means of measurement will serve as a reminder that immunization is a quantitative process.

OTHER POST-WAR VACCINES

In 1947, L. B. Holt, who was a pupil and associate of Sir Alexander Fleming at the Wright-Fleming Institute, London, prepared a new alum-containing prophylactic, which he called *Purified Toxoid, Aluminium Phosphate, P.T.A.P.* It differed from A.P.T. in two particulars: the toxoid used for making P.T.A.P. is highly purified in the first instance in order to reduce the likelihood of reactions, and secondly it is adsorbed on to aluminium phosphate instead of being precipitated with alum and then washed. The immunity induced by two spaced doses of A.P.T. and P.T.A.P. is similar, although the latter is the better antigen when only one dose is given—an undesirable procedure in this type of immunization.

A third vaccine with an aluminium adjuvant was the Danish *Purified Toxoid, Aluminium Hydroxide, P.T.A.H.* Preformed aluminium-hydroxide gel was used as the mineral carrier.

Finally, the crude diphtheria formol toxoid, which is the starting point for all these vaccine preparations, was itself studied by different research teams, and so-called 'pure' preparations were developed. It is of interest that even the most highly purified toxoid was still a complex product with many antigenic constituents. An official *Purified Formol Toxoid, F.T.* is included in a number of combined vaccines, the modern method of mixing various toxoids, etc. in order to reduce the number of injections: this is discussed in Chapter 28.

THE VALUE OF IMMUNIZATION: SOME STATISTICS

The diphtheria bacillus was discovered in 1883-84. In the nineteenth century diphtheria was one of the most devastating diseases of children. After a little over 80 years of research its toll has become negligible almost everywhere. This achievement has been due partly to antitoxin, which came into use around 1894, but mainly to toxoid, which was first used for human immunization in 1923—a surprisingly long delay!

Diphtheria antitoxin reduced the case mortality in hospitals all over the world from perhaps 30 per cent. to 8 per cent. There is at least one recorded series of figures in which the mortality from one of the gravest forms of the disease, namely laryngeal diphtheria, fell from 62 per cent. to less than 12 per cent. Statisticians are of course better pleased when the remedy is given to alternate cases. This procedure was actually carried out by J. Fibiger in 1898: the case mortality of 245 patients not treated with antitoxin was 12·25 per cent., whereas that of 239 patients who received antitoxin was only 3·5 per cent.

Although antitoxin saved many lives there was still an average of 58,000 cases and 2,800 deaths per annum in England and Wales in the ten years before the outbreak of the 1939-45 war. The national immunization scheme of 1940 became effective in 1941-42, and by the end of the war just over 60 per cent. of the child population had been immunized. Great success, leading to the virtual conquest of diphtheria, attended the scheme (see Table).

TABLE

DIPHTHERIA: ENGLAND AND WALES

	Annual cases	Deaths
1930-39	58,000 (average)	2,800
National immunization scheme introduced 1940		
1946	11,986	472
1960	49	5 (4 in unimmunized persons)
1964	20	0

In his Milroy Lectures of 1966, D. Thomson has given the following additional data for this country: 'During the years 1942 to 1944 four out of every five children who had contracted diphtheria had not been immunized, and 29 out of 30 deaths were in non-immunized children, although the numbers of immunized and non-immunized children were approximately equal. The eradication of diphtheria as an indigenous disease was well under way. Since the national campaign began in 1940 up to the end of 1965, 17,754,923 children had received a full course of primary immunization and 11,007,711 had received a reinforcing injection. During the decade 1956 to 1965 there have been only 468 cases of diphtheria in England and Wales, with 33 deaths.'

On the continent of Europe, the main progress has been since 1946, but there is still a need for stepping up immunization in some countries more than in others. To quote Thomson once again: 'While in England and Wales in 1965 there were only 25 cases . . . in France there were 264 cases, in Germany 324, and in Italy 2,630. By contrast there were none in Norway and Sweden.'

CHAPTER 17

I. GEORGE AND GLADYS DICK AND THE SCARLET
   FEVER STORY
II. STAPHYLOCOCCUS ANTITOXIN AND VACCINES—
   PROMISE THAT WAS UNFULFILLED

ALTHOUGH the two main sections of this chapter are concerned with very different clinical conditions, the causal
bacteria are rounded organisms or cocci (haemolytic streptococci and staphylococci respectively); moreover, representative
strains from both groups are capable of giving off 'soluble' toxins
(analogous to diphtheria toxin) for which there are specific or
distinctive antitoxins. The research problems involved in attempting to conquer scarlet fever (and its streptococci) in the first instance stimulated similar studies of a wide variety of diseases due
to staphylococci. It will be seen that immunological procedures
were very successful in the control of scarlet fever: alas, notwithstanding the initial promise, staphylococcal diseases were more
baffling. Today all these infections are dealt with by chemotherapeutic drugs rather than by sera and vaccines.

Most of the research on toxins and antitoxins was done in the
post-1920 period. Earlier work with the causal cocci is surveyed
briefly at the beginning of each main section.

I

SCARLET FEVER AND ALLIED INFECTIONS

Scarlet fever was formerly much confused with other febrile
diseases with a rash, particularly measles. In 1664, Samuel Pepys
the diarist wrote: 'My little girl Susan is fallen sick of the meazles,
or, at least, of a scarlett feavour.' The disease has varied greatly in
severity from time to time. Towards the end of the eighteenth
century, it acquired a malignant tendency; severe epidemics with

many fatal cases occurred in various parts of Europe. At other periods mild forms which were seldom fatal were common. In 1887 Edward Klein, a German who lived in London, suggested that streptococci of the haemolytic variety (round bacteria growing in chains which disrupted red blood corpuscles in culture media) were responsible for scarlet fever. Definite proof of this suggestion was not forthcoming till the 1920s.

Early Antisera and Vaccines.—All the antisera and vaccines prepared before the 1920s gave inconsistent results—promising according to some reports but of no value according to others. Confusion arose because the pioneers, such as Moser and von Pirquet of Vienna and the Russian Gabritchewsky, had no method of standardizing the potency of their preparations. In retrospect, we can be reasonably certain that some batches of crude antiserum contained specific antitoxin, and some vaccines (suspensions of organisms) also contained scarlet fever toxin and therefore could be expected to immunize quite well.

Streptococci are associated with a variety of diseases other than scarlet fever, including puerperal septicaemia, erysipelas and sore throat or angina. Another group of streptococci apparently had some connection with certain types of rheumatism. Inevitably, killed cultures of numerous strains of streptococci were injected empirically as vaccines in the treatment of rheumatoid arthritis, fibrositis, etc. The evidence for their use was never convincing, and other methods have now taken the place of vaccine therapy. It is chastening to find that remedies of this type had a vogue from 1895 for over thirty years. In any review of medical progress, such events are not uncommon, as new and more scientific knowledge displaces outworn theories and practice.

THE CONTRIBUTIONS OF GEORGE AND GLADYS DICK

George and Gladys Dick, who were husband and wife, took up the experimental study of scarlet fever at Chicago and demonstrated conclusively that the haemolytic streptococcus was the causative agent of the disease and not just a 'hanger-on' of the real invader. This and other important discoveries were first published mostly in 1923-24. The Dicks produced clinical scarlet fever by the swabbing of cultures on to the throats of susceptible volunteers. They found that the streptococci produced a soluble toxin which was absorbed into the blood and carried to all parts of the body. It was this toxin which was responsible for the characteristic rash of scarlet fever and for the general poisoning of the system. If the person injected with the toxin possessed scarlet fever antitoxin in his blood, the toxin was neutralized and the rash did not appear.

Like diphtheria toxin, scarlet toxin can be separated from the bacteria by filtration. The Dicks demonstrated that, when suitably diluted and injected intradermally into subjects who have not had scarlet fever or been otherwise immunized, it gave a localized rash. This was the *Dick test*, the small area of rash being a Dick positive reaction. Subjects who had antitoxin in their blood and were immune to scarlet fever gave no reaction to the Dick test—the toxin was neutralized by the antitoxin—and were classed as Dick negative. Practically all scarlet fever patients at the outset of the clinical attack gave a positive response, whereas during convalescence when antitoxic immunity was developed, they gave a negative response. Thus, in certain respects, the Dick test for susceptibility to scarlet fever could be regarded as analogous to the Schick test for diphtheria.

The Dicks also found that a course of injections of toxin could be used to produce active immunity to prevent the disease. In this case it is surprising to note that the vaccine consisted of toxin and not, as was developed in diphtheria, of toxoid or a preparation of toxoid. The reason was that it was not possible to prepare scarlet fever toxoid from the parent toxin: formalin destroyed both toxicity and antigenicity, instead of only detoxicating the toxin while leaving its power to immunize virtually unimpaired—as can be done so successfully in connection with diphtheria.

Scarlet fever antitoxin, analogous to diphtheria antitoxin, was prepared mainly for treatment. Horses were inoculated with a series of increasing doses of toxic filtrates. After bleeding, their serum was concentrated and was of undoubted value in the early toxic stages of scarlet fever, and indirectly it may have reduced the liability to the septic complications. It helped to shorten the length of stay in hospital.

The Dicks also advocated a method of standardization of antitoxin which involved toxin-antitoxin neutralization in skin tests on Dick-positive human beings. Other methods, which obviated the search for suitable subjects and were introduced in this country and elsewhere, were an intravenous protection test and a skin-neutralization test—both in rabbits. Neither the Dicks nor anyone else had succeeded in devising a test in guinea-pigs because these animals are not skin-sensitive to scarlet fever toxin. This explains why the laboratory work on diphtheria toxin could not be applied to the streptococci until the Dicks employed human volunteers as test animals.

Inevitably, one reflects that, in the modern era of Patients' Associations, valuable research like that of the Dicks would be impeded at every stage.

THE CONTRIBUTIONS OF OTHERS

Schultz and Charlton in 1918 had made an interesting observation when they demonstrated that serum from a convalescent scarlet fever case, when injected intradermally into a patient suffering from scarlet fever, produced a local blanching of the rash. Although they did not appreciate its significance at the time, this was in effect a demonstration of the antitoxic properties of the serum. The use of convalescent serum for purposes of treatment was not suggested.

The results of the Dicks were confirmed by A. Zingher and by A. R. Dochez and L. Sherman in New York and by the workers at the Wellcome Laboratories in London.

C. C. Okell and I found that scarlet fever antitoxin prepared in horses could counteract toxaemia in rabbits infected with cultures of streptococci not only from scarlet fever but also from erysipelas and puerperal septicaemia. We postulated that there was a single toxin common to all haemolytic streptococci and therefore also a single antitoxin which might be useful in treating not only scarlet fever but streptococcal diseases in general. Unfortunately, although some successes were reported in human puerperal streptococcal injections and 'surgical sepsis', the effect of serum prophylaxis and therapy was unfavourable in other cases. Allergic reactions sometimes caused trouble. The use of horse serum was abandoned—except for the control of scarlet fever where antitoxin was invaluable.

CONCLUSION

The work of the Dicks was certainly a major advance and contributed to our understanding of a disease with a history of marked cycles in severity. Today, both antitoxin and prophylactic toxin, which were often of great value, have been replaced by chemotherapeutic drugs, especially penicillin. The credit for the control of scarlet fever, which is now a rare disease, belongs to these drugs, and not to protective immunization.

II

STAPHYLOCOCCAL INFECTIONS

In 1881-82 Alexander Ogston, a Scot who studied in Berlin where he was inspired by Koch, found clusters of round bacteria (the *Staphylococcus*) in suppurative lesions. He concluded that these germs often played a causal rôle in inflammation and suppuration, and that they must be differentiated from similar organisms which tended to grow in chains (the *Streptococcus*).

Between 1894 and 1903 various toxic products of staphylococci were studied. These included a haemolysin which disrupted the red cells of rabbit's blood, a leucocidin which was toxic to rabbit's leucocytes or white cells, a necrotoxin which caused necrosis (tissue death) in the skin of the rabbit and could also be lethal when injected intravenously, and finally a coagulase which caused coagulation of plasma and partially explained the localization of staphylococcal lesions. Although an anti-haemolysin was also prepared, this early knowledge of an immune mechanism was not followed up till the 1920s.

BURNET AND ANTITOXIC IMMUNITY

In 1928, F. M. (now Sir Macfarlane) Burnet of Melbourne, Australia, who later became a leading virologist, undertook the investigation of the diphtheria immunization disaster at Bundaberg, Queensland (see p. 98). Staphylococci were isolated from the contaminated toxin-antitoxin mixture. Burnet prepared an important toxic factor called staphylococcus alpha toxin or haemolysin, which was analogous to diphtheria, tetanus and haemolytic streptococcus toxins. There was also a corresponding antitoxin or antihaemolysin. Much of the experimental work was done in rabbits, and horses, as well as rabbits, were immunized with toxoid or toxin for antitoxin production. Immunization of rabbits ensured that subsequently, when virulent staphylococci were injected intradermally, the skin lesions were smaller, or, when the organisms were injected in larger dosage intravenously, the lives of the immune animals were prolonged.

Unfortunately, the treatment of human staphylococcal disease with antitoxin was often disappointing, although the results obtained in rabbits had been most encouraging. It has been pointed out that rabbits may derive certain advantages from antitoxin which are denied to man: the mechanism of immunity in the two species may be quite different. In man, the presence of serum antibodies to the staphylococcus was only one factor in resistance to infection: disease could sometimes persist even when the antitoxin in the circulation was so high that it should have been rapidly curative. The discrepancies from case to case were baffling.

Other antibodies, notably the anti-leucocidin to human (not rabbit) leucocytes were also investigated. However, this type of immunological research is now only of academic importance. The newer forms of chemotherapy are so much more effective than any antiserum.

STAPHYLOCOCCAL BACTERIAL VACCINES

In an earlier chapter (6), attention was drawn to the persistent research of Almroth Wright on the use of suspensions of staphylococci as vaccines. Neither prophylaxis nor therapy with these preparations gave convincing evidence of their value, although inevitably some successes were reported from time to time. No controlled experiments were carried out, the claims being based solely on the doctor's and the patient's assessment of progress in each individual case, often quite regardless of the combined effect of other measures or factors.

Toxoid prophylaxis and therapy were also used on a considerable scale, mainly between 1930 and 1939. Clinical improvement was claimed in many cases of furunculosis (boils) and other subacute or chronic skin infections. However, many experienced dermatologists thought that equally good results had often followed other measures. The results obtained in deep-seated staphylococcal conditions, such as carbuncle and osteomyelitis, were certainly bad.

In an attempt to improve the toxoid, some clinicians tried a *vaccoid* in which a suspension of staphylococci was added to the product. The use of this mixture did not solve the problem.

Conclusion

The rôle of antitoxic immunity in connection with recovery from staphylococcal disease remains a matter for dispute. A thorough well-controlled clinical trial using alternate cases for the assessment of the toxoid was not carried out—the opportunity was lost and is unlikely to recur. In the end, the advent of the sulphonamides in the 1930s, and of the antibiotics a few years later, replaced all serological measures. Staphylococcal immunity certainly exists, but the exact mechanism is unknown even today.

CHAPTER 18

THE CONTROL OF TETANUS: A MAJOR MEDICAL TRIUMPH IN THE 1939-45 WAR AND AFTER

IT will be recalled that tetanus as well as diphtheria toxoids had been used for horse immunization as long ago as 1903. Nearly twenty years later, A. T. Glenny in England and G. Ramon in France were pioneers in research on diphtheria toxoid (French: *anatoxine*) for human immunization. Diphtheria toxin antitoxin and toxoid antitoxin mixtures were gradually replaced in the 1920s and 1930s by other prophylactics. Inevitably, the knowledge acquired through research on diphtheria led to further investigations on tetanus.

INTRODUCTION OF TETANUS TOXOID FOR HUMAN IMMUNIZATION

In 1927, G. Ramon and C. Zoeller of the Pasteur Institute in Paris were the first to immunize man with a vaccine consisting of tetanus toxoid. Their 'guinea-pigs' for this research were soldiers —a natural choice because an army is specially exposed to the risk of tetanus: moreover, the inoculated men could be kept under observation more readily than civilians.

J. S. K. (later Brigadier Sir John) Boyd, who is also well known for his research on bacillary dysentery, and who became Director of Pathology at the British War Office soon after the 1939-45 war, confirmed and extended the French claims. In 1938, he collaborated with Glenny and M. F. Stevens in a study of the tetanus antitoxin responses in the blood serum of British soldiers inoculated with toxoid. It was established that two injections of 1.0 ml. of the vaccine at an interval of six weeks produced protective amounts of tetanus antitoxin in the circulation. Another very satisfactory observation was that reactions such as sore arms, malaise and fever were negligible, quite unlike those following, say, typhoid-paratyphoid vaccine, to which troops on overseas service

were accustomed. Boyd's research was well-timed, for active im-
munization against tetanus became official policy for the British
Army in 1938, one year before the outbreak of the Second World
War.

An Unexpected Sensitivity Reaction

New preparations not infrequently lead to some unforeseen
event, no matter how carefully testing is carried out before their
general release. Tetanus toxoid was no exception: it had been
used by Boyd and many others for about two years when a small
number of cases of anaphylaxis—the severe variety of allergic
reaction—came to light. Acute anaphylaxis is a potential hazard
whenever horse antitoxic serum is injected, but on this occasion
the trouble arose soon after injections of a toxoid which did not
contain horse protein and was regarded as harmless.

Investigations revealed that the cause of the trouble was the
Witte peptone, a protein constituent of the broth culture media
used in preparing the parent tetanus toxin. The remedy was a
simple one. Alternative forms of culture media, without Witte
peptone, were introduced, and there were no more complaints of
alarming reactions. Witte peptone is best avoided in all serological
preparations intended for human use: even in minute amounts
(1 in 10,000) it is an extremely potent allergen or sensitizing
substance.

Toxoid in the 1939-45 War

British Army.—Although every encouragement was given to all
troops to have a course of immunization against tetanus before
proceeding to battle areas, a minority of men refused protective inoculations. This was a mistake on their part, as some
of these objectors developed clinical tetanus after wounding
(see p. 119).

With regard to procedure, the policy of the British War Office
was influenced by an important finding (1941) of David G. Evans
of the Medical Research Council: a third dose of tetanus toxoid
administered 10 months after the original doses rapidly produced
larger amounts of circulating antitoxin than had been observed

previously. The increases were in many instances profound, thus demonstrating the importance of intervals of many months between injections for the best results with reinforcement. From November 1942, annual boosting or reinforcing doses of toxoid were required by the Army Authorities, a modification which ensured the maintenance of protective titres at a high level throughout the war.

There was some official nervousness about discontinuing the use of tetanus antitoxin for prophylaxis, because antitoxin had been a trusty life-saving medicament in the 1914-18 war, whereas toxoid was relatively new and untried. Further, it was known that soldier 'volunteers' for toxoid inoculations sometimes avoided an injection, with the result that protection was less complete than it should have been. A policy of persuasion rather than compulsion (as in the United States Army) had its drawbacks in war-time! Inevitably, there was a directive that a prophylactic dose of antitoxin should be given routinely as soon as possible after wounding. This pepsin-treated (refined) serum was a second line of defence, which could help those who had incomplete or inaccurate records of injections, or who might have been poor responders even to a complete course of toxoid. In retrospect, the toxoid was a more potent and reliable vaccine than appeared possible in 1942, and much less antitoxin could have been used without detriment—and indeed probably with advantage—to the Forces.

The conquest of tetanus in warfare is shown by the following data for the 1939-45 war. The incidence in different British armies or theatres of war varied between 0.43 and 0.04 per 1,000 wounded, compared with 1.47 per 1,000 wounded for the 1914-18 war (see p. 71). The lowest figure quoted above followed the introduction of annual reinforcing doses of tetanus toxoid in November 1942. These results were excellent, but even more significant was the experience of the British Expeditionary Force of 1939-40, which had to be evacuated from Dunkirk. There was no case of tetanus in more than 16,000 wounded men, who had all been actively immunized with toxoid. However, there were 8 cases of tetanus amongst 1,800 wounded men who had not been actively immunized. Owing to the rearguard action there were often unavoidable delays in the cleaning and dressing of wounds. This was a good test for immunization: no cases in the 90 per cent. of men inoculated and all eight cases in the 10 per cent. who had refused protective inoculations!

United States Army.—From 1941, *all* military personnel were actively immunized. The primary course for the Army was three doses of toxoid, spaced by three weeks. The Marines received only two doses of a different vaccine, namely alum-precipitated toxoid, four to eight weeks apart. The Army Authorities also laid stress on reinforcing doses: one was given routinely one year after the completion of the primary course, and others were a requirement for troops proceeding to a theatre of war overseas. Unlike the British, the Americans used no routine antitoxic serum on wounding: instead, they had every confidence in toxoid and gave a further reinforcing dose to meet this emergency. However, antitoxin was available for the treatment of clinical tetanus, and also for prophylactic use for the relatively very few non-immunized persons who might be wounded.

This policy of thorough immunization with toxoid for (nearly) everybody worked well. Only 12 cases of tetanus were recorded in the American Army throughout the 1939-45 war. According to the records, four of the 12 had had all the recommended injections, two had not received a reinforcing dose on wounding, and the remaining six had not been actively immunized at all.

The battle for the recapture of Manila in 1945 has provided most valuable data. Although the American troops on Luzon escaped tetanus (thanks to their immunization), 473 cases occurred amongst approximately 12,000 wounded civilians—an incidence of about 40 per 1,000 wounded. As far as is known, none of these had received prophylactic toxoid. Moreover, there was little available antitoxic serum for either prophylaxis or treatment, and the mortality was 82 per cent.

During the decade before the outbreak of the war, Manila had an annual incidence of 75 to 100 cases.

Canadian Army.—The forces were well immunized mostly with fluid tetanus toxoid combined with typhoid-paratyphoid vaccine. Three cases of tetanus were reported, with only one death.

Australian Army.—Approximately 600,000 soldiers were actively immunized, and there was only one death from tetanus.

French Army.—Owing to the French collapse in 1940, exact data were not kept. The morbidity and mortality from tetanus were virtually nil.

German Army.—Surprisingly, the Germans neglected active immunization with toxoid for their armed forces, except for the air force and a number of parachute troops. Perhaps an early and inexpensive victory was anticipated, which might not have involved tetanus as a major risk. The army had to rely on antitoxin for tetanus prevention after wounding, and for the treatment of established cases. There was much disorganization at times. Both the morbidity and mortality were very high. For example, there were 80 cases of tetanus in the Normandy area, despite the prophylactic use of serum.

These few data for different countries show clearly the advantage of toxoid, which is used primarily long before injury, over antitoxin, which is an emergency measure for the wounded and may be delayed under wartime conditions.

Post-War Immunization

With the cessation of hostilities, it was assumed at first that routine active immunization with toxoid was no longer necessary for the British Army. The practice was discontinued, only to be resumed in 1949 when the possibility of an imminent conflict could not be ruled out completely. The opportunity was taken for a full investigation of tetanus control by Miss M. Barr of the Wellcome Research Laboratories and Major-General A. Sachs, Director of Pathology at the War Office. The Barr-Sachs Report was published in 1955 under the auspices of the Army Pathology Advisory Committee, and contains an immense amount of scientific information about all aspects of tetanus immunization. The main trend of the recommendations was the increasing use of toxoid: with greater reliance on active immunization, the need for antitoxin was much diminished.

The outstanding success of tetanus control in the Armed Forces during the war had its repercussions on the procedures adopted in civil life in many parts of the world. In developed countries vaccination with tetanus toxoid has been used increasingly, and has been effective in controlling tetanus among the immunized. Of course there have been other factors, including better wound surgery and the use of antibiotics. A reduction in incidence has also followed the mechanization of agriculture, and the use of chemical fertilizers instead of stable manure. The disease is still far too common in tropical countries, especially in the newborn (so-called neonatal tetanus) and among children under 15. More than half of all tetanus cases in many countries result from trivial wounds—another reason for a great extension of active immunization everywhere.

The following data give some indication of what has already been achieved and all that remains to be done. According to the World Health Organization, tetanus kills more than 50,000 persons every year all over the world. In England and Wales there are approximately 30 deaths per annum—a relatively small number, thanks to modern measures of control. The incidence of tetanus in the U.S.A. was recently about 400 cases per year, some 60 per cent. of which were fatal. Tetanus is one of the commonest causes of death in rural India, and is responsible for 50 per cent. of the deaths in some Bombay hospitals.

CHAPTER 19

CALMETTE AND IMMUNIZATION AGAINST TUBERCULOSIS

IN 1921 a French vaccine consisting of living tubercle bacilli was administered by mouth to a newborn baby whose mother had died of tuberculosis. The child remained healthy and well: it did not contract the disease from its mother, nor from the vaccine. This was the first human experiment with B.C.G., a preparation which was given subsequently to many millions of people all over the world, and helped to save countless lives. The terrible scourge which, it will be recalled, Bunyan called the 'Captain of the Men of Death', was about to be checked by means of a protective vaccine at last.

THE DISCOVERY OF B.C.G.

It was no easy victory. The scientist mainly responsible for developing the vaccine was Albert Calmette, who worked under Louis Pasteur and Emile Roux in Paris from 1890 till he became director of a research institute in Lille in 1895. In 1917 he returned to the Pasteur Institute, Paris. While in Lille, he collaborated with Camille Guérin in studying the growth needs of the tubercle bacillus and the possibility of making a good vaccine. In 1906, these two scientists attempted to attenuate or weaken a *bovine* strain by repeated subculture in a medium containing ox bile. Their reasoning was on the following lines. In the first place, an attenuated living vaccine rather than a dead one was in keeping with the tradition and practice of their great master, Pasteur himself. Successes with vaccinia, anthrax and rabies all came to mind. Secondly, they knew that Behring had prepared a vaccine of human tubercle bacilli for veterinary use—so why should they not try to make a vaccine of bovine organisms for human use? A bacterial type from another species (cattle) might make it less hazardous for man. Thirdly, they added ox bile to a glycerine potato culture medium, because bile produced changes in the morphology, and reduced the virulence of certain laboratory strains of tubercle bacilli.

Calmette and Guérin were persistent and painstaking. They subcultured their particular bovine strain no fewer than 231 times at intervals of approximately 3 weeks over a period of 13 years, beginning in 1906. The work of subculturing had continued throughout the 1914-18 war, although the Germans had occupied Lille, where they suppressed all experiments on animals, and very nearly executed Calmette because he possessed pigeons! After the war, the strain was considered to be permanently stabilized in the safe, attenuated form.

Testing of course was very important. When the attenuated vaccine was injected into cattle, it produced temporary fever but no evidence of tuberculous nodule formation. Guinea-pigs are very susceptible to tuberculosis, but here again the vaccine strain was quite harmless on injection. However, it undoubtedly induced a high degree of immunity, for vaccinated animals resisted challenge by virulent bovine bacilli. At this stage it was named B.C.G. (Bacille Calmette Guérin).

Early Experience in Man and Cattle

We have seen that B.C.G. was first used successfully in a human infant in 1921. During the next three years the harmlessness of the new vaccine for man, calves and monkeys was amply confirmed. Not only did the vaccinated children or animals suffer no ill-effects from the administration, but they had acquired substantial resistance against infection by virulent bacilli.

In 1924, Calmette felt justified in distributing B.C.G. free of charge to doctors and midwives, specifically for feeding to quite young infants not yet contaminated by tuberculosis in their immediate environment. It is of interest that at this stage he used Pasteur's descriptive term (for rabies vaccine) of *virus fixé*, thus claiming for B.C.G. loss of any capacity to regain its lost virulence. Although there was no statistically controlled clinical trial, it was impressive that, up to the end of 1925, 1,317 new-born babies were treated, of whom 586 had been in contact with cases of tuberculosis.

There were only ten deaths from tuberculosis in this large group at the end of six months of age.

Soon mass vaccination for infants became a popular measure in France. By 1928 over 50,000 French children had been given B.C.G., and Calmette claimed success in protecting a large proportion of them. However, there were inevitable snags. For example, S. A. Petroff, who was a distinguished American bacteriologist, stated that he had isolated a virulent variant from a B.C.G. culture—an observation which excited much controversy. A leading London statistician, Major Greenwood, deplored the continued failure to carry out controlled clinical experiment which would settle once and for all the efficacy of the vaccine. Outside France, many doctors were influenced by Petroff and Greenwood and remained very distrustful of the claims made by Calmette, whose propaganda was probably exaggerated at this stage as a counterblast.

THE LÜBECK DISASTER

In 1930, Petroff's warning concerning the danger of regained virulence of B.C.G. was recalled by a tragedy at the German town of Lübeck where approximately 250 infants were fed with an alleged B.C.G. vaccine, which gave rise to a high incidence of deaths (27 per cent.), clinical tuberculosis with remission (56 per cent.) and tuberculin allergy without disease (17 per cent.). It is surprising that the fatality rate was not even higher as some of the doses administered were massive.

Allegations were widely made that the B.C.G. vaccine must have dissociated, leading to the emergence of virulent mutants. Calmette and Guérin were greatly upset by the tragedy for which they felt a personal responsibility, but they were reassured when a commission of enquiry decided that a virulent human culture had been substituted in error for the stock avirulent bovine vaccine culture. For some extraordinary reason both these strains had been kept in the same laboratory, so that a switch was feasible. The ageing chief of the establishment was sentenced to a term of imprisonment for his carelessness in supervision. Although B.C.G. was completely vindicated, it was a long time before there was a complete restoration of confidence.

This disaster, like some of those described elsewhere in connection with diphtheria immunization (p. 96), emphasizes the truth that the preparation and testing of vaccines, antisera, and many other substances must be the responsibility of a conscientious skilled staff, working under scientifically approved conditions. In the case of B.C.G., this must mean a separate laboratory into which no tuberculous person, animal or culture is permitted to enter.

Alas, Calmette was an unhappy and disappointed man till his death in 1933.

THE ADVANCE OF B.C.G.

Scandinavia.—Scientists in the Scandinavian countries were prominent in extending the use of B.C.G. outside France. A Swede, A. T. Wallgren, initiated the intradermal route of administration (between the layers of the skin) for the vaccine in 1927, and thus obviated the uncertain absorption and variable dosage which were inescapable in the original French method of giving the preparation by mouth. The intradermal injection of B.C.G. is now favoured almost everywhere, because the effective dosage is uniform and the immunity more consistent. Wallgren's results with routine vaccination of infants (done without controls) in Gothenburg were favourable. So were those of the Norwegian, J. Heimbeck, who was a pioneer of the prophylactic immunization of nurses in the 1920s.

Heimbeck was later to base his practice of immunization on the results of diagnostic tests with tuberculin. In his first large series of tests, he found that among 571 nurses who were tuberculin positive, only 24 cases (4·2 per cent.) showed any evidence of tuberculosis during the period of observation and none died. In the same series, among another 275 nurses who were tuberculin negative, 97 cases (35·2 per cent.) showed evidence of tuberculosis and 10 of these 97 died. Thus, a positive tuberculin reaction appeared to be indicative of a useful degree of immunity to the disease. Heimbeck's crucial experiment was to take a further 355 negative reactors and to vaccinate them with B.C.G. Of this group 210 became tuberculin positive as a result of the vaccination: only 1·9 per cent. showed evidence of tuberculosis and none died. Another 102 of the group remained tuberculin negative in spite of the vaccination: 24 of this number (23.5 per cent.) showed evidence of tuberculosis, with three deaths. This confirmed the observation that a positive tuberculin reaction denoted considerable resistance to infection, and that a tuberculin-negative susceptible person could be protected by the living vaccine, B.C.G.

B.C.G. vaccination has now been discontinued in the Scandinavian countries, because the morbidity and mortality from tuberculosis became very low in them.

France and elsewhere.—By 1933, about one French child in every five was being protected by B.C.G. in the first week of life. In this year also it was estimated by French workers that more than 500,000 children outside France had been vaccinated. An interesting statistic was that the general mortality from all causes during the first year of life was only 4.6 per cent. in the vaccinated, compared with 25 per cent. in the non-vaccinated. Re-vaccination at one, three, five and seven years of age was considered to be safe and permissible in order to increase the immunity of all these children who continued to be in contact with cases of tuberculosis and therefore at special risk.

As we have seen, the French began by feeding B.C.G. to babies, and the Swedes introduced intradermal vaccination. About 1947, a scarification method of administration came into use in France and her overseas territories and also in Canada. It was said to induce a tuberculin positive reaction as efficiently as the intradermal method and to produce less troublesome reactions.

United States of America.—In 1938, J. D. Aronson and Carroll E. Palmer of the Henry Phipps Institute, Philadelphia, carried out carefully controlled trials of B.C.G. on North American Indians. Twenty years later, they reviewed the results, having traced over 99 per cent. of 1,551 vaccinated persons and 1,457 controls. Of the vaccinated group 13 per cent., and of the control group 68 per cent., had died from tuberculosis. Vaccination had certainly been worth while.

Great Britain.—The Medical Research Council was responsible for very thorough clinical trials from 1950 onwards. The final report was published in 1963. Over 50,000 healthy schoolchildren were used for the investigation.

TABLE

Tuberculosis: B.C.G. Vaccination
(M.R.C. Trials: 1950-63)

Group	Incidence of Tuberculosis
Unvaccinated	1·91 per 1,000 participants
Vaccinated	0·40 per 1,000 participants

The reduction in incidence due to vaccination with B.C.G. was approximately 79 per cent.

The trials also showed that the benefit of immunization was still substantial after ten years, and that children should be protected from tuberculosis before they left school. This has been implemented widely, using preliminary tuberculin tests.

Between 1956 and 1962, J. Ungar of Glaxo Laboratories and his collaborators introduced a freeze-dried B.C.G. vaccine, which had the great advantage of being stable for distribution and export. Difficulties which had arisen with liquid vaccine were obviated.

World Progress.—The World Health Organization and the United Nations Invalid Children Emergency Fund (UNICEF) have played a major part in initiating mass immunization campaigns all over the world. Between 1951 and 1961, 345 million people were tested with tuberculin in 41 countries, and 130 million who were non-reactors were vaccinated with B.C.G.

VOLE-BACILLUS VACCINE

In 1936, A. Q. Wells of Oxford isolated a special murine type of tubercle bacillus from voles. It is very virulent for voles but does not produce tuberculosis in man. If B.C.G. had not been discovered, its place would almost certainly have been taken by living vole-bacillus vaccine. Wells's strain made an excellent vaccine for guinea-pigs and later also for children in M.R.C. clinial trials. Its only disadvantage was that it gave rise to rather more undesirable reactions than its rival vaccine, B.C.G.

Appendix A

A NOTE ON TUBERCULIN TESTS FOR DIAGNOSIS

The early history of tuberculin and Koch's attempts to introduce this substance for treatment have already been reviewed (p. 30). As a diagnostic aid it has proved invaluable, particularly in connection with the B.C.G. immunization campaign. It is also much used in veterinary practice.

Koch's Original or Old Tuberculin (O.T.), which produced reactions of hypersensitivity, was a somewhat crude glycerinated extract of the soluble products of the tubercle bacillus. After its discovery in 1890, over 100 variations or 'improvements' were launched. Some were more used than others, but none had lasting success.

Real advances were at last made by Esmond Long and Florence Seibert of the University of Chicago and Phipps Institute, who spent many years between 1920 and 1938 in preparing and establishing a *Purified Protein Derivative* of Tuberculin or P.P.D. They studied the growth of the bacillus on synthetic media of known chemical composition, and then Seibert used purification processes in order to isolate three protein preparations. Of these, P.P.D. had the smallest molecular weight and finally replaced the others. The advantages of purified reagents over the original complex mixture of both the active principle and many unimportant proteins, which might themselves sensitize, are obvious.

The allergic response of tubercle-infected persons was investigated by means of many tests from 1890 onwards. The Subcutaneous Test of Koch, and the Conjunctival Tests of Calmette and Wolff-Eisner, were somewhat risky and had to be given up. Moro's Percutaneous or Ointment Test, Vollmer's Patch Test and the Jelly Test were unreliable, because they depended on absorption from the area of treated skin, which in turn was influenced by skin-penetrability, a variable factor in successive tests.

The first test to retain its popularity for several decades was the Cutaneous (Scratch) Test (1907) of Clemens von Pirquet, who was successively Professor of Paediatries at Baltimore, Breslau and Vienna. Like the Ointment Test, it depended on the absorption of tuberculin, this time from a scratch, and thus had the disadvantage of inexact or variable effective dosage from the local site. A red thickened area was read as positive.

The Intracutaneous Test of the Cannes physician, Charles Mantoux, is the most accurate method of measuring sensitiveness to tuberculin, and is the accepted basis by which all other tests are assessed. It was introduced in 1908, 0·1 ml. of a dilution or of a series of dilutions of Old Tuberculin being injected between the layers of the skin. When P.P.D. began to oust Old Tuberculin, another system of dosage had to be worked out. Today, dosage is expressed more accurately in units.

The Multiple Puncture Test (1951) of Frederick Heaf of the Ministry of Health, London, became popular in the United Kingdom on account of its simplicity, convenience and reliability. It requires a special appliance or Heaf 'Gun', which makes fine vertical punctures or stabs into a small area of skin through a film of P.P.D. Like the Mantoux Test it has been much used in connection with B.C.G. campaigns.

Tuberculin Tests in Cattle.—As in humans, Subcutaneous, Conjunctival, and von Pirquet Tests were all tried—and sooner or later discarded—in cattle. The Intracutaneous or Intradermal Test of Mantoux replaced the others. A usual site for injection was the side of the neck. P.P.D. naturally took the place of Old Tuberculin.

In 1952, a good case was made out for the general pasteurization of milk from any but tuberculin-tested herds. However, heat treatment may still be necessary for tubercle-free milk, on account of the risk of other infections, such as brucellosis.

This brief note on Tuberculin Tests is connected only indirectly with immunization, but is included because such tests are an important part of any B.C.G. campaign. Moreover, it should be of general interest to readers of Chapter 4.

Appendix B

Cautionary Note: Tuberculosis Control by Immunization

B.C.G. vaccination is only an important adjunct to improvements in hygiene and living standards, chemotherapy and other measures used for the elimination of tuberculosis. In Britain, the steady progress in the control of this disease is illustrated by the following statistics. In 1855, tuberculosis caused 3,626 deaths per million of the population; in 1905, the mortality had fallen to 1,632 per million and in 1955 to 144 per million—still too many! Complacency must not be allowed to develop.

What has been achieved in this country can be reproduced everywhere. But the problem is immense—and so would be the cost. According to the Office of Health Economics (1962), nearly 1 per cent. of the people of the world are coughing up tubercle bacilli, and there may be 25 million infectious cases. In India alone there are probably 5 million cases of tuberculosis. We have seen that B.C.G. increases specific resistance to tuberculosis. Non-specific resistance is increased by clean air, ventilation, the prevention of overcrowding and raising the general standard of living. Miniature X-ray, treatment with drugs, the tuberculin testing of herds of cattle and the pasteurization of milk are some of the other measures which help. With regard to drugs, Selman A. Waksman, a Russian who migrated to the U.S.A., discovered the antibiotic, streptomycin, in 1943. In combination with PAS and isoniazid, this substance has revolutionized the prognosis in pulmonary tuberculosis.

CHAPTER 20

IMMUNIZATION AGAINST WHOOPING COUGH (PERTUSSIS) AND ENTERIC FEVER: THE VALUE OF CONTROLLED TRIALS OF VACCINES

I. WHOOPING COUGH

WHOOPING cough or pertussis is an infectious disease of wide distribution, which specially affects infants and young children. The causal organism is the minute Bordet-Gengou bacillus, named after its Belgian discoverers, Jules Bordet and Octave Gengou, who first saw it in 1900 but did not succeed in growing it on special laboratory culture media till 1906. Vaccines were made soon afterwards for both prevention and treatment, but assessment of the results was difficult. Statistically controlled trials were not carried out till much later (1946).

EARLY RESEARCH ON VACCINES

Thorvald Madsen of Copenhagen made extensive studies of preventive vaccination in two epidemics in the Faeroe Isles in 1923-24 and 1929. The population was isolated and very suitable for this research, because every five or six years there was an extensive outbreak of pertussis, when nearly everyone who had not had the disease in a previous epidemic, suffered an attack. In 1924 the fresh outbreak had started before the vaccine was ready for use: for this vaccine several recent strains were obtained. The results of the clinical trial were that, out of 2,094 vaccinated persons only five died, while among 627 unvaccinated controls there were 18 deaths. The case-fatality rates were 0.24 per cent. and 2.9 per cent. respectively. The disease was also less severe among the inoculated. In 1929 a recently isolated strain was once more used for the vaccine, and all the inoculations were completed shortly before the epidemic. The results were confirmatory and need not be given in detail. Taking both outbreaks together, the case-fatality rates were 0·15 per cent. for the vaccinated and 2·4 per cent, for the un-vaccinated controls.

Madsen's experience in the Faeroes was often quoted. It en-couraged attempts at repetition by workers in different countries, who were usually less successful than Madsen for reasons which were not apparent at the time.

British and American Progress

In 1931, the British bacteriologists, P. H. Leslie and A. D. Gardner, demonstrated degenerative changes ('roughness') in per-tussis cultures, which could render them inert for vaccine work. As Madsen had done previously, they appreciated the value of freshly isolated strains, with a distinctive cultural appearance called 'smoothness', for the preparation of vaccines.

Between 1926 and 1948, there was considerable activity on the pertussis vaccine front in the United States of America, the lead-ing exponents being Louis Sauer and Pearl Kendrick. Both claimed good protection, whereas other workers in the U.S.A. and in Britain often obtained much less satisfactory immunity. Con-troversy continued for many years. It was felt that the explanation of the conflicting claims was the existence of an effective but un-known agent which was sometimes damaged to a variable degree or even completely destroyed. Naturally, many variations of tech-nique were tried to overcome the difficulty. For example, Sauer pushed up the total dosage of his vaccine course to 100,000 million organisms, compared with Madsen's estimated total of 22,000 million. Sauer also used human instead of horse blood in his culture medium. Another American, J. A. Bell, was a strong advo-cate of an alum-precipitated vaccine, at first on the basis that aluminium had been a good adjuvant for other types of prophy-lactic. At that time an acceptable laboratory protection-test had not been found, so that direct comparison of different vaccines was not feasible and there was much speculation.

The British Medical Research Council's Clinical Trials

During the 13 years between 1946 and 1959, the M.R.C. Whoop-ing Cough Immunization Committee carried out large and statistically controlled clinical trials of different British vaccines and others supplied by Pearl Kendrick of Michigan, U.S.A., who was herself a member of the Committee. In early trials the American vaccines were the best and provided a target for the British manufacturers in the further series of trials. Kendrick disclosed that the bacilli for her vaccines were grown on a culture medium containing sheep blood and were killed slowly by thiomersal, which she regarded as preferable to more drastic methods such as exposure to heat or phenol. She also used a mouse-intracerebral test for the assessment of efficacy: briefly, mice protected by a good vaccine are unaffected by virulent culture given into the cerebrum or brain. The Committee finally established on the basis of their further trials that vaccines from whatever source which came up to the required standard in this Kendrick test in mice had a considerable value in preventing clinical whooping cough. A most striking finding for such vaccines was that the attack rate in children closely exposed to infection in their own homes (e.g. when older brothers or sisters contracted the disease at school) was reduced from 87 per cent. in the unvaccinated group to 14 per cent. in the vaccinated group.

TABLE

Whooping Cough: Reduction in attack rate following vaccination

Group	% developing whooping cough
Unvaccinated	87
Vaccinated	14

Two points should be made. In the first place, there was the generalization that good vaccines by the Kendrick test in mice would confer substantial protection on children. Secondly, it follows from the historical sequence that progress in whooping-cough vaccination was impeded until this laboratory test of potency was devised by Kendrick and thoroughly investigated by the M.R.C. Committee. The earlier research workers (like Madsen) were sometimes making vaccines on the right lines, but there was no certainty about the outcome: a good vaccine strain might be selected, but it could be damaged if it were subjected to unfavourable conditions of growth. The Kendrick test enabled every stage of vaccine preparation to be scrutinized and, if necessary, amended.

The M.R.C. trials owed much to A. (later Sir Austin) Bradford Hill, the leading statistician on the Committee. The reader might be interested to learn that Sir Austin is perhaps best known for his long and very thorough investigation (in collaboration with Richard Doll) of the association of lung cancer with cigarette smoking.

Vaccines in Prophylaxis and Treatment

Young children are immunized either with pertussis vaccine alone or more frequently with a mixed vaccine (see p. 198). The mild general reactions which commonly occur are not regarded as a cause for concern. Occasionally there are more severe complications such as convulsions, which are unpredictable and possibly alarming but hardly ever give rise to any permanent neurological damage: the most serious type (so-called encephalopathy or cerebral disease) is very rare indeed, the incidence being of the order of 1 in 50,000 administrations.

Vaccines were formerly used fairly widely for treatment, but it has now been established that they neither shorten the illness nor diminish its severity.

Antisera

From about 1945 various American workers recommended human antisera as a prophylactic measure for non-immune infants who had been intimately exposed to whooping cough. The sera were usually human convalescent serum or so-called hyperimmune serum, obtained from a pool of the sera of healthy adults who had had whooping cough in the past and subsequently received repeated doses of vaccine. The gamma globulin fraction of this serum was also used. Large doses of these antisera were sometimes recommended for treatment: This would appear to indicate that none was entirely satisfactory.

In Great Britain the use of antisera for either prophylaxis or treatment was never extensive. The results were never dramatic. Vaccines for prevention and antibiotics for treatment have now taken the place of antisera.

Conclusion

Like other infectious diseases, whooping cough has shown a marked decline in severity in modern times. The number of deaths from it in England and Wales in 1925 was 6,038 and in 1964 only 44. Contributions to this reduction have been made by vaccines (in recent years), drugs and other measures.

Pertussis vaccine is now mostly given in the convenient form of a combined or mixed prophylactic (see p. 204).

II. ENTERIC FEVER

The Choice of Strains for Vaccines

In Chapter 12, the use of typhoid paratyphoid vaccine (T.A.B.) was described up to the end of the first World War. At that time it was accepted that the protection conferred was always substantial: there was no concern about any serious variability between different batches of the product.

However, by 1928, bacteriologists were worried about the so-called 'rough' changes they observed in many old strains of typhoid organisms: the bacterial colonies looked rough with a spreading edge. The Rawlings culture, which was a time-honoured favourite for inclusion in the stock vaccines prepared in many countries, showed this trend. As in the case of whooping cough vaccines, colonies with the distinctive appearance called 'smoothness' had to be selected continually in order to counteract this trend towards 'roughness'. In 1932, F. B. Grinnell of Harvard University, Boston, U.S.A. used the laboratory mouse for determining the virulence of typhoid cultures, and also for assessing the protective value of different vaccines against these virulent strains. On this basis he found that the 'rough' Rawlings strain, as it then existed in 12 laboratories, was less suitable (after 27 years of continuous service) than certain other strains: it was less virulent and less effective (antigenic) in vaccines. In 1936 the Americans replaced it by the Panama 38 strain.

In the 1930s, shortly after Grinnell's publication, Arthur Felix and Margaret Pitt of the Lister Institute, London showed that mouse-virulence was due to a special 'virulence' or 'Vi' component of the typhoid bacillus. The British army bacteriologists, H. M. Perry, H. T. Findlay and H. J. Bensted suggested that only virulent smooth strains rich in this antigen should be used for vaccines. The old classical Rawlings strain and also paratyphoid strains were made more virulent for mice by certain methods and their protective value for mice was also enhanced. Improved T.A.B. vaccine came into general use for the British army in the winter of 1933-34.

T.A.B. VACCINES IN THE 1939-45 WAR AND SUBSEQUENTLY

In 1941, Felix recommended the use of alcohol-killed and alcohol-preserved vaccines, because alcohol was less damaging than phenol and heat to the Vi antigen, and so-called alcoholized vaccines protected mice better than the existing phenolized vaccines. His recommendation was adopted, and the new type of vaccine made from Felix's Ty 2 and other selected virulent strains, was gradually introduced into the British army.

The change was made, although J. S. K. (later Sir John) Boyd showed in 1943 that the British heat-killed, phenolized vaccines conferred a high degree of protection on man. This was demonstrated dramatically by the experience of 16-24,000 British prisoners-of-war in Italian hands, who did not develop enteric fever in spite of the presence of this disease and much bad hygiene amongst their captors. On the other hand, Italian prisoners-of-war who had been immunized with their own T.A.B. vaccine—primary course and, where necessary, reinoculations—suffered from enteric fever. This showed that the Italian vaccine was not effective. However, when British army phenolized vaccine was used for the prisoners, the epidemic waned. Although various factors may have contributed to this result, the British army vaccine was rightly assumed to be a valuable preventive agent.

By 1957 doubt had arisen about the value of the alcoholized vaccines in current use. Troops stationed in the Egyptian Canal Zone seemed to be poorly protected against exposure to numerous enteric carriers and bad water hygiene. The Army Authorities were worried. It became obvious that the high-grade protection obtained in laboratory mice was not applicable also to man: the confidence in alcoholized vaccines (based on animal experimentation but without a clinical trial in the field) must surely have been misplaced! Pending controlled investigations, phenolized vaccines came into favour once more and replaced the alcoholized preparations.

Controlled Clinical Trials and Their Value

In enteric fever as in whooping cough, the statistical approach in evaluating vaccines was at last shown to be an essential requirement. For many years after 1954 controlled clinical trials were carried out in Yugoslavia and British Guiana under the auspices of the World Health Organization. The decision of the British army to give up the use of alcoholized vaccine was shown conclusively to be correct. In the Yugoslav trials, phenolized vaccines were superior to alcoholized: in two groups of 5,000 to 6,000 persons observed for five years, the annual average attack rates per 10,000 were 0.4 for the phenolized vaccine group and 5.7 for the alcoholized group.

A later improvement was the introduction of acetone-killed vaccine, which gave even better immunity than heat-killed phenolized vaccine. The attack rates per 10,000 for $3\frac{1}{2}$ years exposure were 41 for a control group (which received tetanus toxoid instead of enteric vaccine), 11 for the phenolized vaccine group and 2 for the acetone-killed vaccine group.

Much controversy in the 1950s concerning the relative importance of vaccination and hygiene with special regard to the water-supply would have been avoided if the great pioneers such as Almroth Wright had paid more attention to the inherent fallacies of their type of field trials. For example, the vaccinated groups often consisted of volunteers; inoculation might be carried out when enteric fever had already broken out; the duration of exposure of vaccinated and unvaccinated groups was seldom or never considered. The modern statistically-minded scientist would have guarded against the error of *post hoc, ergo propter hoc* with regard to his evaluation of any vaccine.

It is of course easy to be wise after the event, but another mistake was made and must be avoided in future: care can now be seen to be needed in recognizing a new and untried laboratory procedure as a reliable means of testing vaccines to be used in man. Thus, Almroth Wright stressed unduly the value of a so-called bactericidal method (involving test-tubes) in introducing the vaccine, and Felix relied quite wrongly on correlation between the results of protection experiments in mice and the protection likely to be obtained in man.

Further, the human fault of over-enthusiasm in launching a new preparation has to be avoided. 'Multiple causes' (protection from the vaccine *plus* improvements in hygiene) might lead to unwarranted claims for the vaccine. The earlier evidence was too often presumptive rather than conclusive. Nevertheless, one can safely conclude in retrospect that the phenolized vaccines in use throughout the First World War and to a large extent in the Second protected well. The alcoholized vaccines that were introduced very gradually and were used side by side with the phenolized in the latter part of the Second World War were much less satisfactory. They had to be given up eventually on the basis of exhaustive clinical trials.

OTHER DEVELOPMENTS: VACCINES AND ANTISERA

For the sake of historical completeness, various other advances and projects deserve brief mention.

Oral T.A.B. Vaccine.—This killed preparation of organisms in the form of a bile-containing pill or saline suspension was introduced in 1920 by Alexandre Besredka of the Pasteur Institute, Paris. It gained considerable popularity in French-speaking countries on account of the ease of oral administration and the relative absence of symptoms after ingestion. Owing to gross uncertainties of absorption, and therefore of effective dosage, all killed preparations of this type are now obsolete.

Extracts from the Typhoid Bacillus.—Various chemical fractions or extracts have been isolated by very different methods from typhoid organisms, and some have proved antigenic and protective for small animals and man. No material has been sufficiently potent to take the place of suspensions of the bacilli themselves.

South African Endotoxoid T.A.B. Vaccine.—About 1927 E. Grasset of South Africa began to develop an endotoxoid, as it was called, which was (with modifications from time to time) the super-natant fluid obtained by centrifuging a heat-killed culture and formolizing it. It was used on a large scale for civilians as well as the South African troops during the Second World War, and reduced the enteric incidence and case mortality rates. In the North African campaign, the results obtained were similar to those reported with the British Army phenolized vaccine. Reactions were fewer and less severe than with whole suspensions. Controlled clinical trials were not carried out.

Intradermal Injection.—Many of the preparations already described in this section were introduced in order to reduce the incidence and severity of reactions, without corresponding loss in protective power: for various reasons they failed to replace whole suspensions.

A much more promising line of research was intradermal vac-cination (injection of vaccine within the structure of the skin), which was introduced primarily for revaccination in the 1930s. Reactions, local and general, were fewer and less severe than after subcutaneous (under the skin) injection, probably due to slower absorption from the injection site. As the method is effective, it has attracted considerable attention in recent years and is often the route of choice for all T.A.B. injections.

Typhoid Antisera.—Many workers from Chantemesse in 1907 to Felix in 1935 introduced antisera, and claimed good protection. Notwithstanding these favourable reports, experienced clinicians were often uncertain about the real value of the products. Trials were not properly controlled, e.g. on alternate cases. With the advent of effective chemotherapy, antisera became obsolete.

CONCLUSION

Phenolized and acetone-killed vaccines confer useful protection, as confirmed in clinical trials under the auspices of the World Health Organization. Vaccine prophylaxis is required for the armed forces, the staffs of isolation hospitals, and for persons resid-ent in, or going to, countries with a high endemic prevalence of enteric fever. The intradermal route of administration has tended to replace the subcutaneous. (The modern outlook on typhoid and paratyphoid vaccination is also discussed on p. 215.)

In this chapter, the need for statistically-controlled clinical trials has been emphasized for both whooping cough and enteric fever bacterial vaccines. The design of the former trials became a model for subsequent evaluations of biological products of this type.

CHAPTER 21

IMMUNIZATION AGAINST OTHER BACTERIAL INFECTIONS

I N this chapter consideration is given to a miscellaneous group of diseases, some of which have already been discussed in the pre-1920 sections of this book. Here we are mainly concerned with more recent developments, although, in those cases where earlier events have not been covered, it has sometimes been necessary to deal with them also in order to complete the account.

The following is the list of bacterial infections under review:

Anthrax
Cholera
Plague
Brucellosis
Cerebrospinal meningitis

Gonorrhoea
Leptospirosis
Pneumococcal Pneumonia
Tularaemia

ANTHRAX

In an earlier chapter (p. 23) much attention was given to the pioneer work of Louis Pasteur on active immunization with attenuated cultures. Successive batches of vaccine were subject to variation both in the extent of attenuation and in the protection induced—a considerable drawback!

There were no significant developments in connection with vaccines till the 1930s. Then, in 1935, Mario Mazzucchi of Milan suspended anthrax spores (round or ovoid forms of the bacillus, resistant to adverse influences) in saponin, and claimed that a stable attenuated vaccine was the result. This prophylactic was much used in veterinary practice in many countries, and the results were regarded as more uniform and favourable.

A major improvement was effected (1939) by Max Sterne in South Africa. His vaccine consisted of avirulent uncapsulated (without protective cover) sporing bacilli, suspended in glycerol saline with the addition of only 0·1 per cent. of saponin. It was used on many millions of farm animals, and protected well. It was safer and caused fewer reactions than previous vaccines. As it was a preparation of sporing bacilli, it was unacceptable for human injection.

A vaccine suitable for man was at last developed (1948) by G. P. Gladstone of Oxford University. It was an alum-precipitated, bacteria-free antigen and was of considerable value. However, there have been certain doubts about the need for active immunization of the human subject, because various antibiotics are effective in the treatment of cutaneous and other forms of anthrax (see also p. 207).

With regard to serum therapy, Sclavo's anthrax antiserum was first prepared in 1895 in sheep, and later in asses. The published results obtained in veterinary and human anthrax in Italy showed considerable variation. Antisera were used extensively in Germany, where G. Sobernheim eventually introduced (1902) a method of combined active and passive immunization—Pasteur's vaccine and serum at different sites—into veterinary practice, again with variable results. In Britain, large doses of antiserum were given in the treatment of human anthrax, along with arsenicals or, later, antibiotics. There was always doubt about the contribution of the serum to recovery: patients were usually given 'multiple therapy'.

CHOLERA

After experience with cholera vaccines in the 1914-18 war, there were abundant opportunities for studying the value of vaccines in affording protection in India. In 1927, A. J. H. Russell in the Madras Presidency reviewed the experience of mass inoculation campaigns. Even a single subcutaneous dose of vaccine conferred considerable protection, but oral vaccine (Besredka) was less satisfactory. (For similar disappointing results with oral T.A.B. vaccine, see p. 139.)

Twenty years later, in 1947, Adisesham, Pandit and Venkatraman of the King Institute, Madras, published further data and made similar claims. However, as Wilson and Miles have pointed out, figures collected during epidemics are open to criticism: only a properly controlled trial will tell us what the real value of vaccination is. Money, staff and time are required for health education and modern sanitation (including the chlorination of water) as well as for mass vaccination. Sir Leonard Rogers, for many years the grand old man of tropical medicine, always maintained that safe water supplies everywhere were the best preventive, but that vaccination also played a part.

Cholera antisera were tried in the treatment of cholera, but they had little or no value and were given up. The established disease is so difficult to influence or control that the main emphasis is on prevention.

PLAGUE

Like cholera, plague was a major problem in India after the 1914-18 war. From 1919 to 1928 the average annual number of deaths it caused in that country was 170,300.

In 1933, J. (later Sir John) Taylor, who was Director of the Central Research Institute, Kasauli, reviewed the data of 13 outbreaks in which Haffkine's type of vaccine was used. The attack rates were 6.5 per cent. and 29 per cent., and deaths were 3.1 per cent. and 23 per cent. for the vaccinated and control groups respectively. There was useful protection for some months after the inoculations.

Although living avirulent vaccines were advocated by workers in the Dutch East Indies, Madagascar and South Africa, the American Army Authorities decided to use a killed vaccine in the 1939-45 war. While it was consistently claimed that living non-virulent micro-organisms immunized better than any killed preparation, there was the understandable fear that sooner or later there might be a return at some stage to dangerous virulence. On balance a dead preparation seemed preferable.

Karl F. Meyer of the University of California was still recommending a dead vaccine in 1953, but he also emphasized the need for repeated vaccination in order to achieve adequate and lasting protection. Clearly, destroying rats was advisable.

Improved hygiene and control of the flea vector with insecticides have made plague vaccination of much less importance than formerly, except possibly for persons in contact with the disease and therefore specially exposed to risk. In 1961 there were only 808 cases of plague throughout the world, excluding the Chinese mainland.

Plague antisera used to be given sometimes in large dosage for treatment, but were given up in favour of antibiotics which were more effective.

BRUCELLOSIS

Living vaccines of *Brucella abortus*, which were introduced in 1906, were successful in veterinary practice (see p. 84). A major advance was made in 1930 when a strain of modified and fixed virulence named S19 was advocated by workers in the Bureau of Animal Industry in the U.S.A. Attenuated vaccines of this type led to healthier farm stock, and therefore to increased milk production. A policy of vaccination, accompanied by slaughter, eliminated bovine brucellosis in many countries. Eradication of the disease in man must surely follow eradication in animals (see also p. 208).

Nucleoprotein extracts called *Brucellin* and *Brucellergin* were formerly used to detect hypersensitivity in man as a preliminary to active immunization with killed preparations: they have now been replaced by more reliable serological tests. In most parts of the world live vaccines were considered to be too hazardous for man, but in Russia they reduced the incidence of the human as well as the bovine disease.

CEREBROSPINAL MENINGITIS

Readers of an earlier section (p. 84) may recall that inflammation of the meninges, the covering membranes of the brain, may be caused by a wide variety of micro-organisms. Epidemics of 'stiffness of the neck' from various causes occurred throughout the ages. Some of these were due to the *Neisseria meningitidis* or meningococcus, which was first cultivated in Vienna in 1887.

Antisera were widely used in treatment from 1905 till 1938. In retrospect, none was completely satisfactory, although extravagant claims were sometimes made at the time. From the late 1930s the sulphonamides and subsequently other forms of chemotherapy completely transformed the picture.

Dead vaccines of meningococci were tried for prevention, mostly in the control of small epidemics. They were of limited value and were ousted by chemotherapy.

GONORRHOEA

This infectious disease, which was at one time confused with another venereal disease, syphilis, is due to *Neisseria gonorrhoeae* or the gonococcus. The reader will correctly infer from its modern, scientific name that the causal organism is related to the meningococcus. In the past a wide variety of vaccines and also certain antisera were used in treatment, and were of doubtful value. As in the case of the meningococcus, all specific measures or remedies directed at the organism are now obsolete.

LEPTOSPIROSIS

Leptospirosis or Weil's disease is typically characterized by jaundice, enlargement of the spleen, and nephritis. As jaundice is absent in about half the cases, many cases are overlooked. Confusion with other conditions, especially yellow fever and infectious hepatitis, has been inevitable. The causal organism is the *Leptospira icterohaemorrhagiae*, which was discovered by the Japanese workers, R. Inada and Y. Ido, in 1915. It is frequently carried by rats, which contaminate water and food, under insanitary conditions, and thus pass on the infection to human beings. In Britain there have been outbreaks amongst mine workers, sewermen and those engaged in washing fish. In the 1914-18 war, all the armies had cases in association with the rat-infested, water-logged trenches.

A closely allied species, *Leptospira canicola*, is normally a pathogen for the dog but has caused a few human cases also.

Japanese, French and British workers established the presence of protective antibodies in the serum of convalescents in human leptospirosis and in the serum of immunized horses (1915-20).

In this country interest in the disease was stimulated in 1925 by C. C. Okell, T. (later Sir Thomas) Dalling and L. P. Pugh, who discovered that *L. icterohaemorrhagiae* was the cause of enzootic canine jaundice, a disease well known in veterinary circles as 'yellows'. The ground-up liver of infected animals produced the characteristic jaundice in guinea-pigs, but this could be prevented by horse antiserum or the serum of convalescent dogs. Horse antisera also had protective and curative properties against leptospirosis in dogs. In man clinical experience tallied with the experimental findings: antisera were beneficial in the preliminary stages of Weil's disease, but were of doubtful value when jaundice had developed. This meant that specific therapy seldom gave striking results because of the difficulties in making a firm diagnosis early enough.

With regard to prophylactic vaccination, dogs have been immunized (1926) with phenolized liver emulsions from infected guinea-pigs. In the 1930s, Japanese and Dutch workers were able to reduce the incidence of leptospirosis in persons specially exposed to risk, and in 1953 Scandinavian workers also claimed a useful degree of protection. Both phenolized and heat-killed vaccines were used for human immunization, and were associated with rather frequent untoward reactions.

In Italian rice-field workers, B. Babudieri claimed (1957) excellent protection with his vaccines, namely an attack-rate of 0.04 per cent. in 5,000 vaccinated persons, as contrasted with 3 per cent. in 5,000 unvaccinated controls.

To complete the record, infections due to about 80 species of this group occur in various parts of the world: they simulate to some extent classical Weil's disease. The strains must be identified before mass immunization can be considered for an affected area.

Pneumococcal Pneumonia

The pneumococcus (*Streptococcus pneumoniae*), which was discovered by Albert Fraenkel in 1886, was the commonest cause of pneumonia. This disease used to occur in devastating epidemics, some of which were associated with a mortality of five per 1,000 living of the community. However, there was much mis-diagnosis in the pre-bacteriological era: certain early outbreaks were probably plague or influenza with pneumonic symptoms.

With this background of tragedy and gaps in exact knowledge, it was natural that the challenge to conquer pneumonia was accepted by leading research workers in many countries. Much

money was made available, particularly for scientists at the Rockefeller Institute, New York, and elsewhere in the United States.
Intensive studies went on from about 1910 to 1942. Towards the
end of this period, specific treatment with antisera was becoming
increasingly successful when it was replaced by various forms of
even more successful, and much less expensive, chemotherapy.
Seldom can so much brilliant and intensive endeavour have been
wasted at a time when steady progress was being made. The story
can only be summarized here.

In 1910, Fred Neufeld and Ludwig Händel in Germany investigated virulent pneumococci from cases of pneumonia. Their
studies included the protective action in mice of antisera made
from different cultures. There were differences between strains,
which suggested a main or typical group of organisms and subsidiary or atypical groups. This work was continued by the Rockefeller team, which included Oswald Avery, A. R. Dochez, Michael
Heidelberger and Rufus Cole. Three well-defined types and one
heterogeneous group (consisting of ill-defined types) were recognized. Antisera were prepared in horses by injecting whole
cultures, usually dead, of pneumococci (1913-17). A few years later,
the biochemists found that the types and also the virulence of the
organisms were due to complex polysaccharides ('specific soluble
substances' or 'S.S.S.') in their capsules. During recovery from
pneumonia, anti-capsular antibody appeared in the blood stream.

The practical outcome of all this research was the preparation
of type-specific antisera (Type I serum for use only in Type I
pneumococcal infection, and so on) for treating pneumonia in
man. Large doses were given intravenously. A 50 per cent. reduction in mortality was claimed for Type I antiserum, but the results
with other types were less encouraging.

Unfortunately, although further research led to better sera, as
shown by protective titres in mice, the hope of improved results
in man was not fulfilled. Then, in 1925, Lloyd Felton introduced
the Felton process, a new method of concentration of the antibacterial antibodies: this removed the cause of severe reactions,
rigors and high temperatures which tended to follow intravenous
injection of untreated serum. Further improvements were still
necessary, and, during the 1930s, the pharmaceutical industry in
the United States invested heavily in producing appropriate anti-

sera against many of the 80 types and sub-types which were finally identified out of the original four classes. About this time, also, Frank Horsfall of the Rockefeller Institute replaced horse antisera by rabbit antisera (1937). The rationale for the change was the relatively small size of the rabbit antibody globulin particle, which should ensure better diffusion throughout the tissue after injection. Moreover, the product was more easily purified. Encouraging results began to come in, but, as each type of pneumococcus might require its separate protective serum, doubts arose about the eventual limits of the project.

As mentioned earlier in this section, the vast therapeutic effort went on into the early 1940s, but the practical benefits were transient and comparatively slight. From 1938 onwards, various forms of chemotherapy began to replace all specific antisera.

Vaccines.—It is not surprising that Almroth Wright of St. Mary's Hospital, London, tried to simulate his work on typhoid vaccine by introducing killed pneumococcal vaccine for prophylactic use in the South African mines (1914). The native labourers worked under conditions that entailed a considerable risk of pneumococcal infection and a high mortality. Although Spencer Lister and others improved the vaccines by using current infecting strains, the immunity attained was probably slight or transient. All the published data were inconclusive. Effective drugs have now replaced vaccines entirely.

TULARAEMIA

Tularaemia is a plague-like disease caused by *Brucella tularense*, and it derives its name from Tulare County, California, where it was first studied in 1910. The infection is transmitted to man by insect bites or contact with infected rodents, including wild rabbits, hares, squirrels and field-mice. Human cases have been reported from the U.S.A., Canada, Japan, Norway, Sweden and Russia. The usual mortality is 5 per cent., but a more severe typhoid type also occurs with a mortality of 50 per cent.

The disease is found mainly among persons exposed to the infection as an occupational or recreational hazard, such as butchers, poultry-men, shepherds, trappers and laboratory workers.

Phenolized vaccines, acetone-extracted preparations, heat-killed glycerinated cultures and even live-attenuated vaccine strains have all been used with some success for prophylaxis. Antisera were available for treatment, but, like those for other infections where antibacterial immunity is of value, have now been replaced by chemotherapy.

V

ACCOMPLISHMENTS—

MAINLY SINCE 1920 (*Continued*):

THE GROWTH OF VIROLOGY

CHAPTER 22

SMALLPOX VACCINATION IN THE TWENTIETH CENTURY

THE LAST BRITISH EPIDEMIC OF VARIOLA MAJOR

IN the closing years of the nineteenth century, the smallpox mortality was low in England and Wales. However, in 1902 and 1903, there was a recrudescence, and this country had its last large epidemic of the classical (severe Asiatic) form of smallpox, variola major. There were altogether 4,203 deaths between 1901 and 1905: the mean annual death rate per million was 25. The worst epidemic year was 1902 with 13,923 cases and 2,464 deaths, the percentage of deaths being 17·7. In 1903 there were 7,383 cases.

The value of vaccination was shown by some data of cases treated during 1901-04 in London hospitals. It is probable that the difference between the vaccinated and unvaccinated groups would have been even wider if the former group had included more persons whose immunity had been 'boosted' by second or third vaccinations.

TABLE

SMALLPOX: LONDON HOSPITALS (1901-04)

Group	No. of patients	Case Mortality
Unvaccinated	2,984	31·57 per cent.
Vaccinated at one time or other	7,749	9·7 per cent.

The unnecessary loss of life makes sad reading: the case-fatality rate of classical smallpox is usually given as 20 to 30 per cent., an estimate to which the above figures roughly conformed. Vaccination effected a considerable reduction, and yet it appears that, in 1901, only 71 per cent. of infants were vaccinated, and in 1905 76 per cent. At least part of the problem was the 'conscience clause' (see p. 59) of the Vaccination Acts Amendment Act, 1898. During the early years after the passing of the Act the implementation of this clause lacked uniformity, because it was dependent on the attitude of the justices who were supposed to be satisfied that a person's conscience was actually troubled. Some justices gave exemption virtually automatically, whereas others went to the opposite extreme and refused to consider any objections on conscientious grounds.

SMALLPOX IN BRITAIN FROM 1906 ONWARDS

Throughout the last 60 years smallpox has been a negligible cause of death. The disease changed radically and was mainly of the European variety, a mild variant of the Asiatic or classical smallpox hitherto described. The mild form is also called alastrim or variola minor, and has a case-fatality rate of 0·1 to 0·3 per cent., instead of the 20 to 30 per cent. of the parent variola major.

Alastrim, as it was popularly called, was recognized in the early years of vaccination in the nineteenth century, and reappeared in East Anglia after the 1914-18 war and gradually spread. It was widely prevalent from 1921 to 1935, the worst period being from 1926 to 1931 when approximately 66,000 cases occurred. The peak year was 1927, with 14,764 cases. After 1931 the outbreak waned until 1935 when it ceased altogether, with a minor recrudescence in 1953. Once again attention is directed to the 'dissociation of fatality from superficial clinical signs': deaths were few, although there were thousands of cases.

Unfortunately the severe variety or variola major was not vanquished, and successive re-introductions from abroad caused much anxiety to the Public Health Authorities of this country. Energetic vaccination campaigns and the surveillance of contacts were necessary to meet each emergency—otherwise the figures given below would have been much higher. Between 1948 and 1952, 54 cases and 16 deaths occurred. The year 1962 was notorious, for there were several importations of Asiatic smallpox from Pakistan, which resulted in 66 British notifications and 26 deaths—the largest number of deaths for any year since 1930 and more than the total of the previous 11 years. It may be noted that India and Pakistan had more than 25,000 deaths annually from the disease at this time.

VACCINATION IN BRITAIN FROM 1906 ONWARDS

After 1905, major epidemics of variola major ceased, which led to popular complacency and partly explains the fall in the percentages of children vaccinated: it will be recalled that the figure for 1905 was 76 per cent. Many would regard the Vaccination Act of 1907 as a retrograde step, for it made the lot of conscientious objectors even easier than was provided in the Amendment Act of 1898. Parents no longer had to satisfy a magistrate that they were conscientiously opposed to vaccination: a statutory declaration sufficed and involved much less trouble. There was also an increasing awareness that vaccination was sometimes complicated by unpleasant side-effects. This inevitable decline in infantile vaccinations is shown by the following random figures: for 1908, 63 per cent. were vaccinated; for 1914, below 50 per cent.; and for 1939, only 34 per cent.

Even the 'conscience clause' ceased to apply in 1948 with the advent of the National Health Service, which put an end to the *compulsory* vaccination of infants. There was a further fall in numbers to 18.2 per cent. in the last six months of 1948. Latterly there has once more been an increase, and in 1961 the acceptance rate was around 40 per cent.

From 1948, vaccination in Britain has been on the same voluntary basis as, say, diphtheria, tetanus and pertussis immunizations. Although some authorities have suggested that routine smallpox vaccination of infants might now cease in Britain, the Ministry of Health has opposed this change in procedure, since intensive vaccination campaigns and the tracing and supervision of contacts to meet each dangerous importation would put an intolerable burden on available resources.

Variola minor never reverts to the fully virulent classical disease, and standard smallpox vaccination affords excellent protection against both varieties. The possibility of a clinical attack within 10 years of vaccination is very slight and considerable immunity persists even after 20 or 30 years.

SOME TECHNICAL ADVANCES

This section is concerned with a series of miscellaneous developments more or less in chronological order.

The Therapeutic Substances Act of 1925, which was described in an earlier chapter (p. 98), led to greater uniformity between batches of smallpox vaccine, most of which were obtained from the Government Lymph Establishment while others came from trade sources. By means of the Regulations of 1931, under the Act, standards of potency, quality and purity were prescribed for the vaccine lymph, as for other serological products for injection.

The Vaccination Order of 1929 was concerned with the technique for using the lymph—*not* with its preparation and testing. It was based on the Report of a Committee presided over by Sir Humphrey Rolleston, the well-known physician at that time. Public vaccinators were instructed to make a single insertion of lymph, instead of four as previously. The scratching of crosses on the arm ('cross hatching') was deprecated on the grounds that reactions were often much too severe. After vaccination in infancy, revaccinations were encouraged at the ages of 6 to 7 and 14 to 16 in order to boost the immunity which might otherwise tend to wane. In a covering letter to vaccinators, emphasis was placed on the timing of primary vaccination, which should be in infancy rather than while attending school or during adolescence. 'Post-vaccinal nervous disease' is a rare complication of vaccination, and this hazard is at its lowest in infants.

In 1931-33, there was another interesting development in the laboratory, which facilitated progress in the whole field of viruses, and ended the lull in productive development after Pasteur's death. Viruses will grow only inside living cells, and early virologists were forced to use animals as a source of cells—a method which was cumbersome, time-consuming and expensive. We owe the major advance to Ernest W. Goodpasture of Vanderbilt University, who found that the developing chick embryo would support viral growth. This led to the use of fertile eggs on a vast scale: obviously the egg is cheaper, smaller and less liable to extraneous infection than the animal. Many viruses have now been grown by this convenient technique. To revert to smallpox, in 1933, the vaccinia virus was cultivated on the chorio-allantoic (yolk sac) membranes of chick embryos by British and American workers. Two years later the successful use of a chick embryo vaccine on seven persons was reported by Goodpasture and G. J. Buddingh.

It will be recalled that the scratch method of vaccination was the technique of choice of the Rolleston Committee of 1929. In 1944 the attention of British vaccinators was drawn to the American multiple pressure method, which had been first described in 1927 by James P. Leake of the U.S. Hygienic Laboratory and was being preferred increasingly in his country. Its main advantage was that it obviated the pain and messiness (from bleeding) of the older scratch technique. Although it involved needle pressure (and not punctures or scratches) through a small area of film of vaccine lymph, it permitted growth of the virus in the superficial epidermal layers of the skin, an inoculation site which gives rise to maximum immunity. In 1947, the new method received official approval from the Ministry of Health. It continues to be preferred by many workers, although some assert that the scratch method is better in their experience.

The British Government Lymph Establishment had been moved to Colindale, London, in 1907, and was transferred to its present site at the Lister Institute, Elstree, in 1946. On this occasion calves ceased to be used as the source of the time-honoured 'calf lymph'. Sheep, which had been tried in the first instance in war-time when there was a shortage of calves, were substituted routinely with complete success.

The next major development was in 1955 when L. H. Collier of the Lister Institute reported that freeze-dried and stable vaccines were being prepared by tissue-culture and other methods, and were more reliable than 'calf lymph', particularly for use in hot climates and for storage for long periods as reserve vaccine against the phenomenal demands caused by epidemics. Progress was also made in improving the quality of smallpox vaccine and the methods for titrating its potency.

ERADICATION OF SMALLPOX

Smallpox is an international problem, and the World Health Organization has initiated (1960) an ambitious scheme for its eradication by means of vaccination. The ideal procedure would be compulsory vaccination and revaccination, but universal and efficient vaccination is of course unattainable. Nevertheless, it is right to raise herd immunity to smallpox as far as possible throughout the world. The vaccination campaign, with all its difficulties and limitations, has made substantial progress and appears likely to reach its objective. A recent resolution of the W.H.O. executive council has appealed to all W.H.O. member-countries to aid in the fight, and has expressed the hope that smallpox could be wiped out in ten years.

Every doctor in this country may have a case of smallpox unexpectedly in his surgery. The health authorities cope with the situation admirably, but the possibility of epidemic spread always occasions great concern. Success in world eradication must be the aim.

Appendix A

A Chemotherapeutic Agent

The introduction of a drug, N-Methylisatin β-Thiosemicarbazone, commonly called Methisazone or 'Marboran', is a fine example of Anglo-American team work: D. J. Bauer and A. W. Downie, the British virologists, collaborated with L. St. Vincent and C. H. Kempe, paediatricians from Denver, U.S.A. In 1963, the results were published of a controlled study in Madras. The main finding was a 94 per cent. reduction in the number of cases of smallpox when the drug was given during the incubation period to intimate contacts of smallpox patients. The excuse for mentioning it here is that it was a more effective short-term prophylactic than vaccination alone.

This was the first chemotherapeutic agent or drug to exercise control over a virus disease—penicillin and all the usual antibiotics had been powerless. The discovery spurred a world-wide search for other anti-virus compounds.

Appendix B

The Use of Antisera

As in other viral diseases, antisera were useless in the *treatment* of smallpox. Secondly, vaccinial antisera of various types, including gamma globulin fractions of these sera, had little or no effect in treating the more severe complications of vaccination.

The value of such preparations in *prevention* was very different. Household contacts of a case of smallpox were at considerable risk if they had not been vaccinated or had only been vaccinated in infancy many years previously. The active immunity following vaccination takes some time to develop, but immediate passive protection could be conferred by gamma globulin prepared from the serum of recently vaccinated persons or convalescent smallpox patients.

If an eczematous subject had to be vaccinated, antivaccinial gamma globulin was useful in preventing the vaccinial reaction from becoming too severe.

Combined active and passive immunization was used by Kempe, Berge and England in 1956. They were worried by the necessity to vaccinate close contacts late in the incubation period—so late that protection could not possibly be achieved. Among 56 contacts who were vaccinated and also given gamma globulin (prepared from the serum of recently vaccinated persons) there were 2 cases of smallpox—1 fatal and 1 modified. Among 75 comparable controls, who were vaccinated only, there were 8 cases of smallpox and 3 deaths. It should be noted that this paper appeared in 1956 and that Kempe was one of the authors of the important article on chemotherapy published in 1963 (see *Appendix A*). Drug prophylaxis would now be the method of choice in these difficult circumstances.

CHAPTER 23

VIRAL VACCINES: DOG DISTEMPER, HUMAN INFLUENZA AND COMMON COLDS

THE scope of this book is primarily human immunization, and the reader may wonder why a disease of veterinary importance has been given prominence in a chapter heading. The reason is that knowledge and skills acquired by British scientists in studying dog distemper led to further success when they were applied to the isolation of the primary causal agents of human influenza. Both these outstanding advances in virology were made by members of the staff of the National Institute for Medical Research, London.

DOG DISTEMPER

In 1923 the weekly journal, *The Field*, raised a fund for research on this highly contagious, and therefore widespread, disease of dogs. This work was undertaken by P. P. (later Sir Patrick) Laidlaw and George W. Dunkin, respectively the medical bacteriologist and the veterinary surgeon at the Institute. Many animal species were investigated, and major progress was made when it was discovered that ferrets were highly susceptible to the filter-passing causal virus. Between 1926 and 1932 technical improvements enabled certain organs of infected dog or ferret, in which the distemper virus was present in high concentration, to be used for vaccine production without much risk of intercurrent infections—an ever-present hazard when distemper-infected animal tissues (instead of pure cultures on special, sterilized food-stuffs) have to be injected as vaccines. Without going into details, the control of canine distemper was highly successful. Considerable immunity was given to dogs, as confirmed by subsequent injections of virus and by exposure to the natural disease.

There is today much overlap between human and veterinary

medicine—for much too long an artificial break-down of a single discipline. An instance of integration was Laidlaw's work on distemper, and his subsequent research on human influenza. One animal species, viz. the ferret, was susceptible to the viruses of both diseases, and provided a clue to profitable research throughout.

INFLUENZA

The early work on bacterial vaccines for this infection has already been reviewed (p. 87). It was unsuccessful, because the so-called influenza bacillus and other bacteria of the respiratory tract were not the primary causes of 'true influenza'. Increasingly, there was a belief in a hypothetical causal virus—minute, filter-passing, invisible with the ordinary bacteriological microscope, and therefore undiscovered till the 1930s.

Virus and its Transmission.—When the research in dog distemper was well advanced towards the end of 1932, influenza broke out in England. Laidlaw and his colleagues, C. H. (later Sir Christopher) Andrewes and Wilson Smith at once tackled this new problem, and searched for an animal susceptible to the unknown virus. At an early stage they tried the clean-bred (specially cared for in order to be disease-free) ferrets, which were already housed at the National Institute in connection with the dog-distemper work. Nasal washings were obtained from patients showing the early symptoms of influenza. After filtration by a special method in order to remove all bacteria, the washings were instilled into the noses of healthy ferrets, which soon developed symptoms similar to those of human influenza. This was the first step in the proof of a specific viral origin of the disease. The British team made their discovery in 1933, and their work was soon confirmed during epidemics in America, Australia and elsewhere. The same influenza virus was apparently isolated everywhere at this time. It was also demonstrated that antibody to this virus was present in the blood serum of patients who had recovered from influenza. The technique used was to mix the serum with virus and then to attempt to infect ferrets with the treated virus. The disease was not produced because the virus had been neutralized by the antibody.

It is of considerable interest that, at the time of the 1918-19 pandemic of influenza, a new disease of swine called swine influenza or 'hog flu' appeared as an epizootic (a widespread outbreak in animals similar to an epidemic in man) in the United States. It was studied by Richard Shope of the Rockefeller Institute branch at Princeton. Many years later, in 1935 and subsequently, the London team collaborated with Shope and discovered a close antigenic relationship between the swine virus of Shope and the human influenza virus A, as it came to be called: this was almost certainly the cause of the 1918-19 pandemic. The suggestion was also made that both viruses arose from a common ancestral stock.

The first human virus strain to be preserved and used for research on making a protective vaccine was isolated by a member of the original team, Wilson Smith—wherefore the classic W.S. strain. The prospects of success in a vaccine project were improved when it was demonstrated that ferrets which had recovered from one artificial infection were completely resistant to a second attack for about three months. Another line of research begun by Wilson Smith was concerned with the behaviour of influenza virus in embryonated eggs.

In these early years it was appreciated that the ferret was not very suitable for large-scale experimentation. Fortunately, it was discovered in 1934 that influenza virus could also be transmitted to the handy and very cheap laboratory mouse, *not* straight from the human patient but after a few 'passages' (transfers from one animal to another) in ferrets. Thereafter, knowledge accumulated rapidly.

Another discovery of general interest in connection with transmission of the virus was the importance attached to the route of infection. Intranasal instillation was necessary in order to produce an attack of influenza in ferrets, mice or swine. Subcutaneous, intramuscular or intravenous administration gave rise to antibody formation, and therefore immunity, without making the animals ill.

Finally, the virus story was strengthened when an experimental ferret with symptoms of the disease sneezed on C. H. Stuart-Harris, a member of the M.R.C. team. He developed the disease—an event which had good publicity value for the research project. Stuart-Harris later became Professor of Medicine at Sheffield University and a virologist of international renown.

Viral Vaccines.—In 1937, Thomas Francis, junior, of the U.S.A., as well as the British team, experimented with living cultivated vaccines, which were injected subcutaneously into human volunteers. As had occurred in animals, circulating antibody formation followed the injections, without evidence of influenzal illness. Although safety seemed assured, these early vaccines were not acceptable for general release as a preventive measure. Incidentally, Francis's virus strain was isolated in 1934 during an influenza outbreak in Puerto Rico—and was widely studied as PR8. It appeared to be identical with the WS strain.

As living vaccines were regarded with some suspicion and even alarm, the British team substituted a vaccine consisting of the lungs of infected mice, which was inactivated by chemical-treatment with formaldehyde. Ferrets were used as the experimental animals in the first instance, and, when they showed a considerable increase in the antibody content of their blood serum, human volunteers were injected. Once again there were encouraging antibody responses.

Mouse-lung vaccines were hardly ideal prophylactics for human injection, even after chemical treatment. Further research was indicated on other sources of virus in quantity. In 1940, F. M. (later Sir Macfarlane) Burnet of Melbourne, Australia, prepared chick embryo cultures, which were invaluable for investigations on immunization, including virus serology and genetics, throughout the 1939-45 war and subsequently. Serological studies were intensified when Thomas Francis isolated another variety of virus from an epidemic in America in 1940. It was named influenza B, because it differed from the original London strain (1933), both serologically and in pathogenicity for animals: the 1933 strain came to be known as influenza A. An attack by one virus type left the patient unprotected against the other.

Since influenza is a disabling disease, the protection of the personnel of the Services with viral vaccines was an important wartime research project, although the scale of operation had to be limited. In accordance with expectation, a single injection of a concentrated vaccine conferred a useful degree of protection—but only if the vaccine strain and the epidemic strain were of the *same* type.

In the U.S.A. influenza vaccines gave good immunity in 1943

and 1946, but were of practically no value in 1947. The explanation was that the epidemic virus A strain had undergone mutation to a type which was not sufficiently closely related to the virus A in the vaccine. About 1948 the variant strains were referred to as A1 or A–prime strains. It was established that the influenza virus shows a pronounced tendency to mutate. A major change in type is now known to occur every 10 years, minor changes being observed at shorter intervals. Clearly mutations have to be kept under observation, and, in 1948, this need led to the setting-up of a World Influenza Centre, with various national sub-centres, to collect information and strains for study. The obvious location for the centre at this time was the National Institute for Medical Research, London, with C. H. Andrewes, one of the discoverers of the virus, as the first director.

Another distinct type of these viruses, called influenza C, was described in 1949 in New York. It was responsible for widespread, but mild and often subclinical, attacks.

Between 1952 and 1958 four Reports on Influenza Vaccine were prepared by a Committee of the Medical Research Council. Some protection statistics were published in the first report: the attack rates were 3 per cent. in the vaccinated as against 4.9 per cent. in the controls. In the second report an attempt to obtain more sustained responses to vaccines was described: mineral oil was a typical adjuvant (or helping) substance, which might afford better protection, but sometimes at the cost of unpleasant and very persistent reactions. In 1957, yet another variant type of virus A caused difficulties for the world's virologists. It began to spread widely from south-western China and overcame any resistance induced by previous A or A1 infection: there was little overlap of protection between the types. The new variant was designated A2 or Asian virus. According to the fourth M.R.C. report, Asian influenza vaccine gave significant protection against Asian virus, for there was a two-thirds reduction in the attack rate compared with controls which received 'standard' influenza vaccines (without any Asian strain in their composition).

The preceding paragraphs illustrate the type of problem involved in preventing influenza by vaccination. The difficulties throughout are complicated not only by the possibility of mutation but by the short duration of the protection, which may be only some months. A reinforcing dose of vaccine may be advised to prolong the immunity.

On the basis that the number of variants is finite, American workers have advocated multi-strain vaccines composed of about four antigenic variants. Research continues, with much work still to be done.

Live vaccines.—In an attempt to improve the protection, live vaccines were used intensively in the U.S.S.R. and also in the U.S.A. with a strain obtained from Moscow. Later, using Asian (A2) strains of virus, a 1·5 to 2·3 fold protection was achieved (1959) in the face of an epidemic. It is of interest that the subcutaneous route of administration was completely safe even when the live viruses were fully active.

CONCLUSION

Influenza vaccines, prepared from current epidemic strains, gave 1·5- to 3-fold protection, when used shortly before the time of exposure to infection. Live viruses did not immunize much better than inactivated preparations.

COMMON COLDS

Research workers are often taunted, and sometimes abused, for their failure to conquer the 'common' ubiquitous cold, which is responsible for so much discomfort (or worse) and the loss of millions of working days every year. The effort expended on abortive investigations has been tremendous, and it will be seen that most criticism is unfair. Scientists are aware of the great extent of the problem, which has many facets. Effective control of colds is unlikely to be achieved in the foreseeable future.

Colds are caused primarily by minute, filter-passing, infecting agents or viruses, as had long been suspected but was first demonstrated conclusively, and independently, in Germany and America in 1916 and 1917. However, the pathogenic bacteria in the nose and throat, which differ from the viruses in being retained by special bacterial filters, play a secondary rôle in determining the severity of the attack and any complications.

Anticatarrhal Bacterial Vaccines.—Between the two World Wars, mixed bacterial vaccines were used extensively. Almost every authority or pharmaceutical firm recommended a different series of vaccine strains—in different proportions. Similar 'stock' vaccines were advised also for bronchitis and pulmonary catarrh, unconnected with colds. When symptoms were chronic, or tended to recur periodically, special mixtures of the patient's own respiratory flora (autogenous vaccines) were sometimes given a trial, perhaps with encouraging results. Subcutaneous injection was the usual route of administration for all vaccines, whether for prevention or treatment. A variation of this route, which became popular and commercially lucrative, was the ingestion by mouth of capsules or tablets, say, twice weekly throughout the winter months.

Many controlled clinical trials with mixed stock vaccines were carried out in England, the United States, Sweden and elsewhere, but the results were almost invariably disappointing. Notwithstanding this background, the popular demand for various vaccines was encouraged by reports of improvement or cure in individual cases. The statistician might scoff, but the uncritical or unscrupulous doctor or drug firm continued to persuade (exploit) gullible victims of colds to use a particular vaccine.

Attention is again directed to the fact that these trials were made with mixed stock vaccines. Many years later, in 1958, the value of *autogenous* bacterial vaccines, prepared from each patient's own respiratory flora, was investigated. In a controlled trial in a factory, the incidence of fully developed colds was six times greater in the control subjects than in the vaccinated. This result came as a surprise to many bacteriologists, and led to research on a wider scale—and some further controversy.

Search for the Causal Virus.—From 1930 onwards, the successful transmission of the common cold to human volunteers was recorded by workers in America and elsewhere. However, all attempts to maintain the virus in culture failed. Strains were readily lost in the early years of virology, and the preparation of a viral vaccine was not possible.

The immensity of the research project was widely appreciated, and the Common Cold Research Unit was established in 1946 at Harvard Hospital, Salisbury, England. This war-time hospital had been provided and staffed by Harvard University, Boston, in 1940, but was no longer required by the Americans after the war. They generously donated it to the British Government, and it became the concern of the Medical Research Council and the Ministry of Health. Work on colds began in the summer of 1946, with C. H. Andrewes who was already well-known for his share in the discovery of the influenza virus in 1933, as its first director.

In investigations on colds human volunteers were inoculated intranasally with nasal secretions from people with colds: all bacteria had been removed from the inoculum by filtration. Mild infections were produced by these virus-containing filtrates in non-immune persons. A great deal of work was done on the cultivation of the viruses. Human embryo lung tissues were the basis for a suitable culture medium which was followed up for a time.

Later, the common cold problem became very complicated, because improved methods of tissue culture led to the isolation of many new respiratory viruses, mostly from children. Media containing monkey-kidney cells, malignant human cells, and human embryonic kidney cells were all used at different times to support growth. Well over 50 different 'cold' viruses have been regularly cultivated since 1961. Some of them, which cause bronchitis, bronchiolitis, croup and bronchopneumonia, might more correctly be designated Acute Respiratory Disease viruses, but this observation does not simplify matters. Details of the classification would be out of place here, but the various technical names used for some of the groups illustrate the complexity: they include adenoviruses, ECHO viruses, Coxsackie viruses, Price's JH virus, para-influenzal virus, Coe virus, respiratory syncytial virus and rhinoviruses. The latter group was recognized and studied by David Tyrrell, the present director of the M.R.C. research team at Harvard Hospital, Salisbury, now a W.H.O. Centre for the study of all respiratory virus diseases.

Viral Vaccines.—Robert Huebner, Maurice Hilleman and other Americans have carried out intensive research on vaccines made of a limited number of adenovirus types. Neutralizing antibodies have been demonstrated in vaccinated persons, who acquired useful protection (60 per cent. and upwards) against the particular virus strains selected. As it is impossible to predict which virus strains will cause colds in a given season, a practical means of vaccination is not in sight.

Conclusion

To date no vaccine can be used with confidence for common cold prevention. The main difficulty is that numerous viruses have been identified at different times as causes of acute respiratory diseases (A.R.D.) in man. Prophylactic viral vaccines give rise to neutralizing antibodies in susceptible persons, but the protection applies only to the corresponding strains—only the fringe of the problem.

There is little justification for the use of bacterial ('catarrhal') vaccines.

Appendix A

Interferon

In 1957, Alick Isaacs and J. Lindenmann of the National Institute for Medical Research, London, published a description of a protein substance which they called interferon (that is, an interfering product). It was first observed in a chick-embryo tissue culture of influenza virus, and has become of great academic interest in virological research.

It had long been known that one virus will interfere with the growth of another. This phenomenon of viral interference was discovered to be the result of the action of a cellular factor induced (for example, in tissue culture) in the course of virus infection and capable of inhibiting virus multiplication.

Further study showed that the appearance of interferon, this protein factor, was a general reaction of animal cells to viral infections—and not merely to human influenza. Interferon appears to limit the spread of such infections; when it was first described, it was hoped that it might be a valuable therapeutic or prophylactic agent against viral disease. Alas, the practical application of Isaacs's research has not proved fruitful so far.

CHAPTER 24

YELLOW FEVER AND TYPHUS FEVER VACCINES

YELLOW FEVER

ONCE again it is necessary to include much earlier but relevant material in a section of this book which deals mainly with post-1920 developments. All the dangerous but fruitful work on yellow fever vaccination was done in the later period, say, from 1927 onwards. Nevertheless, readers would be disappointed if the famous investigations of the great pioneers, which indeed made vaccination possible, were omitted or described in a few lines.

Yellow fever is essentially a tropical disease which has menaced newcomers to the coastal areas of Africa, South and Central America and the West Indies for many centuries. It made the West Coast of Africa the 'white man's grave'. From time to time it has spread into temperate zones. It has also been called 'yellow jack', not on account of jaundiced victims but from the yellow quarantine flag hoisted by shipping to give warning of the presence of infectious disease. Outbreaks have had a considerable popular appeal and have inspired poets and other writers. Perhaps it was yellow jack that smote the ship that carried Coleridge's Ancient Mariner and thus avenged the albatross. It also gave rise to the legend of the Flying Dutchman.

The Yellow Fever Commission.—After the Spanish-American war, Cuba was occupied for a time by United States troops. An outbreak of yellow jack affected large numbers of non-immune foreigners, both American and Spanish. The illness was much dreaded, because its severe form proved fatal after intense jaundice for a few days ('black vomit' disease).

In 1900, a Commission of the U.S. Army was sent to Cuba to

investigate the rôle of the mosquito in disseminating yellow fever. The president was Major Walter Reed. Other members were James Carroll, bacteriologist, Jesse Lazear, entomologist, and Aristide Agramonte, an immune Cuban. Understandably (as the agent is now known to be a filterable virus), no micro-organism was seen in the blood or elsewhere. When the team proceeded to study the means of transmission, human volunteers were not infected by blankets or clothing of yellow fever patients. The mosquito was next studied as the possible vector from man to man: in this connection it was recalled that Carlos Finlay of Cuba felt strongly, in 1881, that the mosquito was the villain of the piece, but he failed to prove his hypothesis. In 1900, Carroll allowed himself to be bitten by a mosquito in a planned experiment, developed severe yellow fever and recovered. Lazear was bitten fortuitously—not a deliberate experiment—by a resident mosquito, and died as the first of a number of martyrs to science in investigating yellow fever. After prolonged enquiry it was established that a special type of mosquito, *Stegomyia fasciata* (later classified as *Aedes aegypti*) conveyed the infection. The research was completed in 1902. Obviously, a war against this mosquito was indicated. Reed's findings were applied by William Gorgas, the Chief Sanitary Officer of Havana: in 1900 there were 1,400 cases in Havana and in 1902 there were none! Gorgas also introduced anti-mosquito measures into Panama in 1904 and facilitated the construction of the Panama Canal, completed in 1914. An earlier attempt to carry out this work in 1882 failed on account of yellow fever and malaria. The United States took over the project in 1904.

Carroll, another member of the Commission, filtered blood from a case and injected the filtrate into three volunteers, two of whom had typical yellow fever (1901). This proved the virus origin of the disease.

The Walter Reed Army Medical Centre in Washington was named after the president of this famous Commission.

The Tragedy of Hideyo Noguchi.—Noguchi was an enthusiastic research bacteriologist at the Rockefeller Institute, New York. He was of Japanese descent. He had done splendid work on the causal organisms of syphilis and leptospirosis, but was unfortunate in his claims for the discovery of a similar causal microbe for yellow fever.

His results in South America could not be confirmed by British scientists in West Africa, where there was no sign of Noguchi's organism. In order to clear up the discrepancy, Noguchi went to Accra, contracted yellow fever and died (1928), 'stricken at once by a sense of failure and the disease that had eluded him'. The crux of the trouble was that leptospiral jaundice (see p. 146) co-existed with yellow fever in parts of South America but not in Accra in Africa. Noguchi had been misled from difficulties in clinical diagnosis and had isolated a leptospiral strain from a non-yellow-fever case. A tragic ending of a distinguished pioneer!

Early Virus Research.—Adrian Stokes, professor of pathology at Guy's Hospital, London, joined a Rockefeller expedition to West Africa in 1927. He and his colleagues, J. H. Bauer and N. P. Hudson failed to demonstrate Noguchi's leptospira or any other organism. However, they conveyed yellow fever to the rhesus monkey —a significant advance, because an experimental animal was now available for their study of the nature and behaviour of the virus. Its transmission to mosquitoes was being investigated, when Stokes was the next victim of this dread disease (1927). Two years later, William A. Young, who was formerly a member of Noguchi's team, also died. A native laboratory technician who had an accidental infection recovered.

In 1929, Paul Lewis of the Rockefeller Institute died of yellow fever in Brazil. In 1930, Theodore Hayne, an entomologist was also a martyr to science—the fifth in three years!

About this time, the African team were making significant progress. A reservoir of yellow fever infection was found to exist in certain species of monkeys and was transmitted by the local mosquitoes, which were different from *A. aegypti*, studied by Walter Reed. A high proportion of the natives in African (and South American) country districts had antibodies against the disease, without having had an obvious illness identifiable as yellow fever. Sub-infecting doses of the virus had immunized them. 'Jungle yellow fever', as it was called, was identical with the urban type previously studied. It constituted a reservoir of infection, which could be transmitted by human beings to towns and cities and then spread possibly by the *A. aegypti* vector. Obviously, the conquest of yellow fever was an immense problem, entailing mosquito control, which might be difficult, backed up by inoculation.

Viral Vaccines.—In 1929, Marshall Findlay and Edward Hindle of the Wellcome Bureau of Scientific Research, London, showed that monkeys could be immunized with a phenolized or formolized vaccine from the liver and spleen of monkeys which were killed when moribund from the disease. Protective antibodies were present in the serum of these vaccinated animals. The serum of a man who had yellow fever 24 years previously was also protective. These investigations on monkeys were very dangerous, and three members of the research team at the Wellcome Research Laboratories, Beckenham developed mild yellow fever.

Meanwhile, in 1930, Max Theiler, a Swiss born in South Africa and a member of the scientific staff at Harvard and the Rockefeller Institute, New York, transmitted yellow fever to mice by an unusual route at that time, namely, intracerebral inoculation. The virus caused intense inflammation of the brain tissue, because it was 'neurotropic' for mice. Infected mice could be protected by convalescent or other immune serum given at the same time as the virus. By examining blood samples, Theiler was able to detect immune humans or monkeys and thus to prepare a world map showing yellow fever areas.

Theiler and other distinguished Americans, including Wilbur Sawyer and A. W. Sellards, then set about preparing a protective vaccine. It involved much patience—serial mouse passage of selected strains followed by prolonged tissue-culture passage. There were some set-backs from insufficient attenuation. Moreover, in 1935, Theiler himself contracted mild yellow fever as a laboratory infection. It was the last attack of this type, for vaccination henceforth put a stop to the risks incurred by the staff of laboratories.

The first effective vaccine was an attenuated strain, together with yellow fever immune (convalescent) serum, which was used (1935) for research workers and later for more general immunization in Brazil. Extension of this work was impeded by difficulties in obtaining sufficient immune serum. The search for a better preparation continued.

In 1937 complete success was achieved with a vaccine from the greatly attenuated virus strain, 17D—a variant from the highly virulent Asibi strain, which had been isolated from Asibi, a West African patient, in 1927. Although passaged repeatedly through mice and various tissue cultures, it still retained the capacity to immunize well. It was also so attenuated that it appeared to be safe without the addition of convalescent serum. Large-scale production was facilitated when Theiler was able to transfer this strain from chick tissue culture to the developing egg itself.

In Brazil, more than one million persons were vaccinated in 1938. The field trials were continued till 1940, different subcultures of 17D being used. During this period and later, some variations were detected in Brazil. While one sub-strain failed to immunize well, another was unsafe since it caused encephalitis at times: both were eliminated.

The stabilized chick-embryo-adapted 17D strain came into use in Britain about 1936. Thousands of Colonial Service employees were successfully protected against yellow fever within the next few years.

Vaccination in the 1939-45 War.—Millions of Allied troops received 17D vaccine, and were completely immune: in West Africa, American and British soldiers did not contract yellow fever although the infection was widespread. In South America, where there were areas of high incidence, vaccination brought the disease under control.

Between March and September 1942, a major and quite unforeseen disaster occurred. Approximately 28,600 out of 2.5 million American troops became jaundiced two to three months after being injected with 17D vaccine, which contained a small amount of supposedly normal human serum as diluent. There were 62 deaths. The obvious suggestion was that the strain had recovered some of its lost virulence. However, the disease was not yellow fever but serum hepatitis (p. 191), the virus of which must have been present in the human serum; this hazard was not fully appreciated at the time. On enquiry, some of the donors of the serum had a history of 'catarrhal jaundice'—in retrospect, suggestive of viral hepatitis. An aqueous base was substituted for human serum, and there was no more trouble.

Theiler was a Nobel Prize winner in 1951 for his work on yellow fever.

The Dakar Scratch Vaccine.—This living attenuated vaccine was developed by M. Peltier and his associates at the Pasteur Institute in Dakar, French West Africa. The virus strain was obtained from a Syrian in Dakar in 1929, and was repeatedly passaged in mice by intracerebral inoculation. The vaccine was mouse-brain tissue in gum arabic solution, and was applied to scratched skin. The scratch technique enabled it to be given combined with smallpox vaccine. The French used the combination for the mass immunization of millions of native populations throughout French colonies in Africa. It gave a good and lasting immunity but occasionally was complicated by encephalitis in vaccinated subjects, especially children. Theiler considered it too virulent for human use, but the French argued that fatal cases in their vaccination campaigns were altogether exceptional.

Conclusion

17D virus vaccine is the most successful attenuated living viral immunization so far 'hand tailored' in the laboratory for use in man. The immunity conferred is of a high order and lasts for many years. Yellow fever vaccines have been invaluable for the protection of travellers, the control of outbreaks and mass prophylaxis.

Typhus Fever

In a previous chapter (p. 85) the early history of typhus fever and the discovery of its causal organism were described. Research on active immunization was not undertaken till the 1920s.

Vaccines against Louse-borne Typhus.—The British workers, J. A. (later Sir Joseph) Arkwright and Arthur Bacot, both contracted typhus while investigating the disease in Cairo (1922). Bacot, who was a distinguished entomologist, died. Lice were fed rectally with human blood from infected patients, and the development of the typhus rickettsiae was studied. This technique of artificial culture determined the trend of much of the earlier researches on vaccines —before cultivation on chick embryo tissue came to be used.

Rudolf Weigl in Poland made a vaccine (1930-33) of louse intestines one week after infection per rectum, phenol or formalin being added to inactivate the rickettsiae. Enormous louse farms were set up, and 200 immune volunteers who had recovered from typhus fever were employed as suppliers of human blood on which human lice thrive. This vaccine was used on a considerable scale and was apparently successful. None of the staff of Weigl's typhus laboratory contracted the disease. According to one series of figures, 160,000 persons who were vaccinated were exposed to typhus: only 30 contracted typhus, in a mild form. During the 1939-45 war, Weigl's vaccine was recommended for the German army in Poland, as well as for Polish civilians.

Much ingenuity was expended by American, French and other bacteriologists in devising other types of vaccine grown in various animal tissues—rat peritoneum, rat lungs, mouse embryo tissue, mouse lungs, etc. The rickettsiae were treated with phenol or formalin or even thiomersal.

In 1938, Herald Cox of the United States Public Health Service grew rickettsiae in the yolk sac of the developing chick embryo. The pooled embryonic tissues were ground up and then treated with thiomersal and formalin. Cox vaccine was convenient for large scale production and met the demands imposed by the 1939-45 war. Immunity lasted about one year and had to be reinforced with further injections.

Several million Allied troops and civilian population received protective doses of Cox vaccine, prepared from either the louse-borne (epidemic) or a combination of louse-borne and flea-borne (murine) strains. The Connaught Laboratories of the University of Toronto supplied almost all the typhus vaccine used in the British Armed Forces for many years. The results were excellent, although, with the establishment of D.D.T. and other insecticides, vaccine has tended to be less used than formerly.

In the 1939-45 war only 64 vaccinated Americans contracted mild louse-borne typhus, all of whom recovered. In the Korean war, the U.S. Army, which had been well vaccinated, had only 28 mild cases. Control measures had obviously been most effective.

Scrub Typhus.—This disease was widely prevalent in many areas of eastern Asia before the 1939-45 war, but came into prominence when its incidence was rising in British troops serving in Burma and elsewhere. The causal agent, *Rickettsia tsutsugamushi*, was isolated from human cases in 1923. Man is infected by a bite of a small larval mite, which lives on voles and other wild rodents and is later found on grasses and soil. Japanese and British soldiers were bitten as they walked through the scrub.

In 1945, a vaccine was made available on a large scale by the British Ministries concerned and the Wellcome Foundation. It was prepared from the lungs of infected cotton-rats, the rickettsiae in the suspension being killed by formalin. Its value was never determined under field conditions, as insect repellents on protective clothing, the clearing of scrub, and the collapse of Japan made active immunization unnecessary. Moreover, effective antibiotics were also coming into use for treatment.

Miscellaneous rickettsial infections.—Other rickettsial diseases such as trench fever, murine or endemic typhus, Mexican typhus fever, Rocky Mountain spotted fever, Q or Query fever, and rickettsial pox have been studied from time to time. Their hosts and vectors are known, and the spread of infection can be controlled by insecticides. Vaccines are sometimes very effective, but their use is limited.

CHAPTER 25

POLIOMYELITIS VACCINE: FAILURE BUT LATER OUTSTANDING SUCCESS

POLIOMYELITIS almost certainly existed throughout the ages and accounted for at least some of the palsies and atrophied limbs in the early records. All such references are vague: accurate descriptions and more exact diagnosis of the disease are a modern development.

Towards the end of the last century small outbreaks occurred in Scandinavia, the United States of America and elsewhere. Because children were usually the victims, *infantile paralysis* became the common name for the infection at that time. In 1916, a major epidemic, which was little understood, attracted much attention in the U.S.A. where 27,000 persons were paralysed and 6,000 died. New York City alone reported 2,000 deaths. Very many of these persons were adults. Public concern was reinforced in 1921 when Franklin D. Roosevelt, who was later to become the war-time American President, contracted poliomyelitis and was left with almost complete paralysis of the legs.

Early experiments on monkeys.—In 1909 successful transmission of the disease to monkeys was reported in Austria and also by Simon Flexner and Paul Lewis at the Rockefeller Institute, New York. The latter team was able to produce infection by specially filtered washings from the nose and throat of a patient, thus demonstrating that the responsible agent was a virus. Secondly, neutralizing substances were found in the serum of monkeys which had recovered from poliomyelitis. This was shown by injecting the serum intrathecally (into the spinal fluid) of other monkeys within 24 hours of the infecting dose. These monkeys were therefore passively immunized with immune (convalescent) monkey serum. Thirdly, active immunity was demonstrated, because animals which recovered from one attack of experimental poliomyelitis tended to be protected against a further inoculation of a virus-containing filtrate.

Antibodies could sometimes be detected in the serum of human beings who had recovered. Although there were certain anomalies that were little understood at that time, this comparative success in experiments on monkeys pointed the way to the use of convalescent serum in the control of clinical poliomyelitis.

CONVALESCENT SERUM IN PROPHYLAXIS AND TREATMENT

At first serum was given intrathecally (1910) to patients in the early, pre-paralytic stage of poliomyelitis: the results were believed to be encouraging. Later, it was tried intravenously (1914), without clear-cut improvement in the findings. In 1915 serum was used for treatment of acute cases: some benefit was claimed.

Between 1930 and 1941, several more papers were published. Although certain reports were favourable, the final conclusion reached was that once a definite diagnosis of poliomyelitis could be made it was too late to give serum. However, there was a revival of interest in 1951-53 when the serum protein fraction known as gamma globulin (immune serum globulin) was tried as a preventive measure for contacts of a patient. Although there was apparent success in individual cases, the over-all results were again disappointing. This globulin was clearly not the answer to the problem of obtaining protection against poliomyelitis.

UNSUCCESSFUL VACCINES

In 1934, John Kolmer of Philadelphia recalled that Flexner occasionally obtained active immunity in monkeys which had been injected with living poliomyelitis vaccine. After further experiments in monkeys, Kolmer and his colleagues introduced a new type of vaccine, namely a 4 per cent. suspension of infected monkey cord in 1 per cent. sodium ricinoleate. It was claimed that this attenuated ricinoleated virus vaccine had been rendered harmless for man by repeated passages through monkeys and by chemical treatment.

About the same time Maurice Brodie and William H. Park of the New York City Health Department also introduced a vaccine of infected monkey cord. It was 'killed' or inactivated by treatment with formaldehyde. Alas, when each of these vaccines was being used on something over 10,000 children, suspicions arose concerning their safety. Nine paralytic cases and five deaths occurred among children who had received the Kolmer vaccine, and three paralytic cases and one death among the Brodie vaccinees. Although there was controversy about the relationship of these cases to the vaccination—poliomyelitis occurred among unvaccinated persons also—both vaccines were withdrawn. Monkey tests indicated (1936) that paralytic poliomyelitis could be produced experimentally by these discredited preparations. There is therefore a reasonable assumption that the human cases were more than a coincidence, as had been claimed.

Cultivation of the Viruses

In 1949, John Enders, Frederick Robbins and Thomas Weller of Harvard University and Boston Children's Hospital cultivated poliomyelitis viruses in human embryonic and adult tissues that did not belong to the central nervous system (brain and spinal cord). They also found abnormalities in the cells of these tissue-cultures—so-called cytopathic changes—which made it possible in subsequent work to recognize the presence of virus, without having to fall back on expensive and time-consuming animal inoculation. The propagation of viruses in non-nervous tissues was a splendid and far-reaching achievement, a tribute to the team's perseverance, and incidentally a reversal of previous findings and beliefs.

The next step was to grow the viruses in various monkey tissues, especially the kidneys. The living cells from these organs are kept alive and made to multiply in a simple type of nutrient fluid: they are the counterpart of the intact animals or fertile eggs used in earlier work in this field. Here was a more accessible source of material in preparing good culture media for large-scale vaccine production and other research projects. All this work gathered momentum and in 1954 the Harvard team shared the coveted Nobel prize for their key discoveries.

In 1949, also, there was a further American contribution. David Bodian and his associates from the Johns Hopkins University, Baltimore, demonstrated three separate types of poliomyelitis virus, each with its own separate antibodies. This finding explained discrepancies in the results of other workers on monkeys and on human subjects: vaccines containing only one strain of virus had sometimes given anomalous results.

INACTIVATED ('KILLED') VACCINES

In 1952, Howard Howe of Johns Hopkins University inoculated formalin-inactivated vaccine incorporating all three types of virus into chimpanzees and six persons. Antibodies were induced and persisted for six months.

Salk Vaccine.—Jonas Salk, who was Research Professor of Bacteriology in the University of Pittsburg, U.S.A., was inspired by the success of Enders in 1949. He began his own research work by confirming Bodian's claim that all strains of poliomyelitis virus belonged to one of three well-defined types. The next stage was the preparation of a vaccine from tissue cultures of monkey kidney or testicle. All three types of virus were included, and were inactivated by formaldehyde. The type 1 strain was the virulent Mahoney culture, which was known to give extremely good antibody responses: it had been isolated from a family of that name in Ohio. The selection for the type 2 strain was MEF-1, isolated from an adult patient in the Middle East Forces in the 1939-45 war. The type 3 strain was a culture labelled Saukett, isolated in Salk's own laboratory. The patient of origin was called Sarkett, but a technician had mis-spelt it as Saukett. The error crept undetected into the literature, by which time it was considered unwise to attempt to rectify it.

This vaccine was given to animals, including monkeys, in the first instance. The safety of the product had to be ensured. Thereafter it was administered to groups of children, who developed good protective titres—as monkeys had done earlier.

In 1954 a nation-wide mass trial of Salk vaccine was undertaken in the U.S.A. This campaign was under the auspices of the National Foundation for Infantile Paralysis, which had been inaugurated by President Roosevelt in 1938. Intense public emotion was aroused by this Foundation's repetitive, high-pressure propaganda to raise funds ('March of Dimes'). The excessive publicity was detrimental

179

to the happiness of the research workers and to the dispassionate conduct of their project. The first experimental stage (1954) comprised 650,000 children, which included a control group of more than 200,000 who received a harmless placebo instead of Salk vaccine. Preliminary data on a few thousand children and adults indicated that all three types of virus were highly effective immunizing agents. The safety of the preparation appeared to be absolute.

A report on the 1954 trial was prepared by Thomas Francis, of the University of Michigan, a well-known virologist who had pioneered influenza vaccine in the U.S.A. (see p. 162). An extremely satisfactory finding was a reduction of the incidence of paralytic poliomyelitis in the vaccinated population to just over one-quarter of the incidence of the unvaccinated controls. However, it was disquieting that the batches of vaccine varied very much in quality, a few being quite useless. The obvious deduction was that Salk vaccine was not a standardized product and could engender false confidence in its efficacy. However, there was no hint of danger associated with its use.

The Francis report was released in April 1955. Soon afterwards there was serious trouble, recalling the tragedy with the Brodie inactivated vaccine in 1935. Two of thirteen batches of vaccine, which were licensed for sale solely on the basis of the manufacturers' safety tests, contained residual living virus: this had been undetected before issue, because the margin of safety permitted by the existing regulations of the National Foundation was too small. Altogether 204 vaccinated persons and their family contacts fell ill with poliomyelitis soon after the inoculations. The vaccine which caused the trouble had been prepared by the Cutter Laboratories of Berkeley, California; all supplies from this source were recalled forthwith. Under the laws of warranty, the Cutter firm was liable for damages and paid over three million dollars in compensation (two million covered by insurance).

Enquiry disclosed that other manufacturers also had difficulties in the processing and testing of Salk vaccine. Much research was carried out on the safety aspects of production. The official regulations were revised, and there was no further trouble. The Salk programme was rightly blamed by Francis and his colleagues (Report, 1957) for the Cutter tragedy of 1955. On the other hand, from 1954 onwards, it led to a vast saving of lives. Readers will recall that other vaccines of great benefit to mankind have also had their set-backs: examples are the prophylactics for smallpox, rabies, tuberculosis and yellow fever.

In 1956, an immunization campaign was begun in the United Kingdom. With the Cutter incident in mind, the authorities used a Salk-type inactivated vaccine, modified by substituting the less virulent Brunhilde strain as the type 1 component instead of the American Mahoney strain. Of course, all other safety precautions were intensified, as was the custom for manufacturers in the U.S.A. Thereafter, good results were speedily obtained. Recorded cases of poliomyelitis were reduced from approximately 6,000 in 1955 to 3,000 in 1956. Then, by 1957, out of a total of 148,684 children between the ages of $1\frac{1}{2}$ and $9\frac{1}{2}$ years who received Salk vaccine, paralytic poliomyelitis occurred in 2.68 per 100,000, whereas in a control group of 1,563,216 children, it was 11.57 per 100,000. A more intensive campaign appeared to be worth while.

During the last decade, Salk-type vaccines have been modified by a process of concentration, thus ensuring much higher and more durable protective titres than were obtained with the old-type 'unconcentrated' preparations. In retrospect, there was justification for some criticism in the early years of the vaccine: protection used to wane rather quickly and require too much reinforcement. All this has been corrected to a considerable extent.

LIVE VACCINES (ORAL)

In 1946, Hilary Koprowski of the Lederle Laboratories, New York, began work on the vaccination of monkeys, preferably with a live vaccine of low pathogenicity. Progress was necessarily slow till Enders succeeded in growing the virus in tissue culture three years later, in 1949. A further three years elapsed before Koprowski and his colleagues, George Jervis and Thomas Norton, published their first paper on the clinical trials of live attenuated vaccine by mouth. The oral route of administration was favoured because it imitated the process by which immunity to poliomyelitis was acquired naturally. The vaccination was completely successful at this stage, because all 20 human subjects showed the production of protective antibodies, and suffered no ill-effects, either immediate or more remote: all remained free from symptoms for one year. The virus was also observed to multiply in the intestinal tract, thus keeping up the stimulus to the body's immunity mechanism. Herald Cox, who is famous for his work on viral growth in chick embryo and for his typhus vaccine (p. 174), was Koprowski's stimulating research director, and one of his 'guinea-pigs' for oral vaccine in January 1950.

Unfortunately for Koprowski and his pioneer work, vaccine trials carried out by George Dick, Professor of Microbiology at Belfast, revealed a possible safety hazard. In this clinical and laboratory research, the first of its kind in Europe, 200 persons were fed with the Koprowski virus by the mouth. Dick made the disconcerting discovery that, while the attenuated vaccine itself produced no paralysis when it was injected into monkeys intracerebrally (into the brain), the same virus excreted from the gut of the vaccinated persons had undergone some alteration during passage: it caused paralysis in some monkeys, indicative of slight reversion of virulence. Although all these human vaccinees showed no ill-effects, the stability of the Koprowski attenuated virus remained suspect: in order to avoid the possibility of even more dangerous reversion, the project was permanently discontinued in the United Kingdom.

Albert B. Sabin of the Children's Hospital in Cincinnati is another enthusiastic American research worker, who had better luck at the right time than his rival, Koprowski. Between 1953 and 1955, he developed attenuated live viruses for use as an oral vaccine. By 1957, it had been thoroughly tested on 10,000 monkeys, 160 chimpanzees, and finally 240 humans, including Sabin himself and members of his family. Antibodies were induced in the blood stream, and, as in the case of the Koprowski vaccine, the attenuated viruses often multiplied in the gut, setting up a carrier state. Since the strains were excreted in the stools, transmission to contacts was possible and indeed inevitable. This meant that contacts of persons vaccinated could also be immunized through viral spread, and develop protective antibodies in their serum. Moreover, when attenuated viruses became well established in the intestinal tract, they played the useful rôle of impeding 'colonization' of the tract by virulent ('wild') viruses which could cause clinical poliomyelitis. Live vaccine thus gives rise to two defensive barriers, namely, antibody production and breaking the chain of transmission of virulent infection. By preventing wild viruses from flourishing, the mass use of vaccine might conceivably eradicate the disease altogether.

Sabin is a Polish Jew who spent the first 15 years of his life in Russia. When he visited that country again in 1956, he was successful in arranging for clinical tests involving millions of people—an interesting achievement at that time as the vaccine had been developed solely in the United States of America! The Czechs and East Germans also used Sabin vaccine in their campaigns. The results everywhere were entirely successful, and a reputation for safety was built up to the detriment of the Koprowski vaccine.

In 1958-59, poliomyelitis virus type 2 was very satisfactory in preventing the extension of a type 1 epidemic in Singapore. This was of special interest because the vaccine and epidemic strains of virus were of different types. Successful control of the disease was ascribed to the attenuated vaccine virus replacing and impeding the virulent wild virus in the community. In 1961 this success was repeated in the control of an epidemic of different virus type in Hull. However, a trivalent vaccine (containing all *three* virus types) was effective in a Dundee outbreak in 1962, and had the additional advantage that it induced antibody formation against all three types.

Supplies of Sabin-type oral vaccine became more generally available in the United Kingdom in 1962, local authorities and family doctors being permitted to change over from Salk-type vaccine progressively. The majority of them did so.

Only 37 cases of poliomyelitis were confirmed in 1964 in England and Wales. In the first year of the campaign, 1957, there were 4,844 notifications. The success of immunization was dramatic.

TABLE

Control of Poliomyelitis: England and Wales

	Cases notified
1957 (1st year of vaccination campaign)	4,844
1964	37

CHAPTER 26

MEASLES ANTISERUM AND VACCINE

MEASLES is a highly contagious virus infection which was first described by the Arabian writer, Rhazes, in the tenth century. It used to be much confused with smallpox and scarlet fever. However, the seventeenth-century physician, Thomas Sydenham, who is known as the 'English Hippocrates', distinguished between these three diseases, and was able to establish measles as a clinical entity. This was the result of accurate observation of symptoms during an epidemic which raged in London about 1670.

Although there has been a substantial decline in the severity of this infection in Britain from 1915 onwards, the mortality has remained high in parts of India, Africa and South America. In this country, while the incidence has shown no tendency to fall, the death rate is as low as one or two per 10,000 notified cases per annum. In Nigeria, the rate may be at least 500 per 10,000 cases (5 per cent.) in some outbreaks, thus making measles the principal killing disease of childhood. There were 84,500 deaths in India in 1959.

It is widely known that devastating epidemics of measles have occurred in virgin communities. In the Fiji Islands in 1875, according to various estimates, 20,000 to 40,000 persons (say, 20 per cent.) in a population of about 150,000 died of measles; the next outbreak occurred 32 years later, when 6 per cent. of the population died. In the Faeroe Islands, after a remission of 65 years, there was a great epidemic in 1846 when about 6,000 (78 per cent.) of the 7,782 inhabitants contracted the infection; none of 98 persons who had had measles 65 years previously had a second attack. This is in line with what we know today, namely, that one attack usually confers life-long immunity.

SERUM PROPHYLAXIS

Passive protection was first demonstrated by the Italian, Francesco Cenci, in 1901. Six children were given serum from a human convalescent case and remained immune although heavily exposed to measles during an epidemic. Obviously this donor who had recovered from an attack had powerful protective substances in his blood. It is now known that, although a convalescent has a potent, long-lasting defence for himself, subjects passively immunized with his serum are given a protection which soon wanes as this foreign protein is eliminated, leaving them, in a few weeks, once again susceptible to the infection. This point is merely a repetition of a fundamental principle of immunization, but the present reminder may assist some readers.

Passive immunization with convalescent serum was studied in greater detail by the French workers, Charles Nicolle and E. Conseil in a small outbreak of measles in Tunis in 1916. Their publication appeared in 1918. In the next few years, American, German and French scientists confirmed their findings. It was also shown that not only convalescent serum, but the serum of adult immunes (persons who had an attack of measles many years before) contained antibodies. The adult serum was less protective than the convalescent variety, and accordingly had to be given in larger dosage to make good the deficiency.

In 1920, R. Degkwitz in Munich described *sero-prevention* and *sero-attenuation* with these products. The idea behind sero-prevention was the complete suppression of an attack, and this could be achieved by injecting the serum prior to the fifth day after exposure to infection. As we have seen, prevention was associated with a transitory passive immunity due to the serum in the circulation: thereafter there was again full susceptibility.

Sero-attenuation (modification) was usually brought about by injecting the serum rather later in the incubation period, say, between the seventh and tenth day after exposure. The attenuated or weakened form of measles which developed had the great advantage of being associated with a permanent active immunity.

Children in a poor state of health were of course given sero-prevention rather than sero-attenuation. The aim of complete suppression was to obviate all the danger inherent in a natural attack which could become severe and even fatal. Infection with measles was postponed till the child was older and presumably at less risk.

Between 1925 and 1927, serum prophylaxis was introduced into Britain by W. S. C. Copeman, who later became a leading rheumatologist.

Placental extract.—As there were certain difficulties in obtaining adequate supplies of convalescent and adult sera, American workers introduced an extract (human immune globulin) from human placentas, that is, after-births, which contain a considerable amount of blood and which are otherwise waste products. This was used in place of serum and proved to be a reliable source of antibodies against measles. Occasionally there was an unpleasant rise of temperature after injection. Although the product was purified considerably, it did not become as acceptable in Britain as it was in the U.S.A.

A Disaster with Human Convalescent Serum.—Batches of convalescent serum, which were prepared for use by mixing individual specimens in serological laboratories, tended to become larger in the 1930s. The aim was to ensure a more uniform content of antibody, such as might result when large numbers of specimens were mixed; a further advantage was the reduction in the time and equipment involved in carrying out the required tests on bulk material instead of on all its constituents. Unfortunately, as was apparent subsequently, one of the donors represented in a particular large batch of measles serum, which was distributed in 1937-38, must have had in his blood the virus of homologous serum hepatitis. This minute organism had been distributed on mixing and had contaminated the entire batch. However, this germ did not show up in any of the official tests, nor in any subsequent tests—which were naturally very exhaustive. The result of the contamination was that jaundice occurred in 37 persons, all of whom were recipients of the serum, and seven died. The disease was little understood in the 1930s. It was only in 1939 that two British investigators, Marshall Findlay and Frederic Mac Callum, first implicated a virus as the probable cause of the trouble (see p. 192).

Gamma Globulin.—An important advance in prophylaxis was the introduction and use of human immune serum globulin—the gamma globulin fraction of the appropriate antiserum, usually convalescent serum. As a reminder to some readers, the common name of this protein preparation is gamma globulin. Purified antibody is present in high concentration, so quite rightly gamma globulin has ousted all other products for the passive prophylaxis of measles. Disadvantages are its relative scarcity and high cost of production.

In the previous section, a disaster was described due to transmission of the serum hepatitis virus in a large batch of measles convalescent serum. Gamma globulin has the outstanding advantage over all other blood products that its use obviates almost entirely this distressing risk.

Edwin J. Cohn of Harvard in the U.S.A. was the pioneer in this field (1944). He used ethanol for the fractionation. In Britain R. A. Kekwick and M. E. Mackay introduced an alternative method in which ether was the precipitating agent.

The successful use of gamma globulin is well illustrated by experience in the highly virulent epidemic which occurred in southern Greenland in 1951. This was a first introduction of measles into a non-epidemic area, and has become a classic in medical history. The attack rate was 99.9 per cent. of the whole unprotected population *at all ages*—surely a record. The mortality was only 1.8 per cent., apparently owing to sero-prophylaxis with gamma globulin, combined with the penicillin treatment of those who developed complications: these measures were rapidly organized from Denmark. The complication rate of those who were not treated prophylactically with gamma globulin was 45 per cent. One can only speculate about the probable case-mortality rate which might have occurred in the absence of specific prophylaxis and chemotherapy. Perhaps the following figures are of some relevance. By comparison with the 1.8 per cent. in Greenland, the mortality rate for parts of Africa today is 5 per cent. and for the Fiji Islands in 1875 it was 20 to 25 per cent., according to some estimates.

The protection afforded by gamma globulin is of course temporary. Only an effective vaccine can give a durable immunity.

EARLY ATTEMPTS AT MEASLES VACCINATION

The first attempt at active immunization against measles was made in 1758 by Francis Home, the first professor of Materia Medica at Edinburgh University. He may have been influenced by the famous anatomist, Alexander Monro, who is said to have suggested the project in the previous year. Home was familiar with the work which was in progress on variolation against smallpox, and set out to attempt protection against measles on similar lines. Pieces of cotton soaked with tears from a patient, or with the fresh blood and tissue fluid from an incision into the rash, were carried round in his pocket-book. When he found suitable recipients he again made incisions and bound the pieces of cotton on the incised area. In 7 of 15 subjects thus inoculated, mild measles developed after an incubation period of about nine days. This method had its advocates for over 100 years. In the present century it has been severely criticized by Ludwig Hektoen of Chicago University on the grounds that both Home and his followers always conducted their experiments during epidemics (when new cases are being infected by natural means) and without any controls.

In 1905, Hektoen was himself the first to demonstrate unequivocally transmission by the subcutaneous injection of human volunteers with blood from measles patients. He also showed that the virus may be circulating in the blood at least during the first 30 hours of the rash.

Little further progress was made for nearly fifty years. Some early experiments suggested that measles was a virus infection which was transmissible to monkeys. Abortive attempts were made at immunizing children by such crude and dangerous methods as giving daily doses of filtered nasopharyngeal washings, or injecting a so-called attenuated egg-passage virus vaccine—at a time when the causal virus had not been definitely isolated. These were interesting milestones but led to nothing of permanent value.

ANOTHER CONTRIBUTION TO VIROLOGY FROM ENDERS

John Enders and Thomas Peebles of Harvard University,

Boston, isolated the measles virus in tissue culture in 1954, and thus for the first time made vaccination a practical possibility. Enders had previously cultivated the poliomyelitis vaccine in various tissues, and he later had to his credit the first isolations of mumps virus, varicella or chickenpox virus, and the first of another group of viruses called the ECHO viruses.

In 1957, with Milan Milovanovic, a Yugoslav working in his laboratory, Enders adapted the measles virus to chick embryos. Many of the earlier tissue cultures contained monkey renal cells, which might be contaminated with latent 'simian wild viruses': chick embryos did not involve this risk. In the following year (1958), Enders passaged a strain, *Edmonston*, and found that after chick-adaptation it was attenuated for man. In the same year with Samuel Katz, he prepared experimental vaccines from it and was able to induce solid immunity to the natural disease during subsequent epidemics: the antibody titres which developed were similar to those found in naturally occurring measles. Katz's own children were among the first to receive the vaccine.

Various Vaccines

Some of the children vaccinated with the early Enders' vaccines developed mild fever and modified measles rash, which were regarded as undesirable side-effects. Further research with different strains and methods of preparation led to many new vaccines of both the living attenuated type and the killed inactivated virus type. The aim throughout was to induce solid and presumable long-lasting immunity with as little troublesome reaction as possible.

One method of reducing the vaccination reaction was to give a minute dose of gamma globulin at the same time as the vaccine but in a different site. Another was to give one or two injections of a killed (formalinized) measles vaccine first, followed by living attenuated vaccine.

However, perhaps the major research project in different countries was to secure better attenuation of the virus by further passage in chick cell cultures or embryos. Most of the work was in fact done with the classical Edmonston strain at various passage levels. Another notable strain was the variant obtained by Schwarz.

189

The potency of inactivated vaccines also received attention. With sufficiently potent preparations and an immunization schedule involving a reinforcing or boosting injection after a suitable interval, apparently good protection was obtained. Whatever the type of vaccine employed, the duration of immunity must be an important consideration.

Much of this research on vaccines is too recent for inclusion in a history of immunization. The consensus of opinion is that vaccination is worth while. The fatality rates in Britain are not high but there is still a considerable risk of serious complications, some of which leave permanent damage of the nervous system or respiratory tract. Mass vaccination is of course most desirable in parts of the world where measles has a much higher incidence than in this country and is a killing disease.

CHAPTER 27

VIRAL HEPATITIS, MUMPS, RUBELLA:
PROGRESS TOWARDS CONTROL

VIRAL HEPATITIS

IT will be recalled that difficulties in diagnosis between yellow fever and viral hepatitis were noted in the American Army as recently as 1942 (see p. 172). The reader will hardly be surprised, therefore, that accounts of early epidemics of 'jaundice' have given rise to doubts about their true nature: only during the last three decades has exact differentiation been possible between three causes of epidemic jaundice, namely, yellow fever, leptospirosis (Weil's disease), and hepatitis or inflammation of the liver of viral origin. The last of these infections is of considerable interest and complexity and must be reviewed here in view of its medical importance.

Two Varieties.—Viral hepatitis exists in two forms, namely infectious hepatitis or 'I.H.' and homologous serum hepatitis or 'S.H.' The former variety is common, and used to be known as 'catarrhal jaundice': it was ascribed erroneously to catarrh or infection extending up the bile ducts from the intestine. Acute damage or destruction of the liver is observed in fatal cases. The causal virus gains access to the body by the gut, its spread from person to person being effected in the same way as in the case of poliomyelitis or typhoid fever. Gross pollution of the water supply by sewage containing this virus caused a serious epidemic of infectious hepatitis in Delhi in 1955. An outbreak of 2,395 cases was recorded in Bristol in 1960-62. Epidemics of this character were also relatively common amongst troops, for example in the Gallipoli campaign of the First World War. In all these outbreaks, high morbidity and low mortality were the general rule.

191

With regard to the second variety, homologous serum hepatitis or 'S.H.' is relatively rare, and was recognized in the 1930s as a sequel to human blood transfusion, blood collection by venepuncture, dental procedures, tattooing and the like. When proper syringe and needle sterilization was introduced, the incidence of this condition showed a dramatic fall. A disaster with a batch of measles convalescent serum in 1937-38 has already been described (p. 186). It was directly responsible for an intensification of research on both varieties of hepatitis, including their virology. The British workers, Marshall Findlay and Frederic Mac Callum, first implicated a virus in 1939, and in the following year Findlay transmitted the disease to three volunteers by the instillation of filtered nasal washings from patients.

Mumps convalescent serum caused similar trouble (1944). In this year Mac Callum and W. H. Bradley, and Mac Callum and D. J. Bauer, finally proved the virus origin of both types of hepatitis. The virus of infectious hepatitis, 'I.H.' or hepatitis A (a more recent name than the others) was found to be widespread and to be excreted in the faeces of acute cases and probably of some symptomless carriers. After ingestion by mouth, the incubation period before the onset of symptoms was 10 to 30 days. Serum hepatitis, 'S.H.' or hepatitis B was caused by a virus in the blood or serum, even of a few normal persons. Very small doses of blood or blood products could convey infection to others. The incubation period could extend from about 60 days up to 240 days—so long as to be a considerable handicap to diagnosis. Inevitably, a history of jaundice has been a bar to the donation of blood: it was estimated that about 1 in 200 persons in this country were carriers of the hepatitis virus.

Viral hepatitis is the most prevalent viral disease after the common cold, influenza and measles.

Prevention.—Although virus A was propagated in tissue culture and embryonated eggs in 1950, no vaccine against hepatitis is as yet in sight. Gamma globulin was found to be effective in affording protection against the homologous type (A antibodies protective against A but not against B, and *vice versa*). Thus, blood recipients may henceforth be protected by a suitable preparation of gamma globulin against the risk of transfusion hepatitis.

MUMPS

As mumps or epidemic parotitis is widespread and is usually characterized by prominent facial swelling due to a virus infection of the parotid and other salivary glands, it is hardly surprising that it was well described between 400 and 500 B.C. by the Greek physician, Hippocrates. Armies in time of war have often been affected. There were major outbreaks in both the American Civil War and the 1914-18 war. The disease is regarded seriously in young adults, as well as in older school children, on account of the complications—orchitis (inflammation affecting the testicle), ovaritis, pancreatitis, and meningo-encephalitis (inflammation of the brain and its membranes). The two former may result in sterility and the third may be a cause, possibly undetected, of diabetes.

Second attacks of mumps are rare, as immunity is substantial after the first illness. Many adults are immune to mumps without having any history of an attack: this means that very small doses of virus have been at work (so-called subclinical infection).

The mumps virus was isolated by two American scientists, C. D. Johnson and E. W. Goodpasture, in 1934. They used it to produce a transmissible parotitis in the rhesus monkey.

During the 1939-45 war, John Enders, who later received a Nobel Prize for his work on poliomyelitis viruses, was engaged on a research project on active and passive immunization against mumps in man. A leading collaborator in this field was Joseph Stokes, junior, of the University of Pennsylvania. There follows a brief account of some of their discoveries.

Diagnostic Test.—A skin test for diagnosis was an early development. A heated suspension of the parotid salivary gland of an infected monkey gave positive reactions on intradermal injection into persons with a history of mumps. A similar suspension from non-infected monkeys gave no reaction. While nearly 100 per cent. in this 'past-history' group of persons were positive, and therefore immune, approximately 50 per cent. of persons with no history of mumps were also positive. This unexpected finding merely signified that many positive reactions were the result of subclinical infecting doses of mumps virus: persons were becoming immune without being ill in the process.

Rather better results with a diagnostic skin test were obtained in 1945-46 by another American, Karl Habel. Instead of monkey parotid, a suspension of egg yolk from infected chick embryos was used as the test reagent.

Vaccines.—The Stokes-Enders team were unsuccessful in their preliminary attempts to grow the mumps virus. They had to fall back on monkeys as virus hosts, and used formalinized parotid gland from infected animals as their first vaccine. Monkeys and later human volunteers were successfully immunized in 1945-46.

There was a break-through in 1948 when Thomas Weller and John Enders grew mumps virus in tissue culture—fragments of chick embryo in a simple maintenance medium, which permits the survival and growth of cells. Later, repeated passage through embryonated eggs attenuated the virus.

In the 1950s both attenuated live-virus vaccines and inactivated vaccines were used with some success in many countries. The inactivating agents included formaldehyde, ultraviolet irradiation and ether. When vaccination was introduced at the start of an epidemic, the duration of the outbreak was reduced, as well as the incidence and severity of cases. Attenuated live-virus vaccines are now preferred to inactivated preparations, as they give rise to more lasting immunity.

The use of mumps vaccine would probably be confined to specific groups of young adult males.

Antisera.—Both convalescent serum and gamma globulin have had some effect in reducing the incidence of orchitis as a complication of mumps.

RUBELLA

In this viral infection the complications (to the embryo)—not the attack itself—represent the major danger.

Rubella is better known to the layman as German Measles: it was first described by German writers, and it is a relatively mild disease which, however, is unrelated to measles! There are few direct complications and the mortality rate is very low. Nevertheless, much publicity has rightly been given in the last three decades to the connection between rubella in the early months of pregnancy and serious harmful effects in the foetus. In addition to congenital abnormalities, there are such calamities as a higher proportion of abortions and stillbirths, and also the birth of an unusual number of babies who have a low birth weight and die in the first year of life.

The pioneer in the field was N. M. (later Sir Norman) Gregg, an eye specialist of Sydney, Australia. In 1941 he first drew attention to the association between maternal rubella and the high incidence of eye cataracts he and others had observed in Australian babies. Later, he and his colleagues found a raised incidence of other congenital abnormalities, including blindness, squint, deafness, dental defects, heart disease, mental disturbance, Mongolism and hydrocephalus. The explanation of course was that the rubella virus, which had not yet been isolated, had a special affinity for certain organs and tissues of the human embryo.

It is now known that the risk to the foetus is greater when the mother has rubella in the first month of pregnancy. After three to four months there is no further hazard. During the early months, however, about 15 per cent. of the foetuses are affected to the extent that they may be expected to show major abnormalities, mainly of eye, ear and heart. Another 15 per cent. would be likely to have minor abnormalities. Occasionally, defects are multiple.

Antisera in Prevention.—As might be expected, other Australian scientists made valuable contributions to our knowledge of rubella, thus following the lead of their fellow-countryman, N. M. Gregg. Between 1947 and 1953 various papers were published concerning the preventive use of gamma globulin from convalescent serum. This preparation was administered to women in early pregnancy, without a history of having had rubella and therefore presumably non-immune. Ideally, it was given as soon as possible after exposure to infection. The development of rash was usually prevented as one result of this early administration. Moreover, the incidence both of clinical disease and of congenital defects appeared to be reduced—the evidence was not absolutely conclusive, possibly because the gamma globulin was not given early enough in certain cases.

Active Immunization.—American workers were responsible for research which culminated in the isolation of the rubella virus. In 1962, Thomas Weller, who had collaborated with John Enders in the cultivation of the poliomyelitis and mumps viruses (as mentioned above), reported similar success with the rubella virus. This achievement was soon repeated by other workers in the U.S.A. and Britain.

After serial passage in tissue culture several attenuated variants of rubella virus were obtained. Live vaccines of such strains produced only minor subclinical infections with apparent protection against the natural disease.

The above development is very recent, and is an improvement on deliberate exposure of female children and young adults to one or more cases of rubella at 'rubella tea-parties'. The results on these occasions were always uncertain in terms of positive 'takes'. The rubella problem has hitherto been complicated by difficulties in diagnosis and by unreliable histories of exposure, past or present: it seems that a previous history of rubella cannot be relied upon. The use of specific tissue-culture virus vaccines is thus a timely development.

VI

MISCELLANEOUS

CHAPTER 28

COMBINED IMMUNIZATION AND
IMMUNIZATION SCHEDULES

COMBINED immunization usually implies the use of mixed, multiple or combined vaccines (two or more antigens in combination). However, it may also mean combined active and passive immunization: a vaccine, usually a toxoid, is mixed with antitoxic serum before injection, or is given along with it into different sites at the same session.

I. MIXED VACCINES

The combining of antigens has the outstanding advantage that the number of injections is reduced, thus making active immunization more acceptable to the general public. From the doctor's standpoint, also, the use of combined vaccines saves time, simplifies the keeping of records, facilitates the tracing of defaulters and persons who have left the district, and therefore ensures the best possible immunization coverage.

Of course there are snags, and the beginnings of the practice of injecting mixtures were slow and hesitant. After some preliminary work in 1909, the project was taken seriously during the 1914-18 war. Typhoid-paratyphoid A and B vaccines (T.A.B.) and to a less extent T.A.B. Cholera vaccines were used for the troops and some civilians as well. However, all further developments were impeded for years because there was an impression that the mixing of vaccines would lead to mutual interference with the antibody responses, possibly through overloading of the body's defensive resources. Further studies revealed that, while there were some grounds for caution, selective very good responses to certain antigens and possibly very poor responses to others, could be kept under control by maintaining a proper balance between the constituents. In various investigations it became clear that the response to a toxoid constituent of a mixture containing organisms in suspension was usually enhanced (rather than depressed, as expected): in technical terms, there were synergic effects due to the bacteria functioning as an adjuvant to the toxoid.

Combined immunization in France.—In 1926 the French immunologist, Gaston Ramon (see p. 93) and his colleague, C. Zoeller, introduced the modern practice of mixing vaccines, mostly diphtheria anatoxine (the French equivalent of toxoid), tetanus anatoxine and typhoid-paratyphoid vaccine, T.A.B.

Preliminary tests were satisfactory and, in 1929, a mixture of diphtheria anatoxine and T.A.B. vaccine was used for clinical trials in several regiments of the French army where diphtheria had been severe. On 21st December of that year a law was passed which made diphtheria immunization compulsory for all soldiers. Later, it was claimed that this measure practically eliminated the disease from the army where it was formerly present all the time.

In 1934 tetanus anatoxine or toxoid was added to the mixture which now became a T.A.B.T.D., representing all five constituents. A certain number of untoward reactions in vaccinated soldiers were regarded as acceptable, and the immunity produced was satisfactory. (This was ascertained by the examination of blood sera before and after immunization.) Therefore, since clinical trials had demonstrated the harmlessness and efficacy of the mixture, the use of T.A.B.T.D. was made compulsory for all land, naval and air forces in France. The measure was successful. Like diphtheria, tetanus was well controlled in the 1939-45 war: it is hardly surprising that exact data are not available, but no cases occurred amongst some 800,000 French soldiers who were properly immunized.

Although immunization against diphtheria and tetanus succeeded in the French Services, where administrative control could be rigidly enforced, a law which made combined diphtheria-tetanus immunization compulsory for children aged 1 to 14 years, was not fully implemented. This was due partly to opposition from some adversaries throughout the country generally, and partly to the inevitable disorganization of the war and the German occupation.

To complete the record, another combined vaccine, T.A.B. T.D.R., was used on a limited scale; it had no fewer than six components—T.A.B. vaccine, diphtheria and tetanus toxoids and typhus rickettsial vaccine.

Combined immunization in the U.S.A. and Canada.—From about 1935, American and Canadian workers were interested in the development of mixed prophylactics. By 1938 combined diphtheria and tetanus toxoids, alum-precipitated, and a combined diphtheria toxoid, alum-precipitated, and pertussis vaccine were available for American children. A mixture of diphtheria and tetanus fluid toxoids (no aluminium adjuvant) was also under investigation. Similar preparations began to be used by the Canadians in order to 'mitigate the ordeal of the many inoculations' required to protect children against diphtheria, pertussis and other infections. Acceptance of combined immunization was slow in some quarters, but diphtheria pertussis vaccine was adopted for general use in Canada in 1943, and diphtheria tetanus vaccine and diphtheria tetanus pertussis vaccine in 1947-48.

The Services in the U.S.A. and Canada made provision for the protection of troops against tetanus and the enteric fevers during the 1939-45 war and subsequently. For many years the mixture used was a T.A.B.T. By 1954, however, there was a preference in both countries for a T.A.B.T.D., the diphtheria addition being a very small amount of purified toxoid. The reason for this modification was that diphtheria on the American continent had become a disease of adults, because immunization campaigns had been concerned almost entirely with child protection: many American and Canadian troops had already received primary courses of diphtheria toxoid. In consequence the small additional dose in the T.A.B.T.D. usually sufficed for 'boosting' or reinforcement of the individual soldier's immunity. The responses to the other vaccines in the mixture were not 'crowded out', and sore arms and other clinical reactions were not appreciably greater.

In 1955, inactivated poliomyelitis vaccine (Salk) attracted worldwide interest. By this time, also, immunization campaigns with multiple vaccines (without a polio constituent) were effective everywhere. Inevitably, consideration was given in Canada to the addition of Salk vaccine to existing mixed preparations. The Connaught

Medical Research Laboratories, University of Toronto, conducted trials of (1) a D.T.P. Polio Vaccine (so-called quadruple vaccine) for infants and pre-school children; (2) a D.T. Polio Vaccine for children of school age, who of course did not require further pertussis immunization; and (3) a Tetanus-Polio Vaccine for adults, particularly in industry. All these vaccines were released for general issue throughout Canada in 1959. In 1962, work was also in progress on a T.A.B.T.D. Polio Vaccine.

In the U.S.A. multiple preparations containing inactivated (Salk) poliomyelitis vaccine were less used than in Canada, because the national policy favoured live, attenuated (Sabin) vaccine which was given alone by mouth: mixtures analogous to the Canadian preparations were not relevant to this programme.

Combined immunization in Great Britain.—In this country, good progress was made in the early 1950s. However, the campaign received a set-back in 1956 when a Medical Research Council Report suggested that mixtures of vaccines (with no poliomyelitis constituent) might provoke an attack of paralytic poliomyelitis (affecting the injected limb). This sequela of immunization was called 'provocation' or associated poliomyelitis. In retrospect, the risk of this complication was emphasized unduly, in disregard of the statisticians' warning that their estimates were 'based on very small numbers of cases'. The hazard is now regarded as negligible.

The British approach to combined immunization was also influenced by considerations of *immunological interference.* Maternally transferred antibodies could give rise to difficulties of this nature, and were the subject of research by Mollie Barr and her colleagues (1949, 1950). This topic is reviewed briefly in *Appendix A.*

In 1953, Barr and Llewellyn-Jones drew attention to another type of interference which is best explained by the following example. When it is proposed to inject a combined diphtheria and tetanus vaccine into children who already have some active immunity to diphtheria but not tetanus, an unsatisfactory response to the tetanus component may be expected (due to interference), unless the injection of the mixture is preceded by one dose of tetanus toxoid four weeks earlier. The preferential or selective behaviour is due to the previous training of the immunity mechanism in respect of the diphtheria toxoid.

Immunization Schedules.—As all these facts were becoming known, there were variations in immunization practice throughout this country. There were no valid reasons for many of the differences, but much confusion resulted. Accordingly, experts of international renown met in London for an interchange of views on relevant topics, including the use of combined prophylactics. The Proceedings of this *Symposium on Immunization in Childhood* were published in 1960, and two schedules were introduced. These were widely accepted at the time, and formed the basis of official schedules issued by the Ministry of Health. Various modifications were introduced subsequently when necessary.

Modern schedules are, strictly speaking, out of place in a book on history. However, I have decided to include them in the form of an *Appendix (B)* at the end of this chapter. The topics of (1) Immunization in Childhood and (2) Immunization for International Travel are covered.

Other Combined Vaccines.—The mixed preparations already mentioned are not a complete list. Perhaps the reader should be reminded of combined yellow fever and smallpox vaccine (p. 173) and multi-strain influenza vaccines (p. 164). Moreover, in the veterinary field several combined preparations have been introduced for the protection of animals. In 1961, a vaccine became available for sheep, which gave protection against seven diseases of sheep and lambs, namely, lamb dysentery, pulpy kidney disease, struck, braxy, blackleg, black disease and tetanus. It has also been possible to immunize dogs simultaneously against canine distemper, hepatitis and leptospirosis.

II. COMBINED ACTIVE AND PASSIVE IMMUNIZATION

Between 1925 and 1940, Gaston Ramon of the Pasteur Institute, Paris, pioneered the giving of diphtheria anatoxine (fluid formol toxoid) at the same time as antitoxic serum. The preparations were either mixed or injected at different sites. In 1941, Alan Downie and his collaborators in this country modified this procedure by using alum precipitated toxoid (A.P.T.) instead of fluid toxoid: their aim was to ensure that the antitoxic serum, which was used in order to give immediate protection, interfered as little as possible with the process of long-term active immunization. In other words, they selected a dose of serum which would afford protection but was not so large that the dose of vaccine must surely be swamped. Without going into much detail, it was found that the response to diphtheria A.P.T. was delayed and slightly inhibited —another type of immunological interference. However, when a second dose of A.P.T. was given some four weeks later, the final degree of immunity was not much inferior to that resulting from active immunization alone. This work on diphtheria antitoxin titres was carried out on medical student volunteers at Cambridge, Oxford and Sheffield.

Later in 1941, simultaneous active and passive immunization by the same procedure proved successful in protecting children exposed to diphtheria. The earlier research was a valuable guide to the adjustment of dosage of both antiserum and vaccine.

The technique for combined active and passive protection against tetanus is similar to that for diphtheria. An absorbed (aluminium-containing) toxoid is given at the same session as the antitoxic serum, the sites of injection of these two preparations being different.

Appendix A

INTERFERENCE FROM MATERNAL ANTIBODIES

In the case of diphtheria, many babies are immune to the disease at birth, because antitoxin in their mother's blood serum is donated passively via the placenta. The amount of this antibody, which can be measured by titrating a specimen of cord blood, varies within wide limits; it may be sufficient to interfere with the antigenicity (the capacity to induce the body cells of the young baby to make antitoxin) of diphtheria vaccine. The maternal antitoxin is eliminated gradually, and the rate of disappearance has been measured with accuracy. In order to obviate interference with antigenicity, it is advisable to wait till this elimination of antibody has proceeded for some months before administering toxoid.

In the case of tetanus, antitoxin is likewise transmitted from mother to child if, as is sometimes the case, the mother has herself been actively immunized with toxoid. Pertussis (whooping cough) immunity, however, is not passed on to any extent from the mother to her offspring. Young babies are fully susceptible to the disease. On the other hand, poliomyelitis antibody is transferred, and the rate of its elimination influences the timing of immunization with live or killed vaccines. With regard to the latter, it must be pointed out that the original Salk-type inactivated poliovirus vaccine has now been replaced by a considerably more potent preparation, which is less subject to interference from maternal antibodies and gives more lasting immunity. Nevertheless, live vaccines are generally preferred to any inactivated preparation.

To sum up, maternal antibodies naturally acquired via the placenta may cause interference with the baby's capacity to respond to a vaccine administered for artificial immunization. This possibility is considered in determining the balanced composition of combined vaccines, as laid down in official regulations, and has also influenced the timing of different items included in immunization schedules.

Appendix B

Immunization Schedules

The following condensed schedule is based on the recommendations of the Ministry of Health (1968):

Immunization in Childhood

Age	Vaccine	Interval
3-12 months	Diph/Tet/Pert + oral Polio (3 doses)	6-8 weeks between doses 1 and 2 6 months between doses 2 and 3
12-13 months	Measles (live)	
13-24 months	Smallpox	At least 3-4 weeks after Measles (live)
3-5 years or school entry	Diph/Tet + oral Polio	
5 years	Smallpox revaccination	

Age	Vaccine
10-13 years	B.C.G. (for the tuberculin negative)
15-19 years (or school leaving)	Polio (oral or inactivated) Tetanus Toxoid Smallpox revaccination

The notes which accompanied the Ministry's official schedule were for the guidance of doctors and others concerned with immunization. They also explained certain modifications of earlier schedules, and are too detailed for inclusion in this Appendix.

However, the point must be emphasized that the aim of a routine programme of this nature must be to achieve effective protection of maximum number of children at risk, with minimum upset, against diphtheria, tetanus, whooping cough (pertussis), poliomyelitis, measles, smallpox and tuberculosis.

The following two unofficial schedules have been devised as a guide to doctors and travellers. *Schedule I* is designed for persons who have sufficient time at their disposal before departure; consequently injections need not be crowded, with the attendant risks of suboptimal responses and undesirable reactions. *Schedule II* is relatively unsatisfactory from the immunological standpoint, but may suffice for travellers in a hurry to depart.

IMMUNIZATION FOR INTERNATIONAL TRAVEL

Schedule I

Week	
1	Yellow fever vaccine Smallpox vaccine Oral Polio vaccine
2	Read result of smallpox vaccination
4	TABT Oral Polio vaccine
10	Tetanus vaccine (adsorbed) Oral Polio vaccine
36	Tetanus vaccine (adsorbed)

It is common practice for yellow fever and smallpox vaccines to be given simultaneously. If given separately, yellow fever vaccine must be administered 4 days before smallpox vaccine.

Cholera vaccine is injected only in special circumstances.

Reinforcing injections should be given as follows:

Yellow fever vaccine   every 10 years

Smallpox vaccine   every 3 years

TAB   yearly, as long as the individual is at special risk. Every 3 years in all others.

Tetanus vaccine   every 5 to 10 years.

Schedule II

Day	
1	Yellow fever vaccine
	Cholera vaccine
	Oral Polio vaccine
5	Smallpox vaccine
	TABT
11	Cholera vaccine
	Oral Polio vaccine
13	Read result of smallpox vaccination
28	Tetanus vaccine (adsorbed)
	Oral polio vaccine

Longer intervals are desirable when the time available permits.

Tetanus vaccine (adsorbed) should be given some months later to complete the tetanus course.

CHAPTER 29

REVIEW: THE PAST, PRESENT AND FUTURE

THE reader who has tried to follow the progress of immunological discovery and practice, often exciting but sometimes dull, must now agree that immunization has contributed to the triumphant conquest of infectious diseases and therefore to mankind's health and happiness. In this final chapter, the position is reviewed, and certain recent information added. The opportunity is sometimes taken to go beyond the confines of history and indicate various trends and lessons for the future. Of course personal opinions and propaganda have intruded more freely into these supplementary notes than would have been permissible elsewhere in this book.

Sir Winston Churchill has aptly condensed in one sentence the whole importance of history as a subject in teaching—'The further one looked back the more one could look forward.'

Diseases are discussed in alphabetical order in this miscellany.

Anthrax.—Effective control measures, which include vaccination, are now available for farm animals and persons specially exposed to risk. The present vaccine for humans in this country is an alum precipitate of the antigen found in sterile filtrates of the causal bacillus. This most effective advance in control is needed only for workers with certain imported animal hairs, wools, hides and bone meal.

Alas, on the debit side, anthrax, with its very resistant spore-bearing organisms, is a disease which has been specially studied in connection with germ warfare. The remote Scottish island of Gruinard was deliberately infected with anthrax during the Second World War: the hazard of this disease was still present in 1966, and it is thought may persist for another 100 years. This biological weapon remains effective far too long!

Botulism (botulinum toxin), brucellosis and plague have all been considered for dissemination during war. However, bacteriological warfare has its limitations and could again be rejected: even deadly micro-organisms are unreliable in comparison with modern chemicals!

Botulism.—This terrifying disease continues to strike in unexpected places throughout the world. The worst outbreak in this country was at Loch Maree in 1923. As previously indicated there are various types of the causal *Clostridium botulinum,* and the toxic filtrates produced are the most powerful of all poisons. Toxoids have a limited use for prophylaxis. In recent research on the distribution of the organism in nature, type E was almost always responsible when the food is imperfectly preserved fish. It is on record that all outbreaks of botulism in the Soviet Union since 1959 have been due to home-canned or home-pickled foods (ham, fish or vegetables). In Canada there was a recent incident which was fortunately controlled by the recall of tins of a product which had been under-processed owing to a misunderstanding.

Brucellosis.—Britain is at last aiming at the eradication of this disease in the cattle population—a project which may take about ten years to complete. The Scandinavian countries have been free from brucellosis for some years, and Western Germany and Bulgaria are virtually clear. Good progress has also been made by the Government of Northern Ireland.

The British scheme is opportune because about 2 per cent. of individual cows in this country excrete the causative organism in their milk. Much undiagnosed human illness is probably compatible with chronic brucellosis: a conservative estimate is that 5,000 people suffer from the disease each year in England and Wales.

Eradication in dairy animals entails a diagnostic test and the slaughter of reactors, with compensation. In some areas the widespread use of S 19, or preferably the newer 45/20, live vaccine in adult cattle would also be indicated. The latter strain is harmless to personnel and is commercially available in some countries.

Cholera.—Vaccination is not as effective as one would like for prevention, and is only an adjunct to proper sanitary services to ensure clean food and water. The W.H.O. is sponsoring work on the production of more reliable vaccines, mainly because cholera is striking back: the new El Tor variant is endemic from the Pacific Ocean to the Caspian Sea and beyond—an unexpected development!

Improvements must entail not only pure food and water, but a social revolution involving all aspects of sanitation and the combating of ignorance, prejudice and apathy. In this regard, most readers will think of so-called backward countries, because cholera is no longer a significant menace in the western world. Once again the W.H.O. helps by epidemiological studies and the provision of instructional material for the affected areas.

Perhaps one can legitimately widen the scope of discussion and point a moral. While living conditions in twentieth century Britain have been improved dramatically, standards of hygiene leave much to be desired. One cannot feel complacent about the low sanitary standards still observed in some food shops, hotels, restaurants and domestic kitchens. Our roads are ill supplied with public conveniences in country districts. Bathing beaches are too often contaminated by untreated sewage. Dog owners may allow their pets to soil pavements, reminiscent of the absence of hygiene in our streets in former times. Much has been achieved in the field of public health through the new sciences of bacteriology, immunology and virology, but public opinion still requires educating and enlightening.

Common Cold and Respiratory Diseases (excluding Influenza).— There is no imminent prospect of obtaining a beneficial vaccine for the common cold. Illnesses of this type in both adults and children are of great complexity, due to the increasing number of viruses which are being incriminated either alone or in combination. It has been shown that one person may contract respiratory infections due to a sequence of different viruses in a relatively short period of time. Inactivated viral vaccines afford a useful degree of protection but only against viruses similar to those included in the preparation injected. The outlook is probably less gloomy for the control of common colds by some form of chemotherapy than by means of vaccines.

Diphtheria.—The diphtheria story has received prominence in this book. In the life-time of many of us, the disease has been virtually overthrown. A point of criticism may be permitted in retrospect: it took the fears of widespread diphtheria outbreaks associated with the evacuation of children during the Second World War to bring in the eminently successful British national immunization scheme —at least 10 years late (the climate of opinion was different in the early 1930s from that which evolved later)! Our American and Canadian friends acted effectively long before we did. However, our own success (although belated) may have been a turning point in our attitude to preventive inoculation in this country.

Apathy is an ever-present risk. Thus, although prophylaxis is feasible and effective, 24 cases of diphtheria were notified in England and Wales in 1966. This indicated that there has been a failure of some parents to have their babies immunized. The problem of maintaining high immunization rates in a community is not peculiar to this country. In New York City, for example, 30 per cent. of infants up to twelve months old, are not immunized against diphtheria, tetanus and pertussis. An 'alert' has recently been launched to remedy the situation, which would otherwise be potentially dangerous.

In 1964 to 1966 no death was recorded for diphtheria in England and Wales.

Influenza.—Inactivated viral vaccines, which were introduced in the 1930s, have sometimes been highly protective in military establishments. However, the results of certain mass vaccination projects involving civilians have been less convincing: perhaps more young children, who spread infection rapidly, should have been included.

Live influenza vaccines tend to become over-attenuated and to lose their immunizing power.

Whatever the type of vaccine used, the protection has been transient. Moreover the influenza viruses mutate sharply. A further difficulty is that a new mutant can be disseminated so quickly all over the world that a protective vaccine against it cannot be prepared in quantity early enough to be effective: six to twelve months may be required for large-scale production. Much has been achieved, but energetic research is being continued to meet well recognized problems still awaiting solution.

In Britain, formalin-inactivated saline vaccine containing influenza A, A2 (Asian) and B antigenic strains is currently available (1967) and should confer some protection for three to six months. Its use has been advised for 'at risk' persons, especially those with chronic lung or heart disease. Research is in progress on inactivated vaccines prepared with new adjuvants.

Measles.—British policy has been influenced by American experience. The Federal government of the United States confidently expects that measles will be *eradicated* in all U.S. children in a very few years. Measles vaccine has been licensed in the U.S.A. since the spring of 1963. Up to the end of 1966 perhaps 20 million doses of *live* vaccine had been administered. Some 8 million to 10 million youngsters—all in the susceptible age group between 1 and 7 years—were due to receive one shot of live, attenuated measles virus vaccine in 1967. (Henceforth the 4 million children born each year will be vaccinated against measles.) This is fast work even allowing for American standards: in the U.S. measles should soon join the ranks of the conquered diseases of childhood.

In Britain there is now an appreciation of the position regarding complications for they are far from negligible. They include severe bronchitis and pneumonia, middle-ear disease (leading to deafness), and neurological disturbances (including convulsions and encephalitis or inflammation of the brain, the remote effects of which may be mental and physical retardation or even permanent disability). About 33,000 complicated cases occur annually in this country, and over 6,000 of these patients would require treatment in hospital. What a lot of unnecessary and sometimes very dangerous illness, and what an unnecessary, time-consuming and expensive burden on the medical and nursing professions and on the whole community!

I have previously indicated that the situation is much worse in some parts of West Africa, India and South America. Given the will and the financial backing, eradication of measles should be achieved. Serious consideration is being given to simultaneous measles and smallpox vaccinations on a large scale in developing countries where medical services could easily be disorganized.

Mumps.—A live-virus vaccine has proved effective for children and adults in the U.S.A. The immunity appears to be lasting. A combined mumps, measles and rubella vaccine is under trial.

Plague.—This major epidemic disease of earlier times is now being well contained in certain underdeveloped countries, and is even being gradually overcome. Money and education are required for its eradication—a matter of international importance and concern.

Poliomyelitis.—Good protective vaccines are available today in Britain: live attenuated vaccines (Sabin-type) are generally preferred to purified and concentrated inactivated vaccines (improved Salk-type). It is therefore disturbing that poliomyelitis showed a considerable increase in incidence in 1965, there being 91 cases in England and Wales compared with 37 in the previous year.

In New York City recent figures show that there has been only one poliomyelitis case since 1964. Nevertheless the Health Department has launched an immunization 'alert', urging the intensification of measures to protect the city's infants. The need for such action was apparent when a survey revealed that 40 per cent. of infants up to 12 months old were not immunized against poliomyelitis: there was no guarantee that the low incidence of cases in recent years would continue for a further period.

Notwithstanding this cautionary note on public apathy and its consequences, the eradication of this disease is quite feasible. Success has been spectacular in some areas: this has resulted from the ease of giving the oral vaccine and from the interest of the peoples concerned.

Rabies.—The quarantine laws of this country have prevented the introduction of infected animals since 1922. However, infected humans coming from an endemic area cannot be excluded: some immigrants have developed symptoms after admission.

Diagnostic difficulties in the early stages of rabies may be expected. Treatment of the established disease is ineffective.

Provided the patient seeks advice after being bitten by a dog suspected of having rabies, prophylactic vaccination can be carried out. The vaccine most used is the Semple preparation, a killed virus suspension of rabbit origin. The long incubation period (usually one to three months) gives sufficient time for complete protection to result, and enables infected persons to enter rabies-free areas.

A rabies antiserum produced in animals, or a concentrated and purified preparation of this serum, should also be considered for such cases. Although an immediate passive protection results, antiserum has the defect of interfering with the active antibody response resulting from vaccines. This interference has necessitated a prolongation of the daily vaccine course, which is already very tedious.

Throughout the world dogs continue to be the main source of infection for man, and a live attenuated vaccine prepared from the Flury strain is satisfactory for dogs. (This strain was isolated from the brain of a girl named Flury.) In most countries greater efforts are required to extend the vaccination of pet dogs and the eradication of stray dogs.

In Central and South America, vampire bats convey rabies: regional projects of control and research are in progress.

Rubella.—In 1964 tens of thousands of infants in the U.S.A. were born with congenital defects for which maternal rubella (German measles) in the early months of pregnancy was the responsible agent. Rubella is the only virus known to act in this way on the human foetus.

A. B. Sabin, the famous virologist of Cincinnati University, considers that an attenuated virus vaccine is desirable for boys as well as girls in order to eradicate the disease. Criteria of its success would include the amount of immunity it produced, the lack of dissemination of the living vaccine virus, and the absence of congenital abnormalities attributable to the vaccine. Research is in progress on this project.

Smallpox.—The eradication campaign (p. 156) is making progress, the keys to success being finance and education. The problem is most serious in some Asiatic countries, including India, Indonesia and Afghanistan. There were over 57,500 cases of smallpox throughout the world in 1966, of which 70 per cent. were in South East Asia. Parts of Africa and South America are also reservoirs of infection.

In this country there is considerable difference of opinion about the need for infant vaccination. Nevertheless, the author agrees with the Ministry of Health's experts, who advise routine immunization during the second year of life, followed by revaccination at 5 years of age and on leaving school.

Travellers require certificates, and the last-minute vaccination of tourists is highly undesirable.

During the last decade importations of smallpox into Britain from Pakistan have shown that fear of the scourge persists: in fact, this fear is shared with other affluent nations, and is a further incentive to providing funds for freeze-dried vaccine, transport and equipment for the developing countries with smallpox reservoirs. It is of interest that liquid vaccine is no longer acceptable because of its rapid deterioration in the tropics. Donations of vaccine must be 'high quality, fully stable and freeze-dried'.

The advent of a needle-less or jet injector ('dermojet gun') has been timely for mass vaccination campaigns, for this vaccinator has reduced the old 'scratch' costs by four-fifths, and has speeded up the operation and made it more acceptable. (With the increasing number of infections that can now be controlled by immunization and vaccination, the perfection of this novel appliance has been timely. Much time and inconvenience are saved.)

Tetanus.—Owing to the risk of anaphylactic shock from the use of horse antitoxin, more emphasis is now placed on prevention by active immunization. In the meantime, serum may still be required for the non-immune injured patient, but credit must also be given to efficient surgery and the wider use of antibiotics. Since any wound (no matter how trivial) may lead to tetanus, everyone should be vaccinated with the toxoid. This is a long-term policy: toxoid is of no immediate prophylactic value.

Especially for childhood immunization, tetanus toxoid mixed with other vaccines is a convenient preparation.

Details of the modern prophylaxis of tetanus after injury are outside the scope of this book. The casualty officer or family doctor decides on procedure with the assistance of the immunization history: records must be accessible quickly. In order to reduce reactions, small supplies of human antitoxic serum have been made available by the Ministry of Health for selected cases.

In 1965 there were 21 deaths assigned to tetanus, and a further 8 in which tetanus was mentioned as a complication, in England and Wales. Before long such deaths should be eliminated altogether.

Tuberculosis.—B.C.G. vaccine had been given to over $4\frac{1}{2}$ million persons in England and Wales up to the end of 1965. Throughout the world approximately 250 million persons have now been vaccinated as an important adjuvant to improved hygiene, chemotherapy and other measures of control. The reduction in morbidity has been greater in technically advanced countries than in tropical developing countries. Further investigations into the reasons for this difference are necessary. However, mass vaccination is worthwhile, although the first administration of B.C.G. may have to be arranged early in life in developing communities.

Freeze-dried B.C.G. vaccine is a British contribution: introduced in 1958, it is now the only antigen used.

As in the case of smallpox vaccination (see p. 214), the dermojet injector is a recent development. Rapid, painless, automatic and effective B.C.G. vaccination has resulted from its use.

Tuberculosis, being a chronic disease, is more difficult to tackle than some other infections reviewed in this chapter. Nevertheless it has been claimed that eradication in America is possible by a combination of methods, though it may take several decades to achieve.

At the end of last century tuberculosis in Britain caused more deaths than any other disease: one in every five deaths was due to it. Decline in mortality has been rapid, especially after 1948, and in 1962 deaths from tuberculosis were down to one in every 80, and most of these were old people.

Typhoid and Paratyphoid Fevers.—It will be recalled that paratyphoid antigens were first added to the typhoid vaccine during the First World War. Reactions to the resultant T.A.B. vaccine used to be a considerable problem and tended to occur earlier and be more severe with each successive injection.

A reduction in the incidence and severity of reactions has been achieved by intradermal injection: antihistamines given a few hours before vaccination may also be helpful.

Since paratyphoid fevers are often mild and less severe than typhoid fever, the United States Army has omitted the paratyphoid constituents from future vaccines: this change of policy would also ensure a reduction in reaction rates. A similar decision is likely to be taken by other authorities.

Vaccination reduces the risk of typhoid by at least 75 per cent. Since the protection is not absolute, unnecessary risks in taking food and drinking water should be avoided by travellers in many countries.

Viral hepatitis.—Although much progress has been made, this infection with its long incubation period is still an unsolved public health problem. The clinical disease is often mild but may be very serious, especially in some adult females.

Gamma globulin should be considered as a protective measure for close contacts, pregnant women and possibly travellers. Local epidemics might also be controlled by this means.

Whooping Cough (Pertussis).—No vaccine has yet approached the efficiency of diphtheria, tetanus or poliomyelitis vaccines. Although mortality from whooping cough has fallen sharply, the case incidence has risen in recent years and considerably in 1967. The disease is 23 times more fatal in infants than in older children.

Vaccines can be improved, and more immunization is required to further lessen the toll.

Yellow Fever.—Medical science in the present century has pointed the way to prevent and combat this 'sword of pestilence'. The first step was the discovery of the U.S. Army Yellow Fever Commission (1900-02) in Cuba that a mosquito, *Aedes aegypti*, was the vector of the causal virus. Effective vaccines began to be developed in the 1920s.

The disease may be eradicated from the whole American continent by 1970, with the possible exception of some jungle areas. The outlook in Africa is less hopeful.

VII

CHRONOLOGY

BIOGRAPHICAL NOTES

A NOTE ON BIBLIOGRAPHY

GLOSSARY

CHRONOLOGY

I: Developments in the Pre-Scientific Age

Pre-history—Disease ascribed to magic: demonic, religious and astrological theories.
Variolation against smallpox in China and India.

5th century, B.C.—Greek influence on medicine: Hippocrates: deduction from observation.

1st century, B.C.—Mithridates of Pontus: 'immunization' against poisons.

1st century—Pliny and rabies 'vaccine'.
Life expectation = 22 years (?).

2nd century—Galen of Pergamum and Rome: evolution of epidemiology: atmospheric changes, individual susceptibility, contagion.

590—First recorded account of variolation.

Middle ages—Infection from living 'contagium'. Leper laws.
Life expectation = 20-25 years.

1349-59—Plague (Black Death): 2 million deaths in Britain (one-quarter to one-half of population).

1664-65—Plague (Great Plague of London): 63,000 to 100,000 deaths.

1683—Van Leeuwenhoek's microscope. Discovery of bacteria and protozoa.

1721—Lady Mary Wortley Montagu: popularization of variolation in Britain.
Cotton Mather: variolation in America.

1750—*Population of Great Britain = 7.5 million.*

1751-1800—Smallpox caused 10 per cent. of all deaths in U.K.—in some years 20 per cent.

1798—*Life expectation (western countries) = 36 years (?).*

18th century—John Hunter, famous London surgeon, advised Edward Jenner: 'Why think—why not try the experiment?'
Dawn of scientific era.
Variolation in several European countries.

II: Developments from Edward Jenner to Paul Ehrlich
(circa 1800-1900)

1798—Edward Jenner: smallpox vaccination.

1800—Jennerian vaccination in the U.S.A.

1801—*Population of Great Britain = 11·6 million.*
(England and Wales = 8·9 million).

1802—Smallpox caused 45,000 deaths annually in U.K. (Statement in House of Commons).

1826—Bretonneau: diphtheria recognized.

1840—Variolation illegal in Britain.

1848-49—Cholera caused 54,000 deaths in England.

1848-55—John Snow: cholera transmissible.

1855—Tuberculosis (Great Britain): 3,626 deaths per million.
Crimean War: three regiments of Guards lost 449 'by ordinary warfare' and 1,713 from disease (enteric fever, dysentery, cholera, etc.).

1861—*Population of Great Britain = 23·1 million.*
(England and Wales = 20 million).

Circa 1870—Staining of bacteria introduced.

1875—Measles (Fiji Islands): 20,000 to 40,000 deaths in population of 150,000.

1876—Modern era of bacteriological and immunological discovery begins.
Robert Koch: anthrax bacillus discovered.
Life expectation (England and Wales) = male 41 years: female 43 years.

1876-80—*Infant Mortality (England and Wales) = 145 per 1,000 births.*

1880—Eberth: typhoid bacillus.
Louis Pasteur: fowl cholera vaccine.

1881—Ogston: staphylococcus.
Pasteur, Roux and Chamberland: anthrax vaccine.

1882—Koch: tubercle bacillus.

1883—Koch: cholera vibrio.
Pasteur: swine erysipelas vaccine.

1883-84—Klebs and Loeffler: diphtheria bacillus.

1884—Nicolaier: tetanus bacillus.

1885—Pasteur: rabies vaccine.

1888—Roux and Yersin: diphtheria toxin.

1890—Koch: tuberculin introduced.

1891—Behring and Kitasato: diphtheria and tetanus antitoxins.
Population of Great Britain = 33 million.

1892—Haffkine: cholera vaccine.

1894—Roux: classical paper on value of diphtheria antitoxin.
Goodall: diphtheria antitoxin in England.

1896—Bacillary dysentery (Japan): 90,000 cases and 20,000 deaths.

1897—Ehrlich: standardization of diphtheria antitoxin.
Haffkine: plague vaccine.
1898—Almroth Wright: typhoid vaccine.
Monckton Copeman: glycerinated calf lymph for smallpox vaccination.
1899-1902—Boer War in South Africa.
Typhoid vaccine given to 4 per cent. of British troops.
1900—*Population of Great Britain = 38·2 million.*

III: ANTISERA AND VACCINES *(1900-20)*

1900-02—Walter Reed: Yellow Fever Commission.
Yellow Fever (Havana): 1,400 cases in 1900 reduced to 0 cases in 1902.
1901—*Population of England and Wales = 32·5 million.*
1901-05—*Infant Mortality (England and Wales) = 138 per 1,000 births.*
1903-05—Brucellosis (Malta): 456 cases per annum in British forces —see 1907-09.
1904—Glenny and Loewenstein (independently): toxoid for active immunization of horses.
Tetanus antitoxin prophylactically in Independence Day celebrations, U.S.A.
1905—Tuberculosis (Great Britain): 1,632 deaths per million.
1906—Bordet and Gengou: cultivation of whooping-cough (pertussis) bacillus.
1907—Von Pirquet: tuberculin (scratch) test.
1907-09—Brucellosis (Malta): 6 cases per annum in British forces.
1908—Mantoux: tuberculin (intradermal) test.
1909—Nicolle: epidemic typhus spread by body louse.
Gibson and Banzhaf: antitoxin concentrated.
1913—British Medical Research Committee (forerunner of M.R. Council).
Schick test for immunity to diphtheria.
Behring: toxin antitoxin mixtures for human immunization against diphtheria.
1914-18—First World War.
Tetanus: prophylactic antitoxin for wounded troops.
Typhoid-paratyphoid vaccine: incidence of enteric fevers reduced.
Park and Zingher: large-scale diphtheria immunization in New York.
1914—Typhus fever (Serbia): 400 cases and 126 deaths amongst doctors.
1916—Da Rocha-Lima: typhus rickettsia.
Poliomyelitis: large epidemic in U.S.A.

1918—Nicolle and Conseil: measles convalescent serum.

1918-19—Influenza: world pandemic: 500 million cases and 25 million deaths.

1918-22—Typhus fever (Russia): 30 million cases and 3 million deaths.

1919—Martin and Pettit: antiserum for leptospirosis.

IV: DEVELOPMENTS SINCE 1920

1921—Glenny and Südmersen: primary and secondary stimulus responses.

Calmette and Guérin: B.C.G. vaccine for tuberculosis.

1921-25—*Infant Mortality (England and Wales) = 76 per 1,000 births.*

1922—Ramon: flocculation test for titrating toxin and antitoxin.

1923—Ramon: diphtheria anatoxine (toxoid) for human immunization.

O'Brien and colleagues: diphtheria toxoid-antitoxin mixtures (T.A.M.).

George and Gladys Dick: scarlet fever toxin and antitoxin.

Laidlaw and Dunkin: research on canine distemper begun.

1925—British Therapeutic Substances Act.

Pope: laboratory work on aluminium as adjuvant.

Copeman: measles serum prophylaxis in Britain.

Pertussis (England and Wales): 6,038 deaths.

1926—Laidlaw and Dunkin: ferrets found to be susceptible to distemper virus.

Ramon and Zoeller: mixing of vaccines for human use.

1927—Glenny and Pope: diphtheria toxoid-antitoxin floccules (T.A.F.).

Leake: smallpox multiple pressure vaccination.

Ramon and Zoeller: tetanus toxoid for human immunization.

1928—Bundaberg (Queensland) disaster with diphtheria prophylactic led to research on Staphylococcus.

Park, Bullowa and Rosenbluth: pneumococcal antiserum (Types 1 and 2) used in U.S.A.

1930—Burnet: staphylococcal toxoid and antitoxin.

Theiler: yellow fever transmitted to mice: research facilitated.

1931—Glenny and Barr: diphtheria alum-precipitated toxoid (A.P.T.).

Therapeutic Substances Regulations.

Leslie and Gardner: pertussis cultures selected to ensure good vaccines.

Goodpasture: fertile hens' eggs introduced for growth of viruses —a major advance in technique.

1931-35—*Infant Mortality (England and Wales) = 62 per 1,000 births.*

1933—Weigl: typhus vaccine.

Sauer: pertussis vaccine.

Smith, Andrewes and Laidlaw: transmitted epidemic influenza to ferrets, which facilitated research.

Tuberculosis (England and Wales): nearly 32,000 deaths.

1934—Kolmer and Brodie prepared first poliomyelitis vaccines—trials unsuccessful.

Felix and Pitt: discovered Vi (virulence) antigen of typhoid bacillus.

Seibert: tuberculin purified protein derivative (P.P.D.).

1935—*Population of England and Wales just over 40 million.*

Infant Mortality (England and Wales) = *57 per 1,000 births.*

1936—Yellow fever: '17D' vaccine.

Kendrick: pertussis vaccine.

1937—Influenza virus vaccines.

1938—Boyd: tetanus toxoid in British Army.

Pope: refined (enzyme-treated) antitoxins.

Cox: typhus vaccine.

Chemotherapy replaced serum therapy of pneumonia, cerebro-spinal meningitis, etc.

Diphtheria (England and Wales): 55,000 to 60,000 notifications and 3,000 deaths annually just before Second World War.

1939-45—Second World War.

Tetanus: toxoid widely used.

Penicillin: production increasing.

1940—Diphtheria: British national immunization campaign.

1941—Gregg: drew attention to congenital defects following maternal rubella (German measles).

Felix: alcoholized T.A.B. vaccine introduced.

1941-45—*Infant Mortality (England and Wales)* = *50 per 1,000 births.*

1943—Waksman: streptomycin for tuberculosis.

Boyd: phenolized T.A.B. vaccine gave good protection against enteric fevers.

1944—Infectious and serum hepatitis due to virus, types A and B.

Cohn: measles gamma globulin introduced.

1946—Diphtheria (England and Wales): 11,986 cases and 472 deaths—see 1938.

Pertussis: M.R.C. controlled trials of vaccine begun.

Common Cold: M.R.C. Research Unit set up at Harvard Hospital, Salisbury.

1947—Holt: diphtheria purified toxoid aluminium phosphate precipitated (P.T.A.P.).

Population of Great Britain = *48.2 million.*

1948—Smallpox: compulsory vaccination of infants ended in Britain under National Health Service Act of 1946.

World Health Organization founded.

Weller and Enders: mumps virus.

1949—Mumps: inactivated virus vaccine.

Enders, Robbins and Weller: cultivation of poliomyelitis viruses in tissue culture (human tissue fragments in the test-tube).

1951—Yellow fever: 17D virus vaccine given to 40 million persons to date.

Population of England and Wales = 43.7 million.

1951-55—*Infant Mortality (England and Wales) = 27 per 1,000 births.*

1954—Poliomyelitis: mass trial of Salk vaccine in U.S.A.

Enders and Peebles: measles virus.

1955—Tuberculosis (Great Britain): 144 deaths per million—see 1855.

1956—Poliomyelitis: Sabin vaccine used in U.S.A.

Tuberculosis: M.R.C. report on B.C.G. vaccine.

1957—Poliomyelitis (England and Wales): 4,844 verified cases in 1st year of Salk vaccination campaign.

1959—Pertussis: M.R.C. controlled trials of vaccine completed—substantial protection.

1960—Diphtheria (England and Wales): 49 cases and 5 deaths.

W.H.O. International Centre for Respiratory Virus Diseases at Harvard Hospital, Salisbury.

Enders: attenuated virus vaccine for measles.

Quadruple (diphtheria, tetanus, pertussis, poliomyelitis) vaccine under investigation.

1961—*Population of Great Britain = 51.3 million.*

1962—Tuberculosis: freeze-dried B.C.G. vaccine.

Poliomyelitis: Sabin vaccine accepted in Britain.

1964—Typhoid: W.H.O. report on vaccines (including acetone-killed).

Diphtheria (England and Wales): 20 cases and 0 deaths.

Pertussis (England and Wales): 44 deaths—see 1925.

Poliomyelitis (England and Wales): 37 cases—see 1957.

Life expectation (England and Wales): male 68 years; female 74 years—see 1st century, etc.

1965—*Population of Great Britain = 54.6 million*—see 1750, 1801, etc. *(England and Wales nearly 48 million).*

Infant Mortality (England and Wales) = 19 per 1,000 births.

This is a record low figure—see 1876, 1901, etc.

Tuberculosis (England and Wales): 1,199 deaths—see 1933.

1966—Tuberculosis: 250 million doses of B.C.G. vaccine used to date all over the world.

BIOGRAPHICAL NOTES

The distinguished scientists included in this series are deceased. (It would be an invidious task to prepare a selection of persons still alive.)

Certain entries are short because they supplement extensive coverage given elsewhere in this book. The length of an entry bears no relationship to the importance of an individual's contributions to immunology.

BEHRING, EMIL (1854-1917)

A pupil and fellow-worker of Koch. With Kitasato (a Japanese), he discovered antitoxin (1890). The first patient to be treated with diphtheria antitoxin was at a clinic in Berlin (1891).

Behring also prepared tetanus antitoxin.

When he was awarded the first Nobel prize in physiology and medicine in 1901, he changed his name to von Behring.

Behring used diphtheria toxin-antitoxin mixtures for human immunization (1913). He was thus a pioneer also in the field of preventive inoculation.

BORDET, JULES (1870-1961)

A Belgian bacteriologist, who was an early contributor to the science of serology and immunity reactions.

He discovered the causal bacterium of pertussis or whooping cough.

BRUCE, DAVID (1855-1931)

British army surgeon, who discovered the causal organism of Malta fever (1887).

Chairman of the Malta Fever Commission (1904-06), which studied mode of transmission of the disease. A spectacular fall in sickness rates followed this work.

He is best known for his investigations of African sleeping sickness or trypanosomiasis.

CALMETTE, ALBERT (1863-1933)

A French bacteriologist of the Pasteur Institutes of Paris and Lille. He joined Pasteur's staff in 1890, and was trained in the spirit and methods of the older man.

With Camille Guérin he prepared a preventive vaccine (B.C.G.) for tuberculosis. Victory over this disease is now a practical possibility, thanks to improved hygiene and various other measures, including B.C.G.

Earlier, Calmette developed an antivenom for the treatment of snakebite.

COLEBROOK, LEONARD (1883-1967)

A British bacteriologist, who was the colleague and biographer of Almroth Wright.

He carried out valuable research on puerperal fever and other streptococcal infections, and was a pioneer of chemotherapy in this country.

He also introduced measures for the successful treatment of burns.

After his retirement he conducted a successful campaign for better guards on gas and electric fires, and he encouraged the use of fireproof clothing for children.

EHRLICH, PAUL (1854-1915)

A German physician of Jewish parentage, who was one of the greatest men that medical science has ever produced.

As he made an all-important contribution to the standardization of toxins and antitoxins (1897), he is sometimes regarded as the first immunologist.

He announced the discovery of salvarsan or '606' for the treatment of syphilis (1910), and was thus a pioneer in chemotherapy.

He introduced new methods of staining blood cells and thus laid the foundation of haematology—the third modern science which he initiated!

He founded and directed the Institute for Experimental Therapy in Frankfurt.

FELIX, ARTHUR (1887-1956)

An Austrian Jew, who settled in England in 1927: he was already an accomplished bacteriologist and serologist.

He worked on the laboratory diagnosis of typhus fever while serving in the Austrian army in the First World War.

In this country he studied the virulence and protective power in mice of various strains of the typhoid bacillus, and introduced a new typhoid-paratyphoid vaccine (alcoholized) in 1941.

FLEMING, ALEXANDER (1881-1955)

A British bacteriologist, and pupil and successor of Almroth Wright.

He worked on vaccine therapy and demonstrated the inefficacy of antiseptics in wound treatment in the First World War.

Later he discovered lysozyme and penicillin.

Fleming shared the Nobel prize for medicine with H. W. (later Lord) Florey and E. B. Chain in 1945.

The Inoculation Department of St. Mary's Hospital, London, became the Wright-Fleming Institute soon after Wright's death in 1947.

FLEXNER, SIMON (1863-1946)

An American pathologist and bacteriologist who became Director of the Rockefeller Institute for Medical Research in New York (1903).

He was a pioneer in research on dysentery (1900) and poliomyelitis (1909).

GLENNY, ALEXANDER (1882-1965)

A British immunologist, who was a pioneer of the principles and laboratory aspects of immunization.

He first used diphtheria toxoid for horse immunization in 1904.

With Südmersen, he described 'primary' and 'secondary' stimuli in diphtheria prophylaxis (1921).

He introduced new vaccines, notably diphtheria toxoid-antitoxin floccules (T.A.F.) and alum-precipated toxoid (A.P.T.).

While Ehrlich was the first scientific immunologist, Glenny laid the foundations of all modern clinical practice in this field.

GOFFE, ALAN (1920-66)

A British virologist, who played an important rôle in the development of vaccines against poliomyelitis, measles and other viral diseases of man.

GREENWOOD, MAJOR (Christian name, not title!) (1880-1949)

A British epidemiologist and statistician, who taught the importance of the application of statistical methods to medical research—a belief which he lived to see widely accepted. His publications related to a wide range of topics and diseases.

He criticized Calmette's conduct of the French immunization programme with tuberculosis vaccine, B.C.G. He was correct in his criticism, but 'the baby was thrown out with the bath water' for many years —a sad set-back to a valuable preventive measure!

Greenwood's influence enriched the intellectual life of a generation of scientific investigators, thinkers, writers and scholars.

GREGG, NORMAN MC.A. (1892-1966)

An Australian ophthalmic surgeon, who correlated German measles (rubella) in a woman in the first trimester of pregnancy with severe physical deformities in her child. This observation led to the effective use of anti-rubella serum for protection and also to the search for a prophylactic vaccine, which now appears to have been successful.

GUÉRIN, CAMILLE (1872-1961)

A French bacteriologist, who collaborated with Albert Calmette in preparing B.C.G. vaccine, the main weapon against tuberculosis in many countries.

Unlike his colleague, who died in 1933, he lived to see the final justification of his painstaking work.

HAFFKINE, WALDEMAR (1860-1930)

A Russian pupil of Louis Pasteur. A pioneer in the production of prophylactic vaccines against cholera and plague.

In India, he began to use cholera vaccine on an enormous scale (1893), and this was followed by plague vaccine (1896).

The research laboratory which he founded in Bombay is now known as the Haffkine Institute.

HARTLEY, PERCIVAL (1881-1957)

A British biochemist, who investigated the production of diphtheria toxin in culture, and the purification of the antitoxic proteins in sera. Later, he became an authority on the principles and practice of biological standardization: he established many International Standards.

ISAACS, ALICK (1921-67)

A British virologist, who succeeded Sir Christopher Andrewes at the National Institute for Medical Research.

For a time he was director of the World Influenza Centre.

He discovered interferon in collaboration with J. Lindenmann.

JENNER, EDWARD (1749-1823)

A Gloucestershire medical practitioner and naturalist, who observed that inoculation with the mild disease, vaccinia or cowpox, produces an immunity to subsequent smallpox inoculation. He also showed that arm-to-arm vaccination could replace cow-to-arm vaccination.

Jenner's experiments led to a practical protection against smallpox and, much later, to the present-day sciences of immunology and virology.

KITASATO, S. (1852-1931)

A Japanese, who was a pupil of Koch and made three major discoveries, viz.

(1) He cultivated for the first time the bacillus of tetanus in a pure state (1889).
(2) With Behring, he discovered antitoxic sera (1890).
(3) He discovered the plague bacillus in human cases of plague and in the dead bodies of rats (1894).

KOCH, ROBERT (1843-1910)

A German bacteriologist.

After graduation in medicine he served throughout the Franco-German war. He started research work in a primitive laboratory at his home while serving as a doctor in Wollstein, a small Prussian town. His technical advances in cultivating and staining bacteria transformed the entire science of infection.

He demonstrated the character and mode of growth of the anthrax bacillus.

He also discovered the tubercle bacillus (1882)—the high point of his brilliant career.

His investigations threw new light on many other diseases.

His pupils and assistants included Pfeiffer, Behring, Kitasato and Loeffler.

He was awarded the Nobel prize for medicine in 1905.

LAIDLAW, PATRICK P. (1881-1940)

A British bacteriologist and virologist, who was a pioneer in the control of dog distemper by vaccination (1923-33).

With Andrewes and Wilson Smith, he first isolated the influenza virus A (1933). His team also initiated clinical and experimental studies of the immunization of human beings against influenza.

LEEUWENHOEK, ANTONI VAN (1632-1723)

A Dutch draper, who was also a surveyor, wine-gauger and 'Chamberlain of the Council-Chamber of the worshipful Sheriffs of Delft'. It was his hobby which earned for him undying fame: he became a naturalist and grinder of lenses, who discovered and drew bacteria, protozoa, red blood corpuscles and many other living organisms.

He was the first great microscopist and microbiologist.

LEISHMAN, WILLIAM BOOG (1865-1926)

A British army pathologist and latterly Director-General of the

Army Medical Service. He was an early collaborator of Almroth Wright, and he supervised a prolonged clinical trial of typhoid vaccine, which he improved.

He introduced Leishman's stain primarily to facilitate tests for the phagocytic power of leucocytes.

He discovered the *Leishmania* group of protozoa, which is responsible for kala-azar and other diseases.

LISTER, JOSEPH (1827-1912)

A British surgeon, who revolutionized the practice of surgery. Inspired by the discoveries of Louis Pasteur, on fermentation and putrefaction, he recognized the comparable rôle of germs in wound infection.

He first used the antiseptic phenol (carbolic acid) in operating theatres in 1865: later he modified the antiseptic method and founded aseptic surgery, which is based on careful cleanliness. He encouraged the use of antitoxic serum in diphtheria (1894).

The memorial to Lister is the Lister Institute, London—in much the same way as the memorial to Pasteur is the Pasteur Institute, Paris. He was undoubtedly one of mankind's greatest benefactors.

METCHNIKOFF, ELIE (1845-1916)

A Russian biologist who worked at the Pasteur Institute, Paris. He originated the doctrine of phagocytosis, and later shared the Nobel Prize award with Paul Ehrlich in 1908 for his work on immunity.

PARK, WILLIAM HALLOCK (1863-1939)

An American nose and throat specialist who became a bacteriologist and immunologist: Director of Hygiene Services in New York City.

Park's laboratory was the first outside Europe to produce diphtheria antitoxin.

With Zingher, he was a pioneer of mass immunization against diphtheria in the U.S.A.

Toxin-antitoxin mixtures were first used for this purpose in 1914. He changed over to toxoid in 1924.

PASTEUR, LOUIS (1822-95)

A French organic chemist, who investigated the causes of the diseases of wines and beer, fermentation, and the diseases of silkworms.

He later developed attenuated bacterial vaccines for fowl cholera, anthrax and swine erysipelas. His best known achievement was to attenuate rabies virus by animal passage and then to prepare a vaccine of treated animal tissue (1885).

His pupils included Roux, Yersin, Chamberland, Metchnikoff and

Calmette. As the founder of modern immunology, he was one of the greatest human benefactors of all time. He laboured without rest, and his constant counsel to his devoted pupils was 'work, always work'. He possessed a will to success. At the opening of the Pasteur Institute, he expressed his creed in these words, which are relevant today: 'Two contrary laws seem to be wrestling with each other nowadays: the one of blood and death, ever imagining new means of destruction and forcing nations to be constantly ready for the battlefield; the other a law of peace, work, and health, ever evolving new means of delivering man from the scourges which beset him. . . . The latter places one human life above any victory, while the former would sacrifice thousands of lives to the ambition of one. . . . Which of these two laws will ultimately prevail God alone knows.'

RAMON, GASTON (1886-1963)

A French immunologist who became assistant to Emile Roux at the Pasteur Institute, Garches (1910).

His persistent advocacy of diphtheria toxoid (anatoxine) for human immunization began in 1923.

He was also a pioneer (1927) in using tetanus toxoid.

He greatly furthered immunization campaigns on the Continent, and was latterly Honorary Director of the Pasteur Institute, Paris.

REED, WALTER (1851-1902)

The American chairman of the Yellow Fever Commission which showed (1900) that yellow fever was transmitted by the mosquito, *Aedes aegypti*.

ROGERS, LEONARD (1868-1962)

A pioneer in tropical medicine, and an outstanding member of the Indian Medical Service.

His achievements included work on cholera, kala-azar, the dysenteries of India, leprosy and snake-bite.

He prevented cholera in pilgrim camps by mass vaccination: this is still the standard method of prophylaxis.

ROUX, ÉMILE (1853-1933)

A pupil and assistant of Pasteur, who proved the existence of diphtheria toxin (1888). He was also the first person to produce diphtheria antitoxin in horses. He delivered a classical paper on serum treatment (1894) which led to the world-wide use of serum.

He was Director of the Pasteur Institute, Paris, from 1904-18.

SCHICK, BELA (1877-1967)

A Hungarian paediatrician from Vienna, who settled in New York (1923).

With von Pirquet he studied the symptoms (manifestations of serum sickness) following the injection and re-injection of horse serum (1902).

He gave his name to a harmless skin test by which the separation of immune from non-immune persons became possible (1913).

SEMPLE, DAVID (1856-1937)

A British pathologist and physician, who worked under Almroth Wright and later founded the Pasteur Institute at Kasauli, India.

He introduced phenolized rabies vaccine, prepared from nervous tissues of hydrophobia-infected rabbits.

SHIGA, KIYOSHI (1870-1959)

A Japanese, who was a pupil of Kitasato.

He described (1898) the causative bacillus of a variety of dysentery which now bears his name. Later he pioneered dysentery antiserum.

SMITH, THEOBALD (1859-1934)

An American pathologist and bacteriologist, who differentiated between the human and bovine types of tubercle bacilli (1895).

He discovered independently the severe type of allergy to serum now known as anaphylaxis (1900-04).

He first suggested (1907) that diphtheria toxin-antitoxin mixtures might possibly be employed for practical immunization in man.

He is best known for his demonstration of the parasite of Texas fever ('Red Water') and its transmission by the cattle tick.

SMITH, WILSON (1897-1965)

A pioneer of virology in Britain.

With Laidlaw and Andrewes he discovered the virus of epidemic influenza in 1933.

TOPLEY, WILLIAM (1886-1944)

A British bacteriologist and experimental epidemiologist.

He was mainly responsible for the Emergency Public Health Laboratory Service which was set up during the 1939-45 war. This new body provided expert bacteriological help in areas that were ill-provided for, and it assisted in the control of epidemics. In 1948, it was incorporated into the National Health Service as the Public Health Laboratory Service (P.H.L.S.).

With G. S. (now Sir Graham) Wilson, he wrote a mammoth text-book on the 'Principles of Bacteriology and Immunity', which has been revised in successive editions by Wilson and Sir Ashley Miles.

WELCH, WILLIAM (1850-1934)

An American pathologist, who introduced the newer bacteriology of Koch and Pasteur to the medical profession of the United States.

He discovered the commonest causal organism of gas gangrene (*Clostridium welchii* or *perfringens*).

As the famous 'Popsie' Welch, he was the teacher of many illustrious American research workers.

WRIGHT, ALMROTH (1861-1947)

A British bacteriologist, who directed the Inoculation Department (later, the Wright-Fleming Institute), St. Mary's Hospital, London, for 45 years.

His work on typhoid vaccine for human immunization (1896) ushered in the (bacterial) vaccine era in this country.

From successful prophylactic inoculation he turned to the use of bacterial vaccines for treatment and to studies of the opsonic index: in the long run these investigations were of little value.

Alexander Fleming, the discoverer of penicillin, was his most distinguished pupil.

G. Bernard Shaw was a friend of Wright, on whom he based the character of Sir Colenso Ridgeon in *The Doctor's Dilemma*.

YERSIN, ALEXANDRE ÉMILE (1863-1943)

A disciple of Louis Pasteur, who was associated with Roux in his research on diphtheria toxin in 1888.

He discovered the plague bacillus in 1893-94, independently of the simultaneous findings of Kitasato, and he also developed plague antiserum.

A NOTE ON BIBLIOGRAPHY

Many references to sources for this book will be found in *A History of Immunization* by H. J. Parish (E. & S. Livingstone, Edinburgh & London, 1965).

The following is a personal selection of histories and other works. It is impracticable to give a comprehensive list:

HISTORIES OF MEDICINE, BACTERIOLOGY, ETC.

BULLOCH, W. (1938). *The History of Bacteriology*. London: Oxford University Press.

FRAZER, W. M. (1950). *A History of English Public Health, 1834-1939*. London: Baillière.

GUTHRIE, DOUGLAS (1958). *A History of Medicine*. 2nd ed. London: Nelson.

HARE, R. (1954). *Pomp and Pestilence*. London: Gollancz.

HOBSON, W. (1963). *World Health and History*. Bristol: Wright.

SINGER, C. and UNDERWOOD, E. A. (1962). *A Short History of Medicine*. 2nd ed. Oxford: Clarendon Press.

WALKER, KENNETH (1954). *The Story of Medicine*. London: Hutchinson.

WILLIAMS, GREET (1960). *Virus Hunters*. London: Hutchinson.

WILLIAMS, HARLEY (1954). *Masters of Medicine*. London: Pan Books.

BACTERIOLOGY, IMMUNOLOGY, VIROLOGY

PARISH, H. J. and CANNON, D. A. (1962). *Antisera, Toxoids, Vaccines and Tuberculins*. 6th ed. Edinburgh & London: Livingstone.

WILSON, G. S. (1967). *The Hazards of Immunization*. London: Athlone Press.

WILSON, G. S. and MILES, A. A. (1964). In Topley and Wilson's *Principles of Bacteriology and Immunity*. 5th ed. London: Arnold.

INFECTIOUS DISEASES

RAMSAY, A. M. and EMOND, R. T. D. (1967). *Infectious Diseases*. London: Heinemann Medical.

GLOSSARY

Adjuvant—A substance which may be added to a vaccine to improve and prolong the immunity.

Aerobe—An organism which grows only in air or free oxygen.

Allergy—A hypersensitive state to foreign protein, e.g. horse serum. Allergic conditions in man include anaphylaxis, serum sickness, food and drug idiosyncrasies, asthma and hay fever.

Anaerobe—An organism which grows best without air.

Anaphylaxis—A condition of hypersensitiveness to certain foreign proteins, e.g. horse serum. A severe form of allergy.

Antibacterial serum—A serum prepared by giving injections of organisms to horses or other animals and subsequently withdrawing the blood in order to obtain the serum, which contains antibodies to these organisms.

Antibiotic—Any specific substance produced *in vitro* by certain bacteria and fungi, which is capable of killing or inhibiting the growth of other bacteria, viruses, etc. *in vitro* and *in vivo*. Examples are penicillin (the first to be used successfully), streptomycin, the tetracyclines and polymyxin.

Antibody—A substance produced in the tissues of man or animal in response to the stimulus of an antigen. It may act against micro-organisms or their products and serve as an antidote to an infection.

Antigen—A substance, such as a component or product of the activity of micro-organisms, which trains the body to produce a special type of response or antibody.

Antitoxic serum—A serum containing an antitoxin.

Antitoxin—An antibody produced against a toxin.

Antiviral serum—A serum containing antibodies to a virus.

Attenuated—Weakened in virulence.

Bacillus—A rod-shaped bacterium.

Bacteraemia—Presence of bacteria in the circulating blood.

Bacterium—A minute, unicellular, living organism, microbe or germ, not including, on the one hand, the protozoa or algae, and on the other, the rickettsiae or viruses. Is held back by an ordinary bacterial filter through which a virus passes freely. Is readily seen by ordinary microscopy.

Broth—Fluid medium for the growth of micro-organisms.

Brucella—A genus of bacteria which includes the causative organisms of Malta and abortus fevers.

Chemotherapy—A specific treatment with drugs of infections due to insects, worms, protozoa, spirochaetes, bacteria, fungi, rickettsiae, and viruses.

Chorio-allantois—The yolk sac in a developing egg on which viruses are grown artificially.

Coccus—A spherical or ovoid bacterium.

Corynebacterium—A genus of bacteria which includes the causative organism of diphtheria.

Demography—Vital statistics, illustrating the condition of communities.

Encephalopathy—Cerebral disease due to various causes.

Endemic—An adjective indicating that a disease or infection is caused by factors constantly present in a community. Usually confined to infections transmitted directly from man to man.

Epidemic—An outbreak of disease in which a micro-organism attacks large numbers of people within a few days or weeks.

Epizootic—A similar term to epidemic, but confined to infections transmitted from animal to animal.

Gamma globulin—The protein fraction obtained from blood in which many of the antibodies present in the original serum can be found.

Haematology—The study of blood and its diseases.

Heterologous serum—A serum from the blood of an animal of another species (*e.g.* horse antitoxic serum injected into man).

Homologous serum—A serum from the blood of an animal of the same species (*e.g.* human convalescent serum injected into man).

Hyperimmune gamma globulin—A globulin obtained from the blood of patients recently injected with certain vaccines, usually viral, to produce effective antibodies.

Hyperimmunization—Immunization to a very high degree.

Immune serum—Serum used in the prevention or treatment of a bacterial or viral disease, usually prepared in animals by intensive immunization with the causal organism or its products.

Immunity—The state of resistance of the living human or animal body to disease.

> *Active immunity* is acquired as the result of contact with a natural or modified disease-producing agent.
>
> *Passive immunity* is conferred by the transfer of antibody-containing serum or other immune mechanism from one individual to another.

Immunization—The production of immunity or increased resistance against disease or infection.

Incubation period—The period elapsing between the time of infection and the time of appearance of first symptoms.

Infection—Invasion of the body by disease-producing micro-organisms and their subsequent multiplication.

Interferon—A substance, produced by cells, which is able to neutralize a virus.

Intradermal—Intracutaneous: within the structure of the skin.

Intrathecal—Within the spinal meninges (membranes).

Leucocyte—A nucleated cell found in the blood: also called a white blood corpuscle to distinguish it from the much more numerous red blood corpuscles, which contain haemoglobin and give blood its characteristic colour.

Maternal antibody—Antibody transmitted from the human mother to the child by the placenta, and not, as in some animals, by the colostrum (the first milk secreted by the mammary gland).

Meningo-encephalitis—Inflammation of the brain and its membranes.

Mycobacterium—A genus of bacteria which includes the causative organisms of tuberculosis and leprosy.

Nephritis—A disease of the kidneys of toxic origin.

Neurotropic—Having a particular tendency towards nervous tissue.

Opsonin—A substance in normal or immune blood which acts on bacteria and enables them to be phagocytosed.

Orchitis—Inflammation affecting the testis.

Pandemic—An epidemic affecting nearly every part of the world within a year or so.

Passage—Transfer from one animal to another.

Pathogen—A disease-producing micro-organism.

Pathology—The study of disease processes, their cause, how they start, how they progress, their termination and how the body reacts and adapts itself to damage or injury.

Phagocyte—A cell that ingests, and usually digests, micro-organisms, particulate matter, etc.

Phagocytosis—The ingestion of bacteria, cells and foreign particles by phagocytes.

Prophylactic—An agent to prevent or ward off an infection.

Prophylaxis—Prevention of the development of disease.

Rickettsia—A group of very small organisms, some of which cause diseases (such as typhus fever and Rocky Mountain spotted fever) in man. Slightly larger than the viruses, with which they are loosely classified.

Septicaemia—Growth of bacteria in the circulating blood.

Serum—Fluid expressed from blood after it clots. It is free from cells and it will not clot again.

The term is also loosely (and wrongly) used for injectable substances, especially vaccines.

Serum sickness—An allergic reaction to serum.

Specific—Acting on a particular causal micro-organism.

Specific serum—A serum containing antibodies to one type of micro-organism only, sometimes to one antigen only.

Spore—A round or ovoid body, produced by some bacteria, which is relatively resistant to heat, dryness, chemicals and absence of food. It affords a means of survival under adverse conditions.

Staphylococcus—A coccus which forms masses like bunches of grapes.

Streptococcus—A coccus which forms chains.

Subcutaneous—Under the skin.

Toxin—A poisonous substance produced by certain bacteria.

Toxoid (Anatoxine)—A non-poisonous substance produced by the action of certain chemical substances, such as formalin, on toxin. The capacity to induce antibody or antidote to toxin is retained.

Vaccine—Any preparation used to produce an active immunity. Originally the term was restricted to the matter or lymph of cowpox or vaccinia (*Latin* vacca, a cow), used as an immunizing agent against smallpox.

Variolation—Inoculation with the virus of smallpox (variola).

Vibrio—Short curved bacterium with flagella (fine hair-like projections as means of locomotion).

Virulent—Capable of causing disease. Also toxic or poisonous.

Virus—Very minute organism so small as to be able to pass a bacterial filter (porcelain or diatomaceous earth); invisible with the ordinary high-power microscope, used with a light beam.

INDEX

INDEX

241

INDEX

Printed in Great Britain by
Northumberland Press Ltd., Gateshead